Praise for Zen Spaces & Neon Places

"This is easily the most enjoyable book on Japan in a long time. It marks an inspiring and timely addition to the critical scholarship of Japanese space, culture and urbanity. With a refreshingly candid perspective, Bharne captures the entire spectrum of Japan's volatile history, through the lens of culture, architecture and urbanity, and sews them together with an erudite mix of professional criticism and passionate voyeurism. Comprehensive, ambitious yet immensely readable, this collection of intimate and tenacious observations by an astute outsider reminds us why Japan continues to be relevant and a reference for our current times."

Eui-Sung Yi, Principal, Morphosis; Director, The Now Institute

"This book will fascinate anyone puzzled by the perceived contrasts between Japan's fanatically ordered calm of temple gardens and the eclectic exuberance of building and urban design since the Second World War. It offers a perceptive yet provocative tour around the history and development of Japan's architecture 'as a cultural continuum between the native and the foreign, between tradition and mutation,' tracing developments from Nara to Tokyo, with plentiful asides along the way. If you have ever wondered what the splendor of Todai-ji Temple and the puzzle of Ryoan-ji Temple have to do with Shinjuku Railway Station, then this is the book for you!"

Michael Greenhalgh, Professor Emeritus of Art History, Australian National University

"Bharne is a highly perceptive flâneur of the Japanese city. On this elegantly written and thought-provoking stroll – from the early beginnings of Japanese architecture in Ise to the neon-lit street canyons of post-industrial Tokyo – he opens up surprising and fresh perspectives on urban Japan and challenges views that have long been taken for granted."

Christian Dimmer, Ph.D., Assistant Professor Urban Design & Urban Studies, University of Tokyo

"This book is an unabashedly ambitious attempt to critically reinterpret the multi-faceted essence of Japan and its myriad apparently-conflicting cultural reference-points, applying the kaleidoscopic twin lenses of architectural theory and urban practicalities."

Ken Rodgers, Managing Editor, Kyoto Journal

Applied Research and Design Publishing
An Imprint of ORO Editons
Gordon Goff: Publisher

www.appliedresearchanddesign.com
info@appliedresearchanddesign.com

Copyright © 2014 Vinayak Bharne
ISBN: 978-1-941806-06-7

Book Design: Orlando Gonzalez
Art Direction: Pablo Mandel
Project Coordinator: Alexandria Nazar
Copyediting: Ryan Buresh

Color Separations and Printing: ORO Group Ltd.
Printed in China.

Text printed using offset sheet-fed printing process in 4 color on 157gsm premium matt art paper
with an off-line gloss aqueous spot varnish applied to all photographs.

Applied Research and Design Publishing has made every effort to minimize the overall carbon
footprint of this project. As part of this goal, AR+D, in association with Global ReLeaf, have arranged to plant two trees for each and every tree used in the manufacturing of the paper produced
for this book. Global ReLeaf is an international campaign run by American Forests, the nation's
oldest nonprofit conservation organization. Global ReLeaf is American Forests' education and
action program that helps individuals, organizations, agencies, and corporations improve the local
and global environment by planting and caring for trees.

For infomation on our distrbution, please visit our website:
www.appliedresearchanddesign.com/distribution

ZEN SPACES AND NEON PLACES

REFLECTIONS ON JAPANESE ARCHITECTURE AND URBANISM

VINAYAK BHARNE

APPLIED
RESEARCH
+DESIGN
PUBLISHING

To my parents – for recognizing my Japan-ness far before I did.

TABLE OF CONTENTS

Preface

This book has been in the making for more than half my life. The thoughts it contains were written over two decades since my first visit to Japan. They represent my intrigue, fascination and love for a culture into which I was not born. But the roots of this intrigue remain close to my birth, because I was introduced to Japanese culture right from my childhood, through my parents' spectacular antique collection. They have gathered artifacts from the world over, but for some reason I was drawn most to the Japanese ones. I wanted to know Japan more than any other place; I guess we all have secret attractions like this. Some of my earliest drawings, my parents tell me, were imitations of their Japanese wall hangings; some of my earliest crafts were replications of their Japanese jewel boxes. My fascination for things Japanese had not escaped them: my father would gift me Japanese artifacts on my birthday; my mother would paint Japanese nature scenes with me. My Japanese journey began with the two individuals who brought me into this world.

It seemed uncanny then, that the first country I would set foot on outside my native India, would be Japan. In 1992, my parents encouraged me to enter the Pride of New Generation Public Speaking Contest, a highly publicized national competition and exchange program conceived jointly by the Indian and Japanese Junior Chamber. Thanks to my father's training, within six months, I beat out more than 50,000 contestants to emerge the winner. In July 1993, as an undergraduate student of architecture, I was traveling – alone – as the Asia Pacific Development Commission Fellow to Japan.

Those two packed weeks in Japan changed my life. I stayed in some of Tokyo's most expensive hotels, gave speeches on Indo-Japanese alliance, met with the Indian ambassador, and was escorted and photographed everywhere I went. I visited ancient temples and monasteries, stayed in traditional Japanese homes, walked to the top of Japan's tallest castle, took in the neon lights of Ginza, and learnt to acquire a taste for raw fish. Japan's dynamic, fierce post-industrial intensity was a literal contradiction to its contemplative traditional gardens and villas. But it was this dramatic juxtaposition, almost schizophrenic at times, that caught me more than anything else. It exploded my simple assumptions about this culture, told me that my ideas were wrong, and overturned my stereotypes. I fell in love with Japan again.

I left India to pursue graduate studies in urban design at the University of Southern California in Los Angeles in 1996. Here, I met Iku Shimomura, who had come to study from Osaka, and it was with her that I published and presented my first ever peer-reviewed paper titled, "The Dilemma of Japan's Street and Square." Encouraged by this success, I went on to write more than a dozen essays on Japanese architecture within a few years of graduation. One of them, an architectural interpretation of Junichiro Tanizaki's 1933 essay "In Praise of Shadows," caught the attention of the University of Ljubljiana that had sought the rights to re-publish this classic into Slovenian, and in 2002, they invited me to write the afterword to this book. I visited Japan many times, and more papers followed – from a comparative history of Kyoto and Rome, to urban examinations of Japanese post-democratic publicness. Many were published by well-respected sources such as the Japan Foundation, Kyoto Journal, Museum of Asian Art (San Francisco), Association of Collegiate Schools of Architecture and Journal of Architectural Education (JAE). I began to receive invitations to lecture on my writings, and opine on scholarly papers and books, most notably by JAE to review the eminent Japanese architect Arata Isozaki's book "Japan-ness in Architecture." Many years had passed since a nineteen-year-old Japan-loving Indian had flown east, and now, so much of me had steeped into Japan, and enough material had gathered to become something more than a scattering of isolated writings.

I have often likened this book, or perhaps more appropriately, this collection of essays, to the fourteenth century Zen monk Yoshida Kenko's "Essays in Idleness." I would not dare to compare my writings to his profound epiphanies, but just as Kenko would instantly pen down his thoughts on pieces of paper, as and how they flashed by him, so have I written these essays, as and how they came to me. They emerged through a variety of inspirations. They were conceived with various states of mind. They were not produced in any sequential order. They were not written with the goal of making a book. Some were outlined in Japanese gardens and streets, and expanded at my home in India and Los Angeles. Others were written in the United States, and polished during my journeys to Japan and other parts of the world. Over the years, I did not fail to notice, however, that there were many common threads that wove them together, that many themes ran through them, and that collectively, they were in fact telling a larger fascinating story. It is this accumulation and interweaving with a few new additions, updates and edits that has brought this volume into being.

This book then is a labor of love. It is my love letter to Japan. It is the culmination of a two-decade-long intellectual and emotional journey that coincidently began in the year of the 61st reconstruction ritual of the Ise Shrine, and now culminates with the 62nd one. It is a chronicle of my reflections and intuitions on Japanese culture as seen through my architectural and urbanist sensibilities. It is an account of what the Japanese built landscape means to me and perhaps what I believe it should mean to others. It reveals what interests me most about Japan. It suggests what does not. It represents my continuing struggle to understand why this isolated archipelago bears an indelible power on me; why it seems like another home that keeps calling me back.

Vinayak Bharne
Pasadena
July 20, 2013 (twenty years since the first day I stepped in Japan)

Acknowledgements

This book is foremost a tribute to my parents Mohanlal and Neela Bharne who started me off on this journey. Were it not for their vision and exemplary parenting, my intrigue for Japan would have never quite blossomed.

I am not a historian of Japanese architecture and urbanism, and have relied on numerous books and papers to deepen my knowledge of this culture. I remain obliged to the scholars and authors who wrote them. Some stand out more than others, because their thoughts and writings have had a deep influence on me: Arata Isozaki, Kisho Kurokawa, Gunther Nitschke and Atsushi Ueda.

Three friends in Japan have served as invaluable critics and advisors for this study: Ken Rodgers, managing editor of Kyoto Journal; Christian Dimmer, Assistant Professor of Urban Design and Urban Studies at the University of Tokyo; and Yu Morishita, Assistant Professor at the Institute of Industrial Science, also at the University of Tokyo. They each painstakingly read my entire manuscript, offered intellectual insights, pointed out factual errors and even challenged me to reconsider some of my positions. This book owes a lot to them.

My close friend Aseem Inam, Associate Professor and Director of the Theories of Urban Practice Program at Parsons The New School for Design, provided insightful comments on the book's introduction, epilog and overall framing. Many of the chapters in this book were originally independent essays, and many colleagues and scholars have reviewed them over the years: Robert S. Harris, Roger Sherwood, Ralph Knowles, Bob Oaks and Iku Shimomura. Additionally many friends and acquaintances within and beyond the academy have served as discussants on various related topics – Yo Hakomori, James Steele, Barton Myers, Stefanos Polyzoides, Andrew Liang, Marleen Kay Davis, Eui-Sung Yi, Zhongjie Lin and Shuji and Karen Kurokawa. Special gratitude goes to Kathryn Smith for her encouragement and mentorship over the past decade.

If Gordon Goff of Applied Research and Design Publishing (AR+D) had not had the initiative to produce this book, I might have not considered making it. He is a publisher of the highest caliber, with a keen eye for quality and detail. He has been a great colleague throughout this project, who understood my emotional connection to this effort, and put up with all my delays and queries. Thanks is also due to his dedicated and talented staff Ryan Buresh, Corrine Evanoff, Jerry Adams, Usana Shadday, and Alexandria Nazar. Pablo Mandel offered some excellent art direction for the book design and composed the book cover. And my good friend Orlando Gonzalez painstakingly composed this volume, spending long nights, as if it were his very own.

Three people stand out for their photographs used throughout this volume: Michael Greenhalgh, Emeritus Professor of Art History, Australian National University; Noboru Asano from Tokyo; and freelance photographer Michael McMorrow from Dubai. Were it not for their keen eye, this book would have been a butterfly without wings. Steve Sundberg generously shared some of his old Tokyo postcards for this book. Malcolm Fairley let me use his image of the historic Kyoto screen. Kevin J. Brown let me use his historic maps of Nara, Kyoto, and Tokyo. And Thiago Valente, Stefan Zwanzger, Michael Mcdermott, and Avni Shah also contributed important images.

Of all the trips I made to Japan, the two most important for this book were the first and the latest. The former happened through the sponsorship of the Indian and Japan Junior Chamber, and I thank them for that life-changing opportunity. The latter came as part of my graduate planning studio at the Price School of Public Policy at the University of Southern California, and I thank Regina Nordhal and Marlon Boarnet for making this a reality. During the writing of this book, I have also thought many times of all the people who hosted me during my various trips to Japan, particularly the Matsuoka family in Himeji, Kenji Hamada in Tokyo, and the Yamamoto family in Shizuoka. I remain grateful for their warmth and hospitality.

The role of my students cannot be underestimated. Yoko Saeki from Tokyo did considerable research with me on Japanese urbanism at the University of Southern California, School of Architecture. It eventually lead to a graduate thesis examining the urban and environmental impacts of the Ise Shrine's cyclic rebuilding during which, we traveled together to Ise and several parts of Japan. Yoko's insights, conversations and efforts helped fill several gaps in this manuscript. Other students did significant research on specific topics that enhanced this text: Winnie Fong on love hotels, Jeffrey Khau on nightlife and yakuza culture, Michael Mcdermott on Japan's train network, Avni Shah on vending machines, Jennifer Bailey on Japanese visuality, Yining Tang and Xin Xin on Tokyo streets, and Nicole Friend and Amber Churches Hathaway on Tokyo's evolution.

I thank my in-laws Nancy and Peter Kemball, for their love and encouragement over the years, and for giving me their cozy home-office in Ottawa to polish the text in its final days. Nancy also served as the much necessary non-architectural critic, reading several parts of this manuscript and advising on its clarity. My two sisters, Simi and Pooja have been witness to my early days of Japanomania, and during this book's making, I have fondly recollected many conversations we had on things Japanese. Finally, this book would have quite simply been impossible without the support and willingness of my wife and most trusted friend Paige. Whether it was reviewing parts of the manuscript after the kids were asleep, or helping me clarify a point through her keen sensibilities as a trained documentary film-maker, I could not have asked anything more from a life-partner. And my two beloved children Sebastian and Portia have played their own invaluable role: waiting patiently for me to wrap up a paragraph during playtime, climbing over my shoulders as I read through the chapters, and most importantly being my inspiration to see this project through.

View of Mount Fuji from Hikone.

Introduction

There is a story in the ancient Indian fables of a man lying motionless in the roadway, his face turned downward. A drunkard passing by assumes that he has fallen intoxicated; a thief suspects he is trying to hide something; a hermit in turn sees a meditating saint and bows in reverence. Each sees in the subject, a bit of themselves. The understanding of Japanese culture over the past century has been similar: each onlooker has seen in Japan what they have wanted to see, or rather seen a bit of themselves. Japan has been a mirror, or as the American architect Charles Moore put it "the dark waters in which Narcissus saw himself."[1]

Since its opening to the world in the Meiji Era (circa 1868) after centuries of self-imposed isolation, the subject of Japan's built environment as such has morphed into a complex intellectual discourse – between what is imported versus indigenous; between what is Japanese versus Western. There are Japan's earliest Chinese influences versus their gradual transformation into distinct Japanese compounds. There is the Euro-American curiosity with Japanese artifacts in the mid-nineteenth century versus Japan's willful embrace of Western architectural styles in the thirties. There is German architect Bruno Taut's 1933 appraisal of the Katsura Villa as the ultimate Japanese archetype versus Kenzo Tange and Yasuhiro Ishimoto's 1960 documentation of the same building as a series of compositions resembling those of Dutch painter Piet Mondrian. There is Metabolism, Japan's response to Western Modernism versus Tokyo's Disneyland.

The question of what is *Japanese* about Japan's built environment has consequently become as bewildering as a Zen *koan*.[2] In attempting to answer this question, one has to drift somewhere between Japan and the West, somewhere between Japan's nostalgia and utopia, and ultimately arrive at no necessarily fixed conclusion. But this cultural complexity of Japan, as a collage of multiple dimensions and nuances, continues to be undermined by outside eyes when compared to the many stereotypes that still dominate how we know it. I for one started my own explorations on Japan with numerous such stereotypes, and my journey in exploring Japan through architecture and urbanism for twenty years has been essentially one of either validating or debunking these stereotypes for my own sake. It has led me to conclude – both as a practicing urbanist as well as educator – that Japan is not very well understood by the larger world, and that many of the deeper lessons it offers us on cultural behavior, architectural expression and city-making lie buried under heaps of clichés.

Through this book, I wish to offer some of my reflections, realizations and perspectives, to instigate a more reflective outlook on Japan as a cultural phenomenon, to dispel simplistic and hasty conclusions about it, to encourage an appreciation of its multi-faceted sides more holistically, for what they are, and with a far more open mind. Japan – seen in this study through the optic of its built landscape – offers profound insights into aspects of cultural resilience, extremes, adaptability, hybridization, isolation, resurrection and refinement that have deep relevance across the world. This book may not be necessarily driven by an overwhelming academic discourse, or the need to dispute the most controversial points of historic or contemporary academic debate on Japan, but it is nonetheless aimed at instilling in readers – particularly outside Japan – a far more sophisticated understanding of its past and present, through what I hope is a delightful and engaged look at key aspects of Japan's built world.

I am myself an outsider to Japan – in that I am neither native Japanese, nor a non-native who has lived in Japan for a major part of his life. But to state that this book is merely an outsider's perspective on Japan would be unfair, because I am not a casual observer of Japan either. I have been deeply engaged with Japanese architecture and urbanism for two decades – through multiple extended visits, serious scholarship, fieldwork, and teaching as a form of learning. I have proposed ideas for Japanese cities, and presented and discussed them with Japanese officials and professionals. Since I end up going to Japan every few years, I notice things that my friends in Japan do not: social changes that take time to evolve or physical transformations that are less dramatic and more nuanced. In turn, I know Japan well enough to see things differently from the relatively obvious aspects that catch a casual visitor. My insights therefore are those of an outsider of a particular kind: involved, evolving, and steeped in punctual and sharp slices of history – and this is why I believe this book stands out.

The Goals of this Book

This book shifts the emphasis on how we choose to read Japanese architecture and urbanism: It focuses on phenomena and meanings rather than objects and form, and prioritizes intentions and legacies over the mechanics of design. The terms "architecture" and "urbanism" in the book's subtitle must therefore be understood in the broadest possible sense: They encompass all aspects that shape the built environment at all scales – buildings, cities, materials, public spaces, rituals, landscapes, processes, perceptions, semantics, urban form, urban life, people – all woven together. They aim to glean more into the spirit of Japan's overall metamorphic ensemble than its individual buildings, and embrace everything that has shaped, or is shaping the Japanese built environment we see today. As a cultural text, architecture and urbanism mean many different things to its authors versus recipients, through various social, political and cultural interpretations. In this book, I intend to trace the historiography of this complex mesh of multiple dimensions. I intend to reread Japanese architecture and urbanism as a creative cultural document of multiple traces, contestations and expressions in time, with its own internal logic.

To accomplish this, the chapters in this book first and foremost seek to capture the breadth of the multifarious dimensions of the Japanese built environment. They traverse Japan's rich, and tumultuous architectural and urban history, shaped by Shinto, Buddhism, wars, earthquakes, democracy, modernism, the economic bubble etc. and open a rich discussion on the entire panorama of how the Japanese built environment has come to be. The places discussed in this book go from the ancient Izumo Shrine to the futurism of the Sendai Mediateque, and from the advent of Kyoto to the ongoing construction of the new island of Toyosu. The name of this book is a conscious provocation of this diversity and breadth, this juxtaposition of Zen and Neon, like Ruth Benedict's classic "The Chrysanthemum and the Sword" (Houghton Muffin, 1946), relatively direct in its idea of seeing Japan as a culture of extremes and contradictions across time.

Secondly, the chapters seek to trace which cultural treads have endured over Japanese history, and which in turn have shifted, transformed, or vanished. Each chapter traces a thematic trajectory connecting past and present, sometimes beginning with traditional concepts and testing how they have survived today, or conversely, starting with a contemporary idea, and seeking its roots in Japanese history. The book's title is also in this sense a metaphor: both Zen and Neon form an intrinsic part of Japan today, blurring the line between its past and present. The goal, in other words, is to negate a history of choice and re-read Japanese architecture as a cultural continuum between the native and the foreign, between tradition and mutation.

Thirdly, the chapters seek to highlight the paradigmatic moments in Japanese architectural and urban history, for either their significant influences on the built environment, or their deep relevance to Japan's future. The various chapter themes largely spring from or engage in such crucial moments, such as the import of the Chinese timber bracket, the introduction of Zen, the Hiroshima bombing, the discovery of neon, the Fukushima Daiichi nuclear disaster, and the 2020 Tokyo Olympics announcement. The goal, thus, is to reflect on Japanese architecture as a phenomenon of multiple epochs or as a series of diverse circumstances with a common cultural ancestry.

In so doing, this volume posits a bigger argument: Inasmuch as one embraces Japan's historical pre-industrial architecture as Japanese, one must also embrace its transitions through Westernization and their mutations into new expressions and compounds – they are and always will be equally Japanese. It is this extreme juxtaposition of seemingly contradictory aspects that makes Japanese architecture such a compelling study. It offers invaluable lessons on how cultures balance and negotiate their past and present, how they reconcile seemingly conflicting cultural meanings, and how cultural identities are reinforced and renewed through successive transformations. This book also seeks to argue that different aspects of Japanese culture, however disparate or inter-related they may seem, can and should be understood on their own terms as co-evolving counterparts of a larger reality. This book claims that the Japanese built environment we see today, despite all its seeming fragmentation and disjunction, is in fact a single unprecedented cultural continuum in which seemingly contradictory things and events seamlessly coexist.

Scholarship on Japanese Architecture and Urbanism

The narrative in this book has been shaped as much by my personal observations on Japan, and innumerable discussions with scholars and citizens, as by the exhaustive and multidimensional scholarship on Japanese architecture and urbanism over the past six decades. First, there are books on Japanese architecture by Japanese architects in Japanese that are relatively less known to the wider world, versus those by foreign scholars written in English that have brought Japanese architecture to the wider world. Second, there are books that prioritize focused studies on a particular era, building or place, versus those that offer broad surveys and reflections. Third, there are books that are meant for introductory versus advanced reading. Fourth, there are narratives that aim at tying past and present through a variety of optics. Fifth, there are personal manifestos by eminent architects, using Japanese traditions as a feedback loop in their own work. And to add to this, all these studies are naturally, period-pieces, in that their commentaries are limited to the specific time in Japanese history in which they were written. Books from the 50s, when Japan was in the infancy of high Modernism, versus those from the 90's and beyond, are significantly different in their extent and tones.

As broad studies on traditional Japanese architecture, three books have served as the touchstones for my experiences and insights. The first is "What is Japanese Architecture: A Survey of Traditional Japanese Architecture" by Kazuo Nishi and Kazuo Hozumi (Kodansha, 1983), a concise compendium of Japanese architecture before the Meiji era, that is, before Western influences began to pour in. Chronological, succinct and less interpretative, this book replaces photographs with meticulous fine-pen freehand plans, sections and sketches, becoming an invaluable beginner's overview on traditional Japanese architecture. The second is "A Short History of Japanese Architecture" by A. L. Sadler (Charles E. Tuttle Company, 1962), a scholarly succinct chronological account of the "growth of Japanese architecture and its connection with the history and culture of the people."[3] By contrast, Arthur Drexler's "The Architecture of Japan" (Museum of Modern Art, 1955), is one of the first attempts by a Westerner to interpret Japanese architectural tradition and expression. The book has three broad sections: Cultural Background, Structure and Design, and Buildings and Gardens, that capture a vast range of places from the Horyu-ji Temple to the Shugakuin Villa gardens. The book's greatest contribution for its time was the publication of several photos of the Ise Shrine and the Katsura Villa, even as it also sought to quickly summarize "some outstanding contributions to the development of modern Japanese architecture."[4] Created by the then-curator of MOMA, the book succeeded in capturing the key aspects of traditional Japanese architecture for a Western audience and in particular Modern architects.

In the genre of numerous focused topical studies, Atsushi Ueda's "The Inner Harmony of the Japanese House" (Kodansha, 1990), and Bruno Taut's "Houses and People of Japan" (Sanseido Press, 1937), remain two seminal classics for their early presentations on the phenomenological dimensions of the traditional Japanese dwelling, a theme that has since been elaborated by many other authors. At the confluence of traditional and Modern Japanese architecture, "Katsura: Tradition & Creation in Japanese Architecture" by Kenzo Tange , Yasuhiro Ishimoto and Wal-

Painting from Seiryo-ji Temple showing Daruma (Bodhidharma), the Buddhist monk who brought Zen philosophy to Japan.

ter Gropius (Yale, 1960) is an unprecedented presentation of one of Japan's most famous traditional buildings as a series of abstract compositions, reinforcing the polemical connection between Japanese and Modern architecture. More recently, Dana Bundrock's "Materials and Meaning in Contemporary Japanese Architecture: Tradition and Today" (Routledge, 2010) focuses on how tradition has been incorporated into contemporary Japanese architecture, through the work of five architects – Fumihiko Maki, Terunobu Fujimori, Ryoji Suzuki, Kengo Kuma, and Jun Aoki. As focused studies on cities, "Tokyo: World Cities" by Botond Bognar (Wiley, 1998) and "Tokyo: City and Architecture" by Livio Sacchi (Universe, 2004) offer sophisticated commentaries on the evolution and significance of one of Asia's most intriguing metropolitan landscapes. Finally, on the subject of Japanese gardens, "Secret Teachings in the Art of Japanese Gardens" (Kodansha, 1987) by David Slawson offers deeper insights into the practical makings of Japanese (particularly Zen) gardens, through his own experience as an apprentice. And Gunter Nitschke's "Japanese Gardens" (Taschen, 2004) provides arguably the most mature assessment to date, on what is a vast and complex topic in its own right.

As interpretative commentaries on the complexity of Japanese architecture, "From Shinto to Ando: Studies in Architectural Anthropology in Japan" (Academy Editions, 1993) by Gunter Nitschke is a thought-provoking collection of numerous scholarly investigations into the deeper socio-spatial aspects of Japanese culture. They range from Ise's rituals, and the spatial manifestations of traditional Japanese concepts such as En, and Ma, to the application of these ideas in contemporary architecture, all based on years of personal fieldwork. The other two are erudite, polemical and advanced anthologies, almost autobiographical manifestos, by two sophisticated minds that have spent almost half a century contemplating the place and larger relevance of Japanese architecture today. In "Rediscovering Japanese Space" (Weatherhill, 1988), Kisho Kurokawa explains his work through his theory of "symbiosis" – between part and whole, interior and exterior, history and present, man and technology – all as extensions of known and less-known traditional Japanese concepts. However, inasmuch as Kurokawa's scholarship on traditional Japanese architecture is thoroughly insightful, his application of these ideas in his built work seems forced and unconvincing. Far more convincing is "Japan-ness in Architecture" (MIT Press, 2006) by Arata Isozaki, wherein he interprets several important places in Japanese history, such as the Ise shrine, the Todai-ji temple and the Katsura Villa along with his own work to explain the continuing "problematic" of defining Japanese architecture in an increasingly fluid milieu. As attempts to dive into the sheer complexity of Japanese architecture, these three books have served as my foremost inspirations, and this is the family of books on Japan that I like to think this one belongs to, although perhaps as a distant cousin rather than an immediate sibling.

The Outline of this Book

Like the complex, interwoven cultural landscape it seeks to capture, the structure of this book is an interwoven sequence of eleven narrative pieces that together create a larger mosaic of scholarly prose. The eleven chapters were selected from a longer list of essays written over two decades, to capture the breadth and diversity of the topic, but also help together make a larger argument. This book can therefore be read as individual reflections on various aspects of Japanese architecture, or as a single meta-narrative on the complex dimensions of Japanese architecture from its origins to the present day. Though each of the chapters move across time and space, I have tried to arrange them to begin with reflections on Japan's rich architectural past, then move into key topics from Japan's pre and post-war era, and end with discussions on Japan's current architectural and urban scene – to add some semblance of structure. Some of these essays focus on place types such as shoin and tea gardens. Others use cultural propensities such as the love for darkness or the consistency of the right angle as springing points for bigger examinations. Some are framed around periods like post-war democracy. Some focus exclusively on urbanity and cities. Different chapters use different intellectual lenses – examining the Japanese built environment today as an extension of its ancient history; reading it through western parameters; analyzing it as an offspring of West and East; and reflecting on it as a contemporary culture-specific pattern. Specific places are used as examples multiple times throughout the book to make different points – like the scroll that shows Mount Fuji more than once along a journey on the Tokkaido road.

Chapter 1 – Between Ise and Katsura: The Forgotten Dimensions of Japanese Architecture strips away the austere, minimalist, monochromatic impression that has remained the foreigner's stereotype of traditional Japanese architecture for decades. It overviews the rich diversity of Japan's architectural accomplishments, from its ancient Shinto origins to the beginning of the Meiji Era, before the entry of Western influences. It shows how the idea of Japanese architecture right from the beginning was a constant dialectic between imports and assimilations.

Chapter 2 – Behind the Culture of Wood probes into Japan's intriguing choice of timber as its traditional building material, whose impermanence and susceptibility to fires and earthquakes, created a history wherein monuments, communities, and entire cities were recurrently destroyed and rebuilt. What was the sense and sensibility behind this tectonic choice? What is the price Japan has paid for it? This study also reveals how this seemingly anachronistic culture is alive in many forms in Japan today, raising complex questions on its future.

Chapter 3 – A View from the Zen Shoin reflects on the two most distinctly Japanese garden types – the *shoin* and the *roji* – as prisms to glean into the ideas and methods of Zen, and vice versa. It traces the behavioral and cognitive experiences brought about by these landscape designs, as both sacred symbols and spatial compounds. It shows how the intentions and reception of these prototypes continue to have deep bearing today, even as they may have found other meanings, applications and guises within and beyond Japan.

Chapter 4 – The Mondrian in the Japanese Room speculates on the striking similarity between the visual tendencies of the traditional Japanese (shoin) interior and the artistic renditions of De Stijl painters like Piet Mondrian. In probing into the possible intentions behind these abstract compositions of straight lines, right angles and flat surfaces, and tracing their parallels to contemporary Japanese visual tendencies, this study surfaces a nuanced side of Japan's east-west discourse that remains relatively unknown to the wider world.

Chapter 5 – Celebrating Time: Transience & Temporality in Japanese Architecture emphasizes the Japanese sensibility to cyclic change and time – from

Top: Landscape in Hikone with Mount Fuji in background. Opposite page: Nightscape in Shinjuku, Tokyo.

changing the picture scroll in the alcove, to reconstructing the Ise shrine every twenty years – not as a nostalgic pattern, but as a cultural blueprint that has endured through Japan's modernization. Whether a Shinto and Buddhist underpinning, or a philosophical response to their fragile geography, this chapter reminds us of the need to understand and engage with the Japanese built environment differently than almost any other culture.

Chapter 6 – Deliberate Dusk: Darkness and the Experience of Japanese Space pays tribute to the 1933 Japanese classic "In Praise of Shadows" by Junichiro Tanizaki, highlighting the traditional Japanese affinity for subdued light, darkness and gloom. Using the European world as a direct counterpart, this chapter traces the origins, meanings and manifestations of this unique cultural trait, and follows upon its subsequent shifts amidst Japan's modernization.

Chapter 7 – Kyoto: A View from Rome celebrates the rich cultural legacy of Japan's former capital for more than a thousand years, by tracing its parallel evolution with its greatest European contemporary, Renaissance Rome. It also highlights the place and role of Kyoto as the cultural epicenter of Japan today, and overviews its ongoing dilemmas and struggles between heritage conservation and post-industrialization.

Chapter 8 – The Japanese Street in Space and Time focuses on the street as the prototypical traditional Japanese container for public life, in contrast to the traditional European city where plazas and squares performed a similar role. It examines the formal and behavioral characteristics of this urban element, and further examines its new guises and identities in Japan today where increasing globalization is bringing other desires and expectations.

Chapter 9 – The Western Genome in Japanese Architecture surveys the shifts in the Japanese architectural milieu from the 1868 Meiji Restoration – when Japan opened its doors to the Western world – to the end of the economic bubble in the 1990s. Looking at more than a century of encounters between Japan and the West, this chapter highlights the key moments and the paradigmatic directions that have emerged from this unprecedented East-West exchange as clues to reflect deeper on Japan's past as well as future.

Chapter 10 – Manifesting Democracy: Publicness and Public Space in Post-war Japan continues the previous chapter's discussion by focusing on the new forms of publicness and concurrent spatial typologies that emerged after a defeated, prostrate Japan suddenly became the first industrialized non-Western democracy in the world. From the Hiroshima Memorial and Tokyo Disneyland to the psyche-delic neon-laden streetscapes of Shinjuku, this chapter traces how Japanese archi-tects flirted with Western ideas as both imports and polemics in a transitional time and culture.

Chapter 11 – Rereading Tokyo contemplates Japan's ultimate urban manifes-tation. It revisits the stereotypical Tokyo hype – its de-regulated evolution, chaotic urban form, hyper-density and mobility, and sex culture – that continues to titillate foreign scholars as a challenge to what cities ought to be. By reflecting deeper on how these various aspects actually shape the everyday ordinary life of Tokyo, this chapter argues for a far more mature understanding of contemporary Japan, beyond isolated first-impressions and exaggerated proclaims.

Finally, an Epilog bookends the narrative – not with a definitive conclusion, but a provocation based on the key questions and insights that emerge from bringing these disparate essays together. What might one take away from this collection? How might one rethink one's engagement with Japan and beyond after reading this book? How might one understand Japan's immediate future as part of the trajectory that has been traced here?

Taken together, the eleven chapters and the epilog build a hypertext that rejects both the biased surveys of traditionalists, as well as the selective viewpoints of mod-ernists. They debunk the assumption that traditions are immune to critical inquiry in their relationship to the multifarious contemporary reality of which they are part, and encourage the reader to re-read Japanese architecture with a far more open mind. The narrative is supported by beautiful photographs, and notes collected at the end of the book serve as a reference source for future scholarship and research.

Finally, before the opening of each chapter, there is a short personal jotting – an epiphany or episode – from one of my numerous trips to Japan over the past twenty years. This is my way of expressing gratitude to those who have picked up this book; this is my tribute to you, my reader.

I walked up for the first time to the Ise Naiku with moist eyes. I had waited twenty years.

I was born in the year of the 60th Shikinen Sengu (the twenty-year-reconstruction ritual of the Ise Shrine). The first time I went to Japan in 1993, the 61st Sengu was underway, but I had neither the knowledge nor insight to understand what I was missing. When I made it in 2013, it was therefore, all the more precious.

The new structures under construction were covered in white canvas; only the sound of hammers and saws affirmed their presence. The Naiku was crowded, so each of us got only a few moments to pray. In turn, I stood at the outer fence facing a white curtain that shrouded my view of the goddess Ametarasu Omikami's inner abode. Then, a tuft of breeze from the other side lifted the curtain for an instant, and with that single glimpse, I felt everything...and nothing.

Walking down the steps, I overheard a guide talking of when the goddess would be moved into her new home later that year. I interrupted him, and insisted on a confirmation. It was October 2, the day I came into this world.

Ise Naiku main shrine covered during reconstruction, circa March 2013.

Nanzen-ji Temple, Kyoto · Detail of bell tower.

Chapter 1
Between Ise and Katsura:
The Forgotten Traditions of Japanese Architecture

"The shrines of Ise are Japan's greatest and most completely original creation in terms of world architecture."
Bruno Taut (Houses & People of Japan), 1937

"Time and again I have been requested to name one extant masterwork on Japanese historical architecture.
The choice is difficult, but I inevitably point to the Nandai-mon of Tadai-ji, not to Ise or Katsura."
Arata Isozaki (Japan-ness in Architecture, 2006)

THE VIEW FROM ISE

It seems like a cliché to begin a discussion on Japanese architecture with the Ise Jingu, but it is unavoidable. The Ise Jingu is the clearest springing point for what this story is all about, not only since it is one of Japan's earliest recorded architectural masterworks, but also one of its most unique places today. This ancient shinto shrine keeps alive a precious cultural thread going back more than 1300 years: Its *shikinen sengu*, the dismantling of the old wooden structures and rebuilding of new ones every twenty years, separates it from any place, sacred or secular, anywhere in the world. There are no precise dates of its origin; records suggest that the first sengu took place in the fourth year of Empress Jito (approximately 686-697 CE), and some speculate that the shrine goes back as early as 4 BCE. Whatever the case, among Japan's 80,000-odd shrines, this mythic place has been and continues to be the most venerated on the entire archipelago.[1]

For a wider audience, however, Ise is a misunderstood place, suggesting by extension, how several aspects of Japanese architecture continue to be misrepresented. For most, the Ise Shrine refers to a modest cluster of impeccably designed thatched wooden buildings within a pine forest clearing – this is how they have been presented to the wider world. In reality, however, the term Ise Shrine refers to two autonomous precincts, the Geku (outer shrine) and the Naiku (inner shrine) located around 5 kilometers apart. Each precinct is centered on a main shrine, with other ancillary objects from storehouses to bridges, totaling more than 60 structures, all of which are rebuilt every two decades. The precincts are connected by a pilgrimage path, with 125 other related shrines located not only within the territory but also outside the boundaries of Ise City (fig 1.1). The complete experience of the Ise shrine and the ceremonies of the sengu thus happen at four scales: 1) that of the regional geography, commemorating the surrounding natural element–mountain, forest, river and agricultural fields; 2) that of the sacred territory bounded by the hundred-odd tutelary shrines; 3) that of the individual sacred precincts and the path connecting them; and 4) that of the main buildings, in which the deity is housed.

Anthropologically speaking, Ise thus reveals some of Japan's earliest philosophical underpinnings, tracing back to the mythic origins of the land itself as

Figure 1.1 The complete Ise Shrine: The main shrines are indicated in red. Ise Geku is in the page center. Ise Naiku is at the page bottom. The preserved Ise forest is shown in dark green. The surrounding larger forest is in light green. The habitat is in grey. The pilgrimage path is in orange. The insets show the clusters of the various shrine buildings with the main compounds in red.

Figure 1.2 Opposite page: Ise Naiku, tutelary shrines.

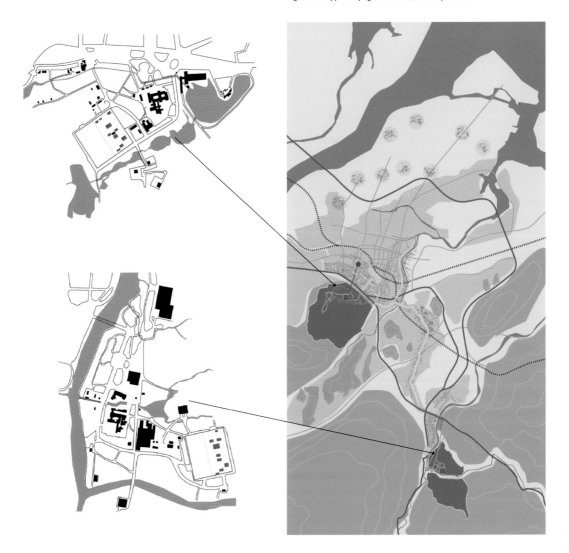

mentioned in its oldest chronicles, the Kojiki and Nihongi. Here, there is mention of *modokim*, a ritual practice of invoking the presence of *kami* (Gods), guided by the rhythms of day and night, sun and moon, the four seasons of the year, and the process of harvest. The twenty year cycle of Ise's sengu commemorates this rhythm while its rituals physically celebrate as part of Shinto belief, various aspects of the natural geography (fig 1.2).[2]

Another reason for beginning at Ise is because its current condition is in many ways emblematic of some of most perplexing dilemmas facing the Japanese architectural world today. While the physical conditions of the shrine precincts are meticulously preserved, the town surrounding the pilgrimage path has been ravaged by random sprawl and insensitive infill. Meanwhile, as we shall discuss later in this book, the sengu itself faces many economic and environmental dilemmas such as timber paucity, raising complex questions on its future. This dialectic between heritage and contemporary realities is a pan-Japanese thematic that is particularly accentuated when seen from Japan's most revered center (fig. 1.3).

Furthermore, Ise Jingu, perhaps more than any other Japanese architectural landmark has also enjoyed significant attention from a foreign gaze, and this has among other things had an indelible effect on the contemporary perception of Japanese architecture at large. While the shrine has always been the prime sacred epicenter throughout Japanese history, not many know that before the 1930s, the architecture of Ise's sublime buildings was read as part of a larger genre of Shinto shrine architecture. The 1927 Nihon Kenchikushi-yo (Summary of Japanese Architectural History), for instance, includes but a short description of Ise, even though it is noted as the "original style" of shrine architecture in Japan.[3] The architectural status-quo Ise enjoys today, both within and beyond Japan, should be attributed, ironically, not to a native but a foreigner, the German architect Bruno Taut.

In 1933, fleeing the hostile political environment of Nazi-dominated Germany, Taut arrived in Japan for the first time, and was taken by some of his former Japanese students to the Ise Shrine and the Katsura Villa. He did not know much about traditional Japanese architecture, and had never seen anything like these two buildings before. The architectural austerity and rusticity of Ise and Katsura made a deep impression on him, so much so, that he proclaimed them as the ultimate

Figure 1.3 Top: Isuzu River within the Ise Naiku precinct. Middle: Original pilgrimage path between Ise Geku and Ise Naiku. Bottom: Steetscape in the town surrounding Ise Naiku showing typical insensitive infill.

archetypes of Japanese architecture, and went as far as comparing the significance of the Ise shrine to the Parthenon of Greece. This proclamation had far reaching impacts both within and beyond Japan. In the 1930s Westernizing Japan, it synchronized perfectly with the emerging architectural generation seeking to break away from historicist attitudes. For the Western architectural world, this minimalism was a breath of fresh air offering a sort of validation to their own evolving minimalist attitudes in Modern architecture. Ise, the ancient Shinto shrine in Mie, and Katsura, the seventeenth century rustic royal villa in Kyoto became the affirmed symbols of authentic Japanese architecture, and for most, the idea of traditional Japanese architecture still begins and ends with austere, rustic buildings and monochromatic tatami rooms, even as one ignores an entire spectrum of architectural accomplishments that span in between. It is against this backdrop that this inaugural chapter strips away the minimalist veneer that has shrouded the richness of traditional Japanese architecture for decades and offers a chronological overview of its pre-industrial accomplishments.

EARLY PERIOD (660 BCE – 540 CE)

In early Japan, with the idea of the emperor as a descendent of the Sun Goddess Amaterasu Omikami, her shrine at Ise occupied the apex of a state-supported hierarchy of Shinto places of worship. But in opposition to this imperial legacy, there was another important shrine, the Izumo Taisha that was seen as a counter-symbol of religious as opposed to political authority. "….of all (Japan) the most holy ground is the land of Izumo," wrote Lafcadio Hearn in his 1895 book "Glimpses of Unfamiliar Japan,"[4] after he learned about it from the Kojiki chronicle.[5] Like Ise, there is no knowledge of the origins of Izumo Taisha, but it is known that in the latter half of the seventh century, Emperor Temmu (631-686) commissioned the Kojiki to be the official history of Japan, and it was completed in 712 CE. Izumo, like Ise, is mentioned in this chronicle as part of Japan's earliest recorded history.

At Izumo, like Ise, the main building is a simple wooden structure raised on pillars, entered by a ladder, with rafters projecting in the form of a crotch above a thatch roof, and timbers bound together with wisteria withes just like those of

Figure 1.4 Izumo Shrine painting circa, 1876. This picture was appended to a request for permission to repair the Grand Shrine at Izumo, on behalf of the Minister of Home Affairs, to the Grand Minister of State, on 17 February in the 8th year of Meiji. Note that the shrine is not on its original raised base. The inset shows a model of the original raised shrine.

the palace. This pattern appears to have established itself in ancient Japan, even withstanding the succeeding influences of Chinese and Indian dominated brick and stone construction that entered with Buddhism in 538 CE. Restraining the use of color and ornament and maintaining the straight line in contrast to the luscious curves favored in China, both shrines retain this primordial form of timber architecture and represent Japan's earliest wooden archetypes. More significantly, according to the Kojiki, Izumo-taisha was considered the largest wooden structure in Japan when it was originally constructed. Legends say it stood nearly 100 meters tall.[6] This can be attributed to early Shinto cosmology, wherein the gods (kami) were believed to be above the human world and dwelling in the most extraordinary and majestic parts of nature. The height of Izumo-taisha could have been an attempt to create a place for the kami symbolically above humans. Nishi and Hozumi have observed how the plan of Izumo's main shrine "resembles that of the Daijoe Shoden, built for the accession of each new emperor" and how the main shrine therefore, preserves a layout characteristic of ancient domestic architecture.[7]

Like other Shinto shrines, Izumo too was cyclically rebuilt–more than twenty five times–but its sheer size raised recurrent construction difficulties, and in response, numerous structural and stylistic changes were introduced with each rebuilding. Over time, even though the floor plan remained virtually unchanged, the shrine's overall outer form changed from the original. Today, its layout consists of eight support pillars arranged to divide the interior into four sections with the entrance off-centered – a significant contrast with the typical symmetry of other Shinto shrines. It is possible that the main structure was built like a less formal domestic space as opposed to a shrine, suggesting a more informal relationship between devotees and their gods (fig. 1.4).

The Japanese architect Atsushi Ueda has rightfully noted that "the history of Japanese architecture is the struggle with the pillar."[8] In this statement Ueda sets forth the basic differences between Japanese timber architecture and its Western contemporaries: in the West, one used the outer and interior walls to bear the load of the building; in Japan, the pillar (post and beam construction) remained the fundamental structural and symbolic element. Conceptually, this early shrine archetype revolved around the idea of a central timber pillar. It symbolized the mythic axis

Figure 1.5 Pagoda at Horyu-ji Temple, Nara.

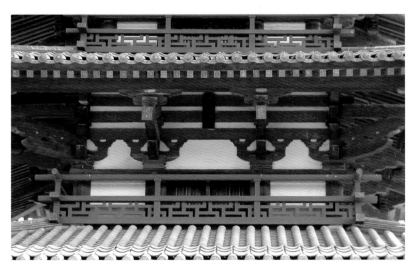

connecting Heaven to Earth and manifested Japan's ancient rituals of tree worship. In ancient Shinto tradition the tree was a *yorishiro*, the means by which Gods descended to the earth.[9] Old trees struck by lightning were revered as evidence of this supernatural event, and this idea of the yoroshiro eventually morphed into the original form of the Shinto shrine. Thus the *shin no mihashira* (esteemed pillar of the heart) under the center of the floor of Ise's main building is significant because it is regarded as a yorishiro in which the Gods reside. It is possible that the existence of timber pillars lining up in a single row in the center of a traditional Japanese building may have evolved through this yorishiro concept as well.

ASUKA PERIOD (540 – 640 CE)

Buddhism entered Japan in 538 CE. But not until the sixth year of the reign of Emperor Bidatsu (578 CE) would the arrival of monks and temple artisans from Kudara (the western part of Korea) and simultaneous support for Japanese Buddhism by the central government bring significant prowess in temple construction. Asukadera was the first temple complex constructed in Japan beginning in 588 CE and completed in 596 CE. It had a *pagoda* (tiered tower enshrining the Buddha's relics) located in the center of an enclosed cloister with golden halls surrounding it on three sides. Like most buildings of this era, nothing remains of this original structure save a few stones and tiles. The *kondo* (main hall), the pagoda, the middle gate and the cloisters of the great monastery of Horyu-ji and the pagoda of Hokki-ji are the only exceptions to this case.

Thus Horyu-ji (built in 607 CE on a different plan, burnt, then rebuilt on the present plan from 670) best showcases the wooden architecture of the Asuka era. It was influenced by the North and South dynasties of China and eventually transmitted through Korea. This combined college, infirmary and temple, was like its contemporaries an enclosed precinct entered through a *Nandaimon* (Southern Great Gate), with the great hall and pagoda, then the library and bell tower, and behind them the lecture hall with the monks' residences to the east and west (fig 1.5).

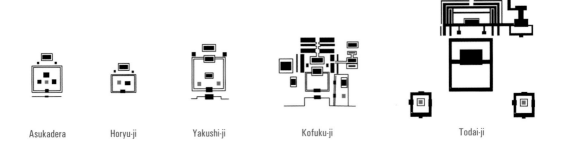

| Asukadera | Horyu-ji | Yakushi-ji | Kofuku-ji | Todai-ji |

Figure 1.6 Above: Evolution of the *garan* prototype. The pagoda locations are shown in red.

Figure 1.7 Opposite page: Todai-ji Daibutsuden, Nara.

HAKUHO PERIOD (640 – 720 CE)

The Hakuho (literally "white phoenix") period saw a significant importation and adaptation of Chinese Tang dynasty ideas, having realized their compatibility to the climate and timber construction techniques of Japan. With increasing relations with the Asian continent necessitating a fixed center of government, the late seventh century saw the building of the splendid new Fujiwara Capital in 694 CE on a plain surrounded by the fabled Unebi, Kagu and Miminashi Hills.

One of the new prototypes of this era was the Tang influenced *shichido garan* or "Temple of Seven Halls." Designed as an enclosed quadrangle like its predecessor Horyu-ji, this model by contrast had two pagodas facing each other, often placed within the enclosure at a little distance from the center line of the buildings through the south gate – as in the case of Yakushiji. The original Yakushi-ji complex was built in Fujiwara-kyō, Japan's capital in the Asuka period, commissioned by Emperor Temmu in 680 CE to pray for recovery from illness for his consort, who succeeded him as Empress Jitō, and completed the project around 698 CE. It has been long believed that the temple was moved to its present location in 718 CE, following the move of the capital to Heijō-kyō known today as Nara. However, excavations of the Fujiwara-kyō Yakushi-ji site in the 1990s suggest that there may have been two Yakushi-jis at one time. Fires destroyed most buildings of the complex in 973 CE, and the main hall in 1528. The main hall was rebuilt in the seventies, and the entire temple has now been restored.

As the fourth of the major temple complexes, the first three being Asuka-dera, Shitennō-ji, and Hōryū-ji, Yakushi-ji's layout illustrates the evolutionary incarnations of the *garan* prototype plan. In the first, the pagoda because of the relics it contained was the centerpiece of the garan , surrounded by three small kondo. In the second, a single kondo stood at the center with the pagoda in front of it. In the third, they were next to each other as seen at Hōryū-ji. And at Yakushi-ji there is a single, large kondo at the center with two pagodas on the sides. The same evolution can be observed in Buddhist temples in China. In other words, pagodas gradually lost their importance and were replaced by the kondo. Because of the magic powers believed to lie within the images the Kondo housed, this idea persisted in the succeed-

ing eras, with Zen sects, which arrived late in Japan from China, doing away with pagoda altogether (fig 1.6).[10]

TEMPYO PERIOD (720 – 780 CE)

The Tempyo Period was Japan's golden age of Buddhist architecture and sculpture. Heijo-kyo (Nara), the new capital, was a city of monasteries and temples with more than fifty pagodas rearing their spires, the two loftiest being those of Todai-ji (320 feet) and Ganko-ji (240 feet). Kofuku-ji was moved to its present location in the second decade of the eighth century with its pagodas moved completely outside the cloister enclosure. Yakushi-ji was rebuilt according to its previous plan, its two pagodas framing a central golden hall. Only its 120-feet high three-story eastern pagoda survives today with its unique double eaves giving it the appearance of a six story edifice.[11]

The evolution of the Tang temple typology in Japan is thus most significant for the evolution of the Japanese pagoda. But it was tectonically a radical departure from its Chinese predecessor. Its construction centered on a single central column made of a massive tree trunk that held cantilevered bracketed members supporting the various tiered roofs. As an urban element, this vertical campanile of sorts served to announce important precincts, either alone as at Horyu-ji and Kofuku-ji, or in pairs at Todai-ji, augmenting urban navigation and engendering a readable visual order with the otherwise horizontal city. And as an autonomous built form, it formalized in a distinctly Japanese manner, the same symbolic meanings as its Indian ancestor, the *stupa*, that had initially covered the ashes of the Buddha.

During the Tempyo period then, the construction and detailing of the colossal Buddhist temple prototype and its ancillary buildings was firmly established, and their aesthetic nuances significantly refined. The Kondo (Great Buddha Hall) at Todai-ji was the largest wooden building in the world, and that of Toshodai-ji with its single *azumaya* roof (hipped with kite-tail details) perhaps the finest architectural specimen (fig. 1.7). But arguably the most outstanding building of this era was the relatively smaller Shosoin, an *azekura* style sacred storehouse made of *hinoki* logs. Standing on circular wooden pillars raised nine feet above the ground, its mem-

Figure 1.8 Above: Shoso-in, located to the north-west of the Todai-ji Daibutsuden, Nara. The inset shows the *azekura-zukuri* detail of another store house at Todai-ji.

Figure 1.9 Opposite page: Kiyomizu Temple, Kyoto. Top: View from temple entry in spring. Bottom: View from east in winter.

bers were joined into three-cornered interlocks that sustained a remarkable climatic rhythm. In summer the heat contracted the logs letting in the breeze through the gaps; in winter the dampness expanded them keeping the interiors dry. This is significant because it enabled the first Nara emperor's priceless and vast collection of treasures and gifts from other rulers to survive in almost climate-controlled conditions until the present day. The Shosoin was an early evidence of the refined combination of structural expressionism and architectural simplicity that would become the hallmarks of Japanese architecture that followed (fig. 1.8).[12]

HEIAN PERIOD (789 – 1190 CE)

The four centuries that saw the shift of the capital from Heijo-kyo (Nara) to Heian-kyo (Kyoto) also saw the introduction of new sects of Buddhism, the decline of the Chinese influence in Japan, and the rise of the Fujiwara regents. The Tendai and Shingon Buddhist sects demanded a different temple prototype. For them, a flat temple precinct within a capital city like Horyu-ji or Todai-ji was no longer suitable for meditation on profound Buddhist philosophies. Remote mountain peaks were the new strategic destinations for spiritual pursuits. On these complex topographies, it was not possible to keep the older rectilinear form of the monastery, and halls had to be sited at varying levels where any small flat land seemed available. The monastery complex was now scattered irregularly, and in some cases built out from the rocks and supported on trestles from below.

The second prototype of this era was a new kind of pagoda, the Daito. Here the usual square lower story and pyramidal roof was superimposed with a round dome called a "turtle belly", eventually crowned by a circular balustrade topped by a roof with a spire supported on pillars. The great temples of the early Heian era were then a combination of these two new ideas. There was Enryaku-ji on Mount Hiei, Kongobu-ji on Mount Koya, Kyoo Gokoku-ji (now called Toji), Ninna-ji, Muro-ji and the Kiyomizudera (fig 1.9). It is amply clear that a decided development of Buddhist shrines and monasteries dominated the architecture of the time.

What the Tendai and Shingon sects did for the first half of the Heian era, the Amida sect did for the second. It sought a new temple prototype to express its

Figure 1.10 Above: Byodo-in Temple, Uji.

Figure 1.11 Opposite page: Itsukushima Shrine with torii in foreground, at low tide. The mud marks at the base of the torii pillars show the level of water at high tide.

central idea of the Pure Land Paradise, the realm where the Amida Buddha dwelled. This Paradise began to be depicted in art as a model of the Imperial Palace, perhaps to incentivize the Fujiwara rulers to fund the temples.

The Imperial Palace in turn had derived its form from the largest residential prototype of this era, the Shinden (literally "sleeping chamber"). It referred to the main south-facing central hall of the building with both sides connected by covered corridors with subsidiary buildings called *tai* (literally "houses opposite"). These two arms enclosed a large central garden, lake and bridges connecting it with either bank. The Byodo-in temple at Uji was one such villa of the Regent Fujiwara Yorimichi which he later turned into a temple (fig. 1.10). The original subsidiary buildings have long since burnt down. The Hoo-do (Phoenix Hall) is the only extant portion deriving its name from the resemblance of its outline to this Imperial bird.[13]

One of the most outstanding buildings of this era is the magnificent Itsukushima Shrine in Miyajima (fig. 1.11). It was incepted in the sixth century, but its current sixteenth century version follows established design from circa 1168. Dedicated to the three daughters of the Shinto deity Susano-o no Mikoto, brother of the sun deity, Amaterasu Omikami (housed at Ise), the red Shinto shrine consists of structures built over the bay, symbolizing the holy status the island once commanded. Commoners were historically not allowed to set foot on the island, approached only by boat and entering through its red "floating" gate.

Aesthetically different, but built round the same time, circa 1164, was Sanjusangendo, the main hall of the Rengeo-in temple, that was dedicated by the retired emperor Goshirakawa as a full-scale temple in itself.[14] It was thirty-three bays long excluding the isles, with a seven-bay porch and enshrined a central image and a thousand life-size images of the Thousand-armed Kannon, along with his Twenty-Eight Protectors. The building was consumed in the great Kyoto fire of 1249, but it is said that the head of the central image, 156 of the thousand other statues, and all the guardians were saved. The current hall was reconstructed between 1251 and 1256 as a replica of the original. It is the longest wooden building in Japanese history, 118.9 meters long, and in the power of its horizontality and rhythmic length, few buildings can match the rustic splendor this Kyoto temple (fig. 1.12).

The rebuilding of Todai-ji also deserves particular mention. Nara's greatest temple had been destroyed in the Gempei conflict in 1180, and reconstruction

Figure 1.12 Above: Sanjusangendo, the main hall of the Rengeo-in Temple, Kyoto.

Figure 1.13 Opposite page top: Nandaimon, the southern gate of the Todai-ji Temple, Nara.

Figure 1.14 Opposite page bottom: Kencho-ji Budsuden, Kamakura. Note the ceiling above the statue that hides the true roof.

began the following year under the leadership of the monk Shunjobo Chogen, who having visited Song China as many as three times, chose a Song style of architecture for the rebuilding (Discussed further in Chapter 2). Today three structures remain from that endeavor, the *kaizando* (Founder's Hall), the *hokkedo* (Lotus Hall) and the one that particularly stands out, the *nandaimon* (Great South Gate). This gate, rebuilt on the same location as its predecessor, is unique in its multiple tiers of brackets sunk directly into the great columns and stabilized by lateral ties extending the entire façade length. Many of the structural members being the same size are easily mass produced, and thereby well suited to efficient rebuilding on a massive scale (fig. 1.13).

KAMAKURA PERIOD (1190 – 1340 CE)

The Kamakura period marked Japan's transition to feudal land-based economies and advanced military technologies in the hands of a specialized fighting class. But it was also a period of prolific religious activity. To the Six Sects of Nara and the two more esoteric sects of Heian were now added six more–Zen, Ji, Shin, Nichiren, Jodo and Yuzu Nembutsu. With them came new architectural prototypes derived from the flourishing Chinese Sung dynasty of the time. But with its increasing adoption by the dominant military class in these war-filled times, it was Zen that would exert the most influence on the buildings of this era.

As such the most distinctive prototype of this era was the Zen temple complex. It was quite different both in plan and detail from its predecessors. One now traversed axially from the south through a two-storied *sanmon* (literally "gate of liberation"), past the *butsuden* or Buddha Hall, the *hatto* or Doctrine Hall and the *hojo* or Residence, with the *tosu* (latrines) and the *yokushitsu* (bath house) to the left and right replacing the two pagodas of their Nara age predecessor. The first of these new prototypes were Nanzen-ji and Daitoku-ji. They were followed by Tenryu-ji, Sokoku-ji, Kennin-ji, Tofuku-ji and Manju-ji in Kyoto, and Kencho-ji, Engaku-ji, Jufuku-ji, Jochi-ji and Jomyo-ji in Kamakura, all different variations in plan and detail of the same basic concept (fig. 1.14).[15]

Figure 1.15 Top: Kinkaku-ji, Kyoto
(Golden Pavilion).

Figure 1.16 Opposite page:
Fushimi Inari Shrine, Kyoto. Red
torii path.

The Zen monastery also introduced a new layer of architectural detailing: the *kato-mado* (literally "flower-headed") ornamental window with an ogival top, the *ebi-koryo*, a new kind of curved tie-beam, and more importantly the Kara style where ceilings within the sanctuary were not coffered but flat with no colored decoration. This new aesthetic preference would exert great influence on Japanese architecture, but only the Shariden (Relic Hall) of the Engaku-ji stands today as a testimony to it.[16]

MUROMACHI PERIOD (1340–1570 CE)

The Muromachi era saw Zen exert its influence on building types other than temples. The most dominant of these was the *shoin* (literally "study"), the library of the Zen temple. The increasing attraction of Zen in the military class nurtured the need for a meditation room in their residences eventually acquiring the name. The *tokonoma* or monastic study alcove containing a picture of Buddha or Daruma along with a small table holding a candlestick, flower vase and censer now became a prominent part of the mainstream Japanese residential interior.

Simultaneously, it had become something of a vogue for the aristocrats to build fine mansions in carefully planned landscaped gardens. The Kinkaku of the Kaen-ji (Golden Pavilion) was one such villa redesigned by the Shogun Ashikaga Yoshimitsu in 1398 on the site of the feudal lord Kintsune's Shinden style residence (fig. 1.15). This blend of residence and temple designed as a three-story pavilion represented a new prototype in its fusion of older Chinese and newer Zen influences into a single building. The ground floor reception room for guests had an open plan like the Shinden-style palace. The study on the second floor and the Zen temple of the third with its bell-shaped windows drew their inspiration from the architecture of the Zen temple. The villa had thirteen buildings arranged within a lake setting where the Shogun could escape from courtly matters to emulate the lifestyle of a Zen monk.

The Muromachi era can claim no great architectural innovation. But the Fushimi Inari Taisha in Fushimi-ku, Kyoto is unique in several respects (fig. 1.16). While its exhibition of bold red color was nothing new for Shinto precincts, what is unique

Figure 1.17 Top: Himeji castle.

Figure 1.18 Opposite page: Fushimi castle.

at Fushimi Inari is the meandering sequence of blood red *toriis* (Shinto gates) creating a three-dimensional serpentine corridor winding atop the sacred hill. The earliest structures were built in 711 on the Inariyama hill in southwestern Kyoto, but the shrine was re-located in 816 on the request of the monk Kukai, and the main shrine structure was built in 1499, the exact same year attributed to the infamous dry Zen garden of Ryoanji. (Discussed in Chapter 3)

MOMOYAMA PERIOD (1570-1616 CE)

The most significant buildings of the war-filled Momoyama era were not religious edifices but palatial villas and military mansions. There was the Shishinden, Seiryoden and Senyoden where the original Shinden prototype was merged with the Buddhist one. There was Toyotomi Hideyoshi's lake villa, the Hiunkaku (Flying Cloud Pavilion) appearing like an exaggerated three-storied version of the Ginkaku-ji. But it is for the establishment of two new contradictory architectural prototypes that this era stands out the most: The *soan* (Tea Hut) was a symbol of solace during these tumultuous times, the *donjon* (castle) a symbol of power.

The soan was where the Zen ritual of Cha-no-yu (Tea Ceremony) was performed. It added a new dimension to Japan's timber traditions with an even greater discrimination of timber less for its structural and more for its aesthetic sensibilities as we shall discuss further in the following chapters. The donjon in turn brought two new concepts to Japanese architecture. First, after sixteen centuries, it introduced earth and stone as dominant building materials. For purposes of defense, the castle bases were giant ramparts not always of stone, but more than often of tamped earth. Second, it introduced the idea of plastering timber for protection against fires. To avoid the danger of being torched, early wood plank walls gradually changed first to earthen walls, then into the *tsuji hei* or mud walls with a wooden framework covered by a small roof, eventually seeing the application of lime stucco.

The era of the Japanese castle began in 1576 with the building of Nobunaga's Azuchi castle on the eastern shore of Lake Biwa. Nothing remains of it today save the foundation stones. But it once stood on a stone base seventy feet high with seven stories rising over a hundred feet above it. It was followed by Hideyoshi's

Fushimi-Momoyama castle in the Momoyama Hills, his Juraku mansion in Kyoto, and his castle of Osaka. The five story keep of the Osaka castle had a seven-mile circumference, and is said to have used stones measuring up to twenty-five feet in length. Other notable castles of this age were the Hikone (1606), Himeji (1609), Matsue (1611), Himeji being the grandest surviving example of this building type. The era ended in 1615 with Ieyasu's destruction of the Osaka castle and the establishment of Edo as the new cultural and political capital of Japan (fig. 1.17, 1.18).

EDO PERIOD (1616 – 1860 CE)

Until about 1700 CE, with Momoyama craftsmen continuing their building patterns, the Edo era hardly saw any change save one major social pattern. The Samurai or military class now forbidden from trading by Shogunal mandate became poorer while the trading classes became richer and more influential. Crafts became

Figure 1.19 Top: Toshogu Shrine, Nikko.

Figure 1.20 Right: Detail of front gate at Toshogu Shrine, Nikko.

Figure 1.21 Opposite page: Katsura Villa, Kyoto.

hereditary repressing any originality and emphasizing technical skill. Yet with commoners now better off under the orderly Tokugawa government, new building types were emerging: theatres, inns, colleges, public baths and restaurants. In Edo, as in other cities, there were now various quarters for specific activities—one with theatres, another with restaurants and brothels—all surrounding the castle, the political and symbolic core of the wooden polis.

When Tokugawa Ieyasu, the founder of all this peace and prosperity died in 1616, his deified status as Toshogu Dai Gongen (Great Manifestation of Buddha Resplendent) needed a suitable shrine. It produced one of the best known works of the period in the shrine of Nikko (fig. 1.19, 1.20). It introduced a new architectural paradigm in combining the Buddhist temple, Shinto shrine and Stupa tomb. The timber building was not only unapologetically colored, it was also bedecked with a riot of golden ornament. Begun in 1634, its present appearance was primarily the result of a far reaching renovation project of Ieyasu's grandson Iemitsu, who added a second complex in 1653. The two mausolea accompanied by a variety of other establishments displayed a sense of Japanese "baroque" unseen elsewhere throughout the country.

Antithetical to the splendor of Nikko stood the austerity of the Katsura Detached Palace. It represented the largest expression of the *sakiya* style, combining the spatial precedence of the Shoin with the increasingly appealing rustic aesthetic of the Zen influenced Tea Hut. Located in the south-west of Kyoto, its Old Shoin was built in 1616, the Middle Shoin in 1641 and completed and remodeled with a Music Room and New Palace in 1660. This private Xanadu with five Tea Houses allowed unimpeded relaxation to Toshihito, Toshitada and their guests (fig. 1.21).[17]

Meanwhile, just as Rome had introduced the thermae (public bath) and the arena as new contributions to its public heritage, Edo introduced the *sento* (bath) and the Kabuki theater (fig. 1.22). Though hot-baths and springs were prevalent even before the Heian period, their distinct form as a public bath house emerged only during the Edo era. The sento (literally "one cent hot water") consisted of a large room with an entry space for clothes and a high seat for the custodian atop a partition that separated the men from the women. It gradually evolved a second story where liquor and light refreshment was served.

Figure 1.22 Kabuki-za, Tokyo. Originally built in 1889, it was destroyed in 1921, restored in 1950, demolished in Spring 2010, and re-opened in March 2013. This photograph was taken in July 2013.

By the mid-eighteenth century, the Kabuki drama became the most popular form of entertainment among the commoners. Kabuki theatres built on a majestic scale found a new challenge in spanning their large interiors. A print of the Ichimura Theater from 1739 reveals ceiling beams supported in the middle by vertical posts rising from the audience boxes. But these central pillars disappear in the Torii Kiyotada print of 1743 of the Nakamura theater showing beams supported by intermediate posts fronting the second-floor tier of the audience boxes and reinforced further by diagonal trusses projecting from the side wall.[18] These intermediate posts in turn disappear in the 1830 print of the Nakamura theater eventually leading to a new construction type, the *kikkobari* (tortoise-shell beaming). These parallel ceiling beams were considerably shorter than the hall width and assembled into a huge rectangular frame with its corners resting on four diagonal beams stretching across the hall. All these theatres were destroyed in the great Ansei-era fire in 1855. Only the Kompira Oshibai in Kotohira around 75 feet wide, 110 feet deep and 35 feet high remains testimony to the achievements of Kabuki architecture.

From a strictly historic standpoint, this concludes the pre-industrial overview of Japanese architecture. In 1868, the Tokugawa Shôgun who ruled Japan in the feudal period, lost his power and the emperor was restored to the supreme position. The emperor took the name Meiji ("enlightened rule") as his reign name and this event came to be known as the Meiji Restoration. It moved the capital from Kyoto to Tokyo, and sought to create a centralized state with the emperor as the symbolic impetus for citizen unity and modernization. To transform the agrarian economy into an industrial engine, many Japanese scholars were sent abroad to study Western science and languages, while foreign experts were brought in to teach. Japan opened its doors to the West and with it the isolated phenomenon of Japanese architecture, spared of any large external influence came to an end.

THE NATIVE & THE FOREIGN – INTERPRETING PRE-INDUSTRIAL JAPANESE ARCHITECTURE

The panorama of pre-industrial Japanese architecture can be seen, as H. Mach Horton has noted "in terms of two poles, the native and the foreign."[19] Buddhist architecture and its subsequent manifestations were essentially built upon imports from

Figure 1.23 Five aesthetic attitudes of traditional Japanese architecture. Clockwise from top right: "primitivist" (Himukai Daijingu), "structuralist" (Nandaimon at Taodai-ji), "pictoral" (Heian Palace), "minimalist" (Kodai-ji Shoin interior), and "eclectic" (Toshogu, inner shrine, Nikko).

Figure 1.24 Opposite page left: Column detail in storage hall at Seiryo-ji. Right: Bracket detail at Ninomaru Palace.

China. In fact Japan is the only place where ironically, examples of these Chinese forms still remain. On the other hand, these Chinese imports were recurrently tempered by indigenous developments with Japanese carpenters combining elements from the Great Buddha and Zen style antecedents to new effects. Throughout this process however, there was a bed-rock of consistencies, a pattern of similar traits that allows us to embrace all the above mentioned examples as traditional Japanese architecture. The most obvious is the choice of wood as building material, one of the traits that separates Japanese architecture from its Chinese predecessors as well as the West. The primary structural system is also consistently the column and the beam, with walls as non-structural partitions. Spatially, the flexible Japanese interior with movable walls, transparency of interior and exterior, lack of fixed furniture, all represent shared characteristics that lend an underlying unity to Japan's pre-industrial architectural traditions.

Within this larger frame, one must now read the multiple aesthetic attitudes of Japanese architecture that have surfaced over time.[20] For instance, a "primitivist" attitude is evident in the early Shinto shrines of Japan, and later in the Soans as well as the Katsura Villa (fig. 1.23). Rustic, rural but not raw, the aesthetic expressions of Ise or Izumo stem from exposed timber, thick thatched roofs with refined touches of formal decoration.

A "structuralist" attitude is evident in the early works of the Asuka and the Tempyo eras. Here a masculine aesthetic of colossal exposed and uncoated timber elements–columns, beams, brackets and eventually the framework of the gigantic roof dominates the architecture. It is through their extraordinary size, scale and structural poetics as seen at Todai-ji's Daibutsuden, Nandai-mon and Shosoin that one encounters an architectural structuralism parallel to the great Gothic cathedrals of the West.

A "chromatic" attitude, wherein the building is dominated by a single saturated color, and appreciated as a pictoral contrast to a natural background is seen in the unmistakable redness of the Fushima Inari Tiasha, the Itsukushima shrine, the gilded profile of Kinkaku-ji, and the white plaster of the Hime-ji castle.

The Zen influenced "austere" attitude is evidenced in the shoin interiors, where there is tendency for subdued monochromes, empty surfaces, and abstract forms and compositions.

Figure 1.25 Details of karamon gate at Nishi Honganji Temple, Kyoto.

An "eclectic" attitude dominates the rich baroque of the Nikko and Gokogu shrine, or the splendor of Nishi Honganji's "Cloud Pavilion" that combines "the aristocratic shoin style with the rustic thatched hut style to create the sukiya style" or the Kabuki architecture of the Edo era.[21] Here traditional canon is amalgamated with playful grafts, ornaments and filigrees bringing about an air of wit and personalization into the reading (fig. 1.24, 1.25).

What this ultimately suggests is that while it seems like Japan secluded itself from the outside world, and even found it expedient to withdraw into this natural sequestered state, in reality, it did not shut itself off completely. "Japanese ships ranged widely, bringing back trade and new goods, ideas, arts, and techniques from many countries" even as Japan remained closed to other cultures.[22] This "semi-seclusionism" was intrinsic to its traditional architectural complexity within a larger identifiable set of thematics. It was this complexity that Bruno Taut's influential proclamation on Ise and Katsura skewed at large. And not until the eighties would this simplistic stance meet with its appropriate rebuttal, largely from architects who were transcending their Modernist training, and rediscovering the rich, expressive decorative aesthetic running through the Azuchi-Momoyama and Edo-period castles, through the shoin style, to the extravagancies of Kabuki theater and the Toshogu mausoleum in Nikko. As Kisho Kurokawa noted, "These hallmarks of decorativism are not anomalies, idiosyncratic flashes of color against a monochrome ground. In fact when one looks for this decorative aesthetic in Katsura and Ise, it is there to be found – if we have the eyes to see it."[23] The complexity of Japanese architecture was being increasingly noticed beyond Ise and Katsura, debunking after five decades, its simplistic monochromatic perception with a complex and contradictory one. It is this complexity that we shall delve into deeper in the chapters that follow.

Years ago, I walked along the pond of the Byodo-in Temple in Uji, across Amida Buddha's Paradise on the other bank. There is a magical moment when you see the golden face of the meditating Buddha through the circular window in the hall's front screen. When I visited Byodo-in in 2013, the hall was caged in scaffolds. It has been under repair since September 2012, scheduled to be completed in 2014.

I had to catch up with Amida Buddha at Kotoku-in, in Kamakura where there is no hall to be caged. The original statue was made of wood and sheltered in a temple, but both were destroyed by a storm in 1248. It was recast in metal, covered in gold leaf and sheltered in a new hall. That hall was destroyed in 1334, rebuilt, damaged again in 1369, rebuilt yet again, and washed away in the tsunami of 1498. Since then Amida has meditated in the open air. As I caught a faint glint of his last remaining golden skin near his sagging ears, I recalled some lines from Rudyard Kipling's "Buddha at Kamakura:"

"A tourist-show, a legend told,
A rusting bulk of bronze and gold,
So much, and scarce so much, ye hold
The meaning of Kamakura?

But when the morning prayer is prayed,
Think, ere ye pass to strife and trade,
Is God in human image made
No nearer than Kamakura?

Close-up of Buddha statue in Kamakura.

Kiyomizu Temple Pagoda.

Chapter 2
Behind the Culture of Wood

I t is not easy to rationalize Japan's traditional choice of timber as a building material. Anyone who has seen Japan's ancient burial mounts or pit dwellings can attest to their primordial rendezvous with earth construction. Anyone who has noted the construction precision at the base of its nine surviving *donjons* (castles) can affirm their knowledge and skill of building with stone (fig. 2.1). The magnificent white castles soaring above these massive plinths, however, are made not of stone but wood. The Japanese chose for their dwellings, temples, and even their bulwarks of defense, a building material that was less resistant and more vulnerable to the perils of fires and natural disasters. Stone and earth, better suited to mediate the climatic extremes of humid summers and dry winters was ignored.

Justifiably, the comparative lightness of a timber building did make it less damaging within Japan's seismic climate. Other cultures have also pursued similar wisdoms. The Anasazi in the American southwest for instance built their dwellings with heavy earth walls to keep away the heat and cold but always had a light wooden roof that could be easily reconstructed after its collapse due to snow. Also as Jared Diamond has pointed out, Japan has high rainfall, and high fallout of soil-replenishing volcanic ash nurturing rapid tree growth. Its natural wildlife had no goats or sheep whose grazing activities have devastated forest landscaped in other cultures. The abundance of seafood also relieved pressure on forests as sources of both food and fertilizer.[1] Japan's incredible culture of wood must therefore also be understood within its geographical and environmental advantages.

Even so, the Japanese obsession with an impermanent building material and their willful acceptance of the recurrent damage to timber construction wrought through fires and typhoons seems counterintuitive to other cultures that have always sought to build for permanence. Thanks to this, there is no traditional building standing in Japan today that has not been rebuilt. The idea of monuments, communities, indeed entire cities being recurrently destroyed and built again seems not only unsustainable but irrational by today's standards. Even as late as the Edo period, when the great Kyoto fire of 1781 destroyed the Imperial Palace yet again, the eleventh Shogun, simply ordered its reconstruction on an even grander scale, only to be burnt again in 1854 and replicated to its current form. And when the Shogunate mandated Edoites to use clay tiles on roofs as a protection against fire,

Figure 2.1 Top: Details of stone base at Osaka Castle.

Figure 2.2 Opposite page left: Shinnyo-do Temple pagoda, Kyoto. Right: Hoki-ji Temple pagoda, Kyoto.

they responded by covering only the visible portions of their dwellings, leaving their cheaply built townhouses to be burnt by the next disaster.

The philosophical underpinnings nurturing Japan's timber architecture then are unique in human history. They genuinely embrace the sentient materiality of wood, accepting cyclic renewal as a natural activity in the making of the built environment. Wood is a material that lives and dies. This explains the Japanese resistance to nails, so as to not hurt wood or wooden components, as well as their willful acceptance to timber's decay through natural processes. Even today, in both the cyclic rebuilding rituals of many of its shrines, as well as the periodic preservation of its wooden monuments, Japan's remarkable culture of wood forms an important part of the larger dialog on its contemporary built condition. In this chapter, we go behind the scenes of this timber culture, and reflect on the multifaceted forces that shaped it. What was the sense and sensibility behind this culture of wood? What did it take to build these colossal timber buildings? How did Japan sustain this culture for a thousand years? What is the price it has paid for it? And what is its place and presence today?

STRUCTURE: COLUMN & BRACKET

In his 1893 essay "Horyu-ji Kenchiku Ron" (On the Architecture of Horyu-ji), Chuta Ito famously speculated that the entasis, that is, the slightly convex curve given to a column to correct the illusion of concavity produced by a straight shaft, in the wooden columns of the Horyu-ji Temple in Nara, one of Japan's oldest monumental buildings, had originated in Greece.[2] Whether this is true or not, one cannot help but compare the scale and size of timber members of Japanese temples with their Hellenistic stone counterparts. The monumental structuralism of Japan's Buddhist temples, dominant from the sixth to the twelfth centuries deserve special attention and what stands out here is the timber pillar—the structural core of traditional Japanese architecture and the symbolic epitome of its rituals of ancient tree worship.

The pagoda for instance has a single central column resting on a stone foundation with other wooden elements cantilevered from it. Thus despite introducing

a completely new vertical paradigm in Japanese architecture, the pagoda was based on the same structural concept as its predecessors. The earliest wooden buildings in Japanese history were the thatched dwellings of the Yayoi era (circa 300 BCE – 300 CE) characterized by a tent like timber roof covering a circular pit. These dwellings rested on a central row of pillars loosely embedded into the earth, creating a hinge joint to provide flexibility and stability during an earthquake. This idea conceptually appears to have persisted through the evolution of Japanese architecture: *minka* (farmhouses) and *machiya* (townhouses) were typically constructed with a main pillar called *daikokubashira* at the center of the building supporting most of the roof weight. This pillar held the status of an object of worship as the dwelling place of the God of the household. Even today in old households, children are not allowed to lean against the central pillar and on New Year's day, it is decorated with pine fronds and a straw rope and revered with offerings of *sake* (rice wine) and *mochi* (pounded rice) (fig. 2.2).

The massive scale of Japanese temples also reveals the architectural shift through the advent of the timber bracket. With this Chinese import, buildings could now become larger objects with longer spans and spaces. The evolution and stylistic diversities of the bracket is an elaborate discussion in itself but fundamentally a bracket complex, *kumimono* or *tokyo*, was made of two basic parts—the bearing block *masu* and the bracket arm *hijiki*.[3] The bearing block, a square or rectangular cube beveled at the bottom, could be set directly into a column to become a *daito* (large block) or on a bracket arm to become a *makito* (small block). The outward support of the bracket complex was provided by bracket arms typically beveled at their projecting ends. The entire network directly supported the purlins above. Here was the ingenuity of pure wooden joinery devoid of any nails thereby creating a looser hinge connection to absorb shocks during earthquakes. Just as the buttress represented for Gothic architecture the aesthetic outcome of a structural intention, enabling the walls to have larger punctures, the timber bracket could be thought of as the Japanese equivalent, enabling the roof eaves to stretch beyond the vertical columns (fig. 2.3).

Figure 2.3 Timber bracket details. Clockwise from top left:
Todai-ji Daibutsuden Precinct, Todai-ji Daibutsuden, Hoto-ji
Temple, Ohara Shoin-in.

Figure 2.4 Opposite page: Todai-ji Daibutsuden ceiling.

AESTHETICS: LIGHTNESS & RUSTICITY

The lightness of a chopstick is peculiar to Japan and could be compared to the lightness of the *shoji* screen. There are chopsticks in other cultures, but they are heavier, made of ivory, silver or other metal; there are sliding doors in many cultures, but the ability to slide a door with the tip of a finger is unique to Japan. The evolution of the shoji began in the early Nara period when boards were used as room dividers with the addition of thick opaque paper. Gradually this paper began to get increasingly translucent and evolved into the shoji with *washi* (rice paper) stretched across a grid of wooden pieces. The aesthetic of the shoji stems as much from its distinctive lattice as its perceived softness. It is the aesthetic antithesis of the colossal structuralism of Japanese temples.

While many of these early temple forms were fundamentally derived from Chinese examples, there were recurrent refinements and shifts that gradually made them distinctly Japanese – an elaboration on the theme of the foreign and the native. One such feature that deserves particular mention is the *noyane* or "hidden roof" because it had a significant impact on the aesthetic and spatial experience of a temple interior, and also took temple architecture beyond its Chinese predecessors.[4] Before its introduction around the tenth century, it had been impossible to build wide spaces without having a steep drop in the roof rafter angle over the building's peripheral sections. The hidden roof made it possible for the pitch of the roof underside to be independent of the exterior, allowing gently inclined exposed rafters along the periphery, thereby eliminating heavy shadows and enhancing the horizontality and repose of the exterior spaces (fig. 2.4).

The architecture of the tea huts in the Momoyama era (1573-1603) brings another aesthetic dimension in putting a premium on the rusticity and the beauty of knots in the wood, with materials chosen scrupulously on a discriminating aesthetic sensibility. Such an approach probably took its origins from the aesthetics of modest timber huts, evolving unique standards that allowed natural characteristics such as bark and crude surfaces to be used. In some instances, the wood employed in tea rooms came from a variety of trees, including Japanese cedar, red pine, chestnut and bamboo, due to which a process of coloring was employed where the wood sections

of the building were coated with a pigment mixed from a red cosmetic resin called *ni* and soot–so that the wood became nearly black while simultaneously the knots and other natural features in the wood remained visible (fig. 2.5).

PEOPLE: THE WORLD OF THE SHOKUNIN

The lives and methods of the *shokunin*, the craftsmen who built the colossal timber temples and shrines is best seen through illustrations on folding screens, woodblock prints and picture scrolls, and they reveal many significant subtexts in understanding Japan's timber culture. For instance, in the eighth through the twelfth centuries, lumber was split with a wedge and then smoothed with an *adze* and a long-blade plane, but began to get sawed in the Heian Era, making it easier to make thin planks and delicate wooden components. As the medieval age wore on, the scarcity of massive lumber necessitated the use of smaller trees, in turn contributing to the development of new tools and methods, for instance the *oga* (two-man saw) that operated vertically, allowing much thinner planks. The Japanese architectural expressionism of various periods can thus also be understood through the lens of the shokunin, and their evolving innovations and advances in carpentry (fig. 2.6).

As seen in the Ishiyamadera Engi (Picture Scroll of the Legends of the Ishi-yamadera Temple), lumber was brought to the site in ox carts. Large planks were pulled by men using rope and rolling logs. In Kuwakata Keisai's Shokunin Zukushi E (Pictures of Tradesmen) painted in 1804, we see wood carvers producing delicately rendered floral patterned panels for a shrine, plasterers kneading clay into balls and tossing them to others who flatten them against the walls with trowels, and tatami-makers weaving straw mats and sewing the decorative strips on the sides. With few tools surviving to this day, the Wakan Sansai Zu E (Sino-Japanese Illustrated Encyclopedia), dating circa 1713, is now an invaluable source in this regard, with pictures of contemporary carpenter tools and explanations.[5]

The shokunin always worked under the leadership of an appointed project leader, and in the case of many a temple, these figures were monks. One can attribute the massive scale of Todai-ji, the largest timber building in the world in its time, to the monk Shunjobo Chogen, just as the Eiheiji Temple in present Fukui

Figure 2.5 Opposite page: Interior of Ryogen-in Tea House.

Figure 2.6 Top: Roof details of Himukai Dajingu. Bottom: Toji Temple Main Hall.

prefecture to Eihei Dogen. If the shokunin were the hands that manifested the building, then it was these leaders who laid out the political and economic strategies necessary to enable the inner workings of these massive operations. Not unlike Ross King's descriptions of the construction of Brunelleschi's Duomo in Florence, it was not just about the construction of the building, but the seeking of the materials, the props for their transportation, and more importantly, the political navigation in obtaining them.[6]

Figure 2.7 Todai-ji Temple. Top: Daibutsuden. Opposite page: Details of Nandaimon.

POLITICS: CHOGEN & TODAI-JI'S DAIBUTSUDEN

Arata Isozaki's essays on Chogen's reconstruction of the Todai-ji daibutsuden reveals several lesser known behind the scenes aspects on what it took to build such colossal timber temples.[7] In 1180, a sixty year-old Chogen visited the burned down Taodai-ji daibutsuden and took up the role of fundraiser and construction commissioner for its rebuilding. Todai-ji was the largest wooden building of its time; each of its columns was around 1.5 meters in diameter and per the Chinese Sung principles upon which its architecture was based, each column had to be a single tree trunk. Further the maximum horizontal beam length was a thirty meter span (fig. 2.7). The daibutsuden's remaking would thus not only take significant material, but also the political savvy to make it happen in times of civil disturbance and war.

Chogen soon realized that the sizes of the timber logs needed for this building were no longer available in the Yoshino hinterlands that had originally supplied wood for the temple. Such timber reserves were now only available at the Ise shrine, that was then preparing for its own periodic reconstruction. Subsequently, Chogen devised a political strategy to "syncretise the people's worship of Ise with that of Todai-ji in support of his reconstruction."[8] He gathered an aggregation of sixty

Figure 2.8 Top: Kiyomizu Temple, Kyoto. Opposite page: Detail of timber supports holding up one of the temple decks.

monks to formally offer a new hand-copied text of the Mahaprajnaparamita Sutra (Sutra of Great Wisdom) to the revered Shinto shrine with hopes of winning their favor. But while this choreographed pilgrimage received tremendous public attention, Chogen's failed to win Ise's timber reserves.

But Chogen had a backup plan. He bought the Suo timberlands (today in Yamamguchi prefecture). The challenge now was to transport the colossal trees from the mountainside to the city of Nara. Water seemed the best means of transportation: The trees "were flushed down the Sawa River for about thirty kilometers, transported by raft via the Set Inland Sea to the mouth of the Yodo River near Osaka, then guided upstream along the Kizu River, and finally delivered overland through the Narazaka highlands."[9] Records claim that more than a hundred temporary dams were constructed along the Sawa River, strong hemp rope was secured from across the country to aid in transportation, and a special roller called *rokuro* was invented to help the thousands of men move the hundreds of logs to the site.

It is now known through excavation that Chogen reused the original column foundations of the daibutsuden whilst enlarging its original span of seven by three bays, to eleven (twelve columns) by seven (eight columns) bays. Chogen could have taken a far more convenient route. Like the Edo builders in the eighteenth century – when large trees were no longer available–he could have chosen to laminate pillars with metallic bands or conversely retain the original building size and spans. He was no architect, but as manager of his carpenter team, he had the discretion to decide the model for the new building. Knowing all the inherent challenges, he instructed his team to build per the Sung tectonic that enabled the significant enlargement of the temple. Chogen's accomplishment at the Todai-ji daibutsiden therefore was not so much in his aggrandizement of one of the largest structures of his time, but his political savvy and unswerving determination to see the project complete without any apparent personal gain.

CRISIS: DEPLETION & REFORESTATION

The Japanese attitude to wood, their Shinto love for nature, Buddhist idea of transience, and zeal for renewal and rebuilding does not necessarily paint the prettiest

of pictures. It is unimaginable to estimate the sheer amount of forest that must have supplied timber for these great architectural endeavors (fig. 2.8). Timber was needed not just for construction and reconstruction, but for heating houses, cooking, industrial uses such as making salt, tiles and ceramics, smelting iron, and transporting timber through ships themselves built of wood. In his book "Collapse", Jared Diamond has provided a detailed account of the lesser known timber crisis and its aversion during the Tokugawa Era (1603 – 1867), when a number of Tokugawa shoguns kept the country free of war and outside influence.[10] Peace and prosperity had resulted in a population and economic explosion and a consequent building frenzy. By 1720, Edo was the most populous city in the world. Beginning in the late Muromachi era around 1570, the various *diamyos* seeking to impress each other through the size of their temples and castles led the way to as many as 200 castle towns and cities built under Hideyoshi, Ieyasu and the succeeding Shogun.

But "just the three biggest castles built by Ieyasu required clear-cutting about 10 square miles of forests."[11] In 1582–to compensate for the timber scarcity in his own domains – Hideyoshi is known to have demanded it from all over Japan taking control of various daimyo forests and private lands, and spreading logging over Japan's three main islands. The years from about 1570 to 1650 marked the peak of the construction boom and consequently that of deforestation. By 1710 the most accessible forests on Japan's three main islands (Honshu, Shikkoku and Kyushu) had been destroyed, with old-growth forest surviving only on steep slopes or areas inaccessible for Tokugawa era logging. With wildfires, soil erosion, snow-melt, flooding and earthquakes consequently on the rise; and with simultaneously increasing disputes amongst villages over timber, fuel, and the use of rivers, deforestation had begun to hurt Tokugawa Japan.

The 1657 Meireki fire that consumed half of the Edo capital and some 100,000 lives exposed Japan's depleting timber supply. Consequently, amidst an urban population explosion, the next two centuries saw a multitude of policy shifts in limiting timber consumption and accumulating reserves to avert a grave crisis: There was an increased reliance on sea food, a near zero-population growth between 1721 and 1828, and the replacing of wood fuel with coal in the 17th century. There were top-down woodland management policies – from detailed forest inventories, strin-

Figure 2.9 Top: Okihiki-zome-shiki is a ceremony to transport timber logs to the Ise Geku for the shikinen sengu. This photograph was taken at the 62nd sengu in 2013. Yakugi log for the Okihiki-zome-shiki ritual at the Betsugu Taka-no-miya Sanctuary of Toyoukedaijingu at the Ise Geku. This photograph was taken at the 62nd sengu in 2013.

gent timber shipment monitoring, laws limiting the amount of timber to be used in buildings and products, and the rigorous promulgation of silviculture since the 1600's. The Tokugawa Shoguns had gradually developed a method of plantation forestry on a national scale to solve a crisis in which they ironically had played one of the biggest roles. With plantation and forestry becoming widespread between 1750 and 1800, by the early nineteenth century, Japan's long decline in timber production had been reversed.[12]

A more recent parallel to such visionary policies is the forest regeneration efforts by outstanding Japanese scholars using the most advanced global forestation practices. The lush forest of the Meiji Jingu, one of the few remaining natural forests set against the backdrop of Tokyo's skyscrapers was created by 110,000 volunteers who planted more than 100,000 donated trees in 1920. The site, barren eighty years ago, has been transformed into a man-made woodland reviving the Japanese idea of the divinity of trees. The forest has since flourished due to its association with the revered shrine.

SHIFTS & ADAPTATIONS: BEHIND THE SHINKINEN SENGU

How has Japan adapted to such crises and to what degree have they shifted the core values of the culture? The various *Sengu*, or cyclic reconstructions at several Shinto shrines across Japan are the best optic to discuss this question. Such reconstructions symbolize a reverence to the deity by cleansing his/her household, but they must also be read as the pragmatic need to intermittently maintain and renew parts of a timber building or complex. Of these, the shikinen sengu, the 1300 year-old reconstruction ritual of the two Ise Shrine complexes, the Geku and Naiku, every twenty years is by far the most elaborate, and therefore the focus of discussion here. Some thirty-five rituals are enacted during this elaborate construction, with workers in white garbs reconstructing over sixty structures (fig. 2.9).[13]

Originally, the trees needed to reconstruct Ise's shrines were available within their surrounding forests called Jingu Birin. The forests had specific areas with trees labeled for use in specific parts of the shrine's re-building. Today, the forest has become a National State Forest and occupies a quarter of the city of Ise with an

area of 5500 hectares. It has three areas: The first is the 1000-hectare scenic forest visible from the path to the shrines that is carefully maintained and controlled. The second is the 93-hectare historic forest from the Muromachi Period (circa 1300 CE), where fallen trees from the 1970 Ise Taihu (hurricane) remain untouched. The third is the 4400-hectare area reserved exclusively for the reconstruction of the Ise Shrine every twenty years. Here, bombing, wars and industrialization have lowered soil quality, and the tree-yield is now far lower both in quantity and quality. Much of the Sengu's timber supply – some 14,000 pieces of timber and 25,000 sheaves of miscanthus reeds–now comes from distant forests, transported by trucks, and needing significant infrastructure and cost.[14] The larger environmental context framing the Ise Sengu has thus significantly changed (fig. 2.10).

Simultaneously, contrary to popular perception, there are significant differences between the original shikinen sengu and the one we see today. Originally, most of the shrines besides the Geku and the Naiku were rebuilt with recycled timbers from the previous sengu. Workers besides carpenters helped with various construction related processes, and locals living near the shrines were also required to participate. Thus the number of shrines rebuilt with new timber was less than what it is today. This new timber was cut from the preserved forest directly surrounding the shrines, and the high quality of timber took only four years to stain instead of the eight years it does today. The duration of the sengu was thus much shorter. Today, select timbers of Ise's dismantled shrines are reused in parts of other contracted Shinto shrines around Japan. The sengu, meanwhile, has added sixteen more shrines to the previous list of the two main and fourteen other reconstructed shrines, bringing the total to over sixty structures, including gates, bridges, and storage spaces, with the total building reconstruction taking over eight years.[15]

Further, while traditional hand tools continue to give final shape and finish to the shrine parts, the carpenters use electric saws and sanders for rough work within the work yards (though never within the sacred sites.) This hybridization saves the shrine significant money while not violating the authentic eventual look of the shrine. And since even the minutest dent on the shrine made by a falling object is considered a defilement necessitating the piece of wood to be replaced, the shrine has opted to have its suyane, the traditional temporary shed over the construction

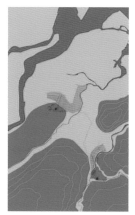
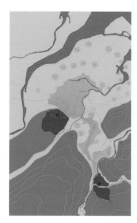
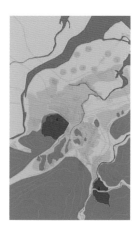

Figure 2.10 Diagrammatic analysis of forest depletion around the Ise Shrine. The grey shows the increasing habitat footprint. The dark green indicates the boundaries of the now preserved forests around the shrines. Opposite page: Forest path within the Ise Naiku precinct.

site, to be made of prefabricated modern materials for better protection of both the building and the workers during the shrine's disassembly.

Meanwhile, bigger changes have happened at other shrines. The Izumo Shrine has a similar ritual called the shikinen senza, performed once every sixty years. But here, reconstruction is limited to only a few shrines rather than the entire complex. As noted in Chapter 1, the main shrine was originally lifted high off the ground with gigantic wooden columns. Today, the shrine structure is much smaller, its columns are slimmer and shorter, and it sits closer to the ground.[16] At the Katori shrine, the shikinen senza is performed every thirty years with the reconstruction limited to mainly the roof structure, and many other Shinto shrines have in fact stopped the ritual of shikinen senza altogether. At the Osaki shrine, the structural material for the shrine's renovation has been changed to Beech, Japanese Judas, and Japanese Chestnut, with proximate land reserved to grow these trees. And the rituals have been opened to the public to enhance cultural education.[17] All these changes are responses and adaptations to the timber production availability of our time.

This crisis of timber seen at Ise is at once ironic and laudatory. It holds on to an ancient tradition with neither its original symbiotic sacred, social and environmental interrelationships, nor a decisive strategy towards adaptation for a new time. During the Meiji era, there were discussions over timber deficiencies leading to propositions for changes in the Ise sengu such as a concrete foundation that could expand the shrine's lifespan. The emperor however denied such suggestions, and the construction method and amount of timber is still the same as in the past, incurring an enormous amount of cost. After the early Meiji's Restoration policy, the government in fact planted more trees to preserve the Ise forest for the succeeding sengus, but until today, this has not been successful. There are concerns about the future of the shikinen sengu because timber production within Japan has been decreasing on the whole, with few remaining preserves able to produce the vast amounts of cypress used as the main structural material for the shrines.

CONCLUSION

Long shielded from any exterior influence – save its early Chinese precedents – Japan's timber architecture was an insulated cultural phenomenon, whose epochs and accomplishments were only as great as its repeated destruction. Seen from a chronological standpoint, it was also arguably a relatively lethargic phenomenon. Unlike European stone construction that transformed from the Roman arch, to the Gothic vault and buttress to Brunalleschi's vertical ribs and double dome at the Duomo, in Japan, there was little tectonic or structural innovation after the great Buddhist temples had mastered the timber column and bracket. Much of what followed was a variation on that theme, with architecture remaining largely preoccupied with spatial and aesthetic concerns. One exception to this, the donjon (castle) elevated the timber edifice over a stone base, and introduced the use of plaster for fire protection, and this idea was adapted to other succeeding monuments or habitats. Whether a cultural lethargy, or a blindfolded adherence to ancient cultural bents, the Japanese seemed resigned to accept the continuous destruction and rebuilding of timber architecture for centuries to follow.

Japan's timber culture lives on through the ongoing preservation of its numerous monuments. The Amida-do, the main hall at the famous Byodo-in temple in Uji is currently caged in scaffolding and a temporary roof, and under repair till March 2014. At the Kiyomizu Temple, the Koyasu-no-to pagoda just completed an overhaul in March, 2013, regaining its original color, and temple authorities, expecting the need to rebuild the main hall in the distant future, have already begun planting trees (fig. 2.11).[18] But simultaneously, an objective assessment of Japan's traditional timber culture raises many complex questions. In a time when Modern build-and-scrap practices pose a global threat to the environment, one can argue that components of demolished wooden buildings should resurrect themselves through reuse in their modern counterparts. Or that the contemporary Japanese wooden structure must redefine itself with concrete foundations, and substitute the tradition of joinery with less skill-demanding connections, with its structural distribution relying more on the rigidity of its outer faces than a single pillar at its core. One can argue, in turn, that the continuity of Japan's timber traditions might

Figure 2.11 Koyasu Pagoda at the Kiyomizu Temple, Kyoto, during and after restoration.

be more through process than product; that contemporary building techniques such as exposed concrete–a popular tendency in Post-Modern Japan–relies heavily on a similarly meticulous precision for the formwork to ensure the aesthetic uniformity of the eventual surface, thereby keeping the culture alive. But then, with modern construction workers using power tools, there is, particularly for those that treasure Japan's authentic traditions, the apparent danger that modern labor and cost efficiency can undermine that contemplative and patient process integral to the refined timber culture of Japan's past.

The story of Japanese timber culture then remains a contradictory one: If its Shinto reverence for nature offers a reading of spirituality and sublimation, then the Shogunal megalomania of depleting entire forests reveals another extreme. One cannot afford to dismiss the deep-rooted philosophical dimensions or the master carpentry that gave us the magnificent daibutsuden at Todai-ji, or the delicate Shokin Tei tea hut. But at the same time, one must also remain unapologetic towards reading this culture's environmentally destructive and eventually impractical dimensions. They in particular, can serve as cautionary barometers towards assessing Japan's post-industrial condition.

The Cha-no-yu (Tea Ceremony) is special when performed in the night hours. There is something about the combination of wet moss, cricket cries, moonlight and bitter tea that transcends words. When Mrs. Matsuoka, the Zen priestess who hosted me, finished the ceremony, I was overcome with emotion, because it was my last night at her house. The following morning I would catch the Shinkansen from Shizuoka to Tokyo.

I sat past midnight talking with her daughter. She is a trained calligrapher, so I could not help but request that she paint me a scroll, a message, a memory I could take. I did not sleep much that night. The smells of tatami and the sound of trickling water seemed all the more special. Tomorrow, I would be back amidst the fierce lights of something called Tokyo.

Early next morning, Mika handed me the scroll half way down the wooden stairway. Due to my over-emotional goodbyes, we missed the first train, so I got to spend a little more time with her before I caught the next one. I was impatient to see the scroll, but it was too delicate for a quick unroll. Throughout the two-hour train ride, and then a cab ride to the hotel, it was the only thing on my mind. What was the message? I finally opened it in my hotel room. On a five feet long white paper were a few simple brush strokes in black ink. They said "Patience."

Chan-no-yu: tea and a sweet snack.

Dry garden at Ginkaku-ji Temple, Kyoto.

Chapter 3
A View from the Zen Shoin

Circa 1191 CE Japan adopted Zen from Chinese Chan, a form of Mahayana Buddhism characterized by its rejection of temporal and scriptural authority, refusal to commit itself to words and emphasis on moral character. It taught self- discipline and meditation as a means to *satori* or enlightenment, not as the ultimate goal of a life-long journey, but as a sudden flash of revelation that could come anytime, any-where, even during the most mundane of acts.[1] This entry of Zen was welcomed by the shogun and samurai alike. Its emphasis on spiritual discipline and intuitive understanding appealed to the warrior mind. Amidst the tumultuous Kamakura (1190 – 1340 CE) and Muromachi (1340–1570 CE) eras plagued by internal conflicts and civil wars, the political power had passed from the shoguns to the samurais, shifting the focus of cultural life from palaces to the samurai residences and Zen monasteries they sponsored. Architecture affected in its scale and social function now transformed from the shinden-zukuri residential paradigm of the Heian palace with its symmetrical buildings, ceremonial courts and central ponds, to the new image of the Zen temple.

The architecture of the Zen temple was like its predecessor, the Great Buddha style, developed in Sung China, yet quite different in design. The complex was generally axial in plan and roughly bilaterally symmetrical, reflecting the regimentation of a Zen monk's daily life. Core architectural components such as the entrance gate, lotus pond, main gate, Buddha hall, lecture hall, bathhouse and toilet were strictly aligned along a north-south axis, surrounded in less disciplined arrangement by numerous autonomous sub-temples. These sub-temples were separated from each other as well as the main temple by court-yards with high walls and it was in these enclosed courtyards that both Japanese interior and landscape architecture were to find new architectural paradigms (fig. 3.1). The interior of the room began to be designed as a *shoin* (writing room) gradually crystallizing its predecessor, the Kamakura era *kaisho* (Assembly Hall for festivities and gatherings) into the shoin-style of architecture. The *tsuke-shoin* (a low wooden desk built into an alcove with a window) now became the central feature of the monastic interior along with the *tokonoma* (alcove), the *chigaidana* (built-in shelves), the *chodaigamae* (painted sliding doors), the *fusuma* (opaque room to room partitions), and the *shoji* (latticed outdoor to indoor partitions) (fig. 3.2). Beyond these sliding partitions was an *engawa* (verandah) that overlooked an enclosed garden that perpetually accompanied the room.

Figure 3.1 Top right: Painting of Tofuku-ji complex showing various sub-temple clusters with their courtyards.

Figure 3.2 Opposite page: A shoin interior in the Kodai-ji Temple, Kyoto.

These gardens adjoining a *hojo* (abbot's residence) or *kyakuden* (guest hall) were also radical departures from their Heian predecessors. Their ponds were not meant for boating, and their paths were not meant for walking. Large or small, virtually inaccessible by foot, they were created exclusively for contemplation from a fixed set of vantage points. Designed to relate to their adjoining rooms inasmuch as the interiors were to frame garden views, their landscapes–from representations of natural sceneries, to entirely dry compositions of rocks and sand–though employing the same natural materials as before, increasingly "abridged nature almost to the point of abstraction", like a painting seeking to "imitate the inner essence of nature, not its outward forms."[2]

These Zen monastic gardens are arguably the most peculiar, if not the most significant of all landscape prototypes Japan has produced. They incepted the Japanese garden's departure from its Chinese influenced predecessors and paved the way for new Japanese garden ideologies to follow. These gardens deserve a closer look also because the means and methods of experiencing these abstract landscapes offer us glimpses into the profundity of Zen. My interest in this chapter is not to delve into the history of these landscapes, but to reflect on how they have been experienced, how they are meant to be experienced, or in turn how they elicit certain experiences. These experiences, I would posit, offer us alternative interpretations of reality, alternative engagements with the physical world, and alternative prisms to assess our own states of mind. This is why these landscapes remain as relevant today as they were then.

SITTING ZEN

The static experience of a shoin garden, in that it is perceived through absolute stillness from a single vantage point, is nothing new to practitioners of the Zen meditation technique of Zazen. During such an act, one sits motionless (Za implies sitting without moving, like a mountain) often facing a wall, the pelvis tipped forward, the knees pushed against the floor, and the spinal column straightened. This visual dissociation from the surroundings is said to bring about an interior revolution, a deep wisdom whose essence is unattainable through logical thought alone. The visual experience of many shoin gardens is in this sense a kind of Zazen, the meditation platform replaced by an engawa, and the frontal wall replaced by a natural mural.

The *karesansui* (dry garden) of the Ryoanji Temple (1499) sits in a rectangular yard about 248 square meters enclosed by a mud wall[3] (fig. 3.3). There is no water within the confines of this enclosure, no plants, no trees and no flowers, nothing associated with a conventional garden save the abstract tranquility of dry sand and fifteen rocks of different sizes laid out in groups of 5,2,3,2 and 3 from east to west. They are per-ceived either individually or collectively always against the backdrop of the intermediate mud wall that separates the foreground from the trees beyond.

At Ryogen-in (1502), a sub temple of Daitoku-ji adjoining the abbot's residence are five gardens according a Zen view on all sides of the shoin: The Ryogintei located to the north has a continuous bed of moss with a stone arrangement; the Isshidan to the south has a bed of raked sand with rocks, one group within an oval moss island. The Nakaniwa to the east in turn is much smaller with raked sand and

Figure 3.3 Ryoan-ji dry garden, Kyoto.

Figure 3.4 Ryogen-in, a sub-temple
of Daitoku-ji Temple, Kyoto.
Opposite page: Isshidan Garden.
Bottom: Nakaniwa Garden.

rocks, and enclosed by a verandah on three sides as opposed to the others than can only have two. There are two other enclosed gardens to the south-east and west. The shoin thus becomes a transparent object floating within a larger outer frame, and the garden becomes a mural surrounding the room. The shoin can be opened to different gardens at different times of the day, or seasons, eliciting multiple frames for meditation (fig. 3.4).

There is an old Zen saying, "Don't just sit there. Sit there." It bears a connection to the very origins of Zen: One day the Buddha came late to his daily sermon, holding a white lotus in his hand. He sat looking at the flower, saying nothing. Even as his disciples gazed anxiously at each other, only one laughed out loud. The Buddha called him, and gave him the flower. The interpretation of this episode is one the foundations of Zen. Buddha was giving his greatest sermon that day, a sermon that was beyond words, and that sought to demonstrate the ultimate state of mind of being completely in the moment. Only one disciple understood its significance. The notion of sitting still in front of a Zen garden is not only about self-discipline, but about mental dissociation with everything else, save the few rocks, shrubs or raked sand that lie in front.

BORROWED SCENERIES

The idea of *shakkei* (borrowing scenery) is one of the most distinctive concepts of Japanese garden design. Here, the perceived limits of the enclosed garden are stretched far beyond its immediate boundaries to a distant natural or man-made feature of the geography. Using various devices–from stone lanterns and bridges to composing frames–such views are "humanized" and captured as integral parts of the garden. Shakkei was codified in the oldest extant Japanese garden manual, the eleventh century Sakuteiki ("Records of Garden Making"). Its origins are unclear, but the concept is probably Chinese, as the concept is found in the Chinese garden manual Yuanye.[4] Its earliest adoption in Japan is seen in the Tenryu-ji Temple garden in the Kamakura era drawing Mount Arashiyama into its composition. Whether as an augmenting device to the introverted confines of the shoin garden, or a reverence for the natural countryside, shakkei transforms the view from the shoin from intimacy to infinity.

Figure 3.5 Top: Shoin garden with Mount Hiei in the distance, Entsu-ji Temple, Kyoto.

Figure 3.6 Opposite page: Shoin garden with Mount Hiei in the distance, Shoden-ji Temple, Kyoto.

At the Entsu-ji Temple (1639) is a slightly tiered, oblong garden to the east of the temple's shoin. Here, Mount Hiei is captured using a technique of successive planes (fig. 3.5). A hedge forming the garden enclosure serves three purposes: as a backdrop for the rock composition; as a trim line to separate the garden from the numerous trees just beyond; and as the lower part of the frame that includes the distant mountain as a live backdrop. A thick wall of bamboo provides the middle plane forming the sides of the frame. Beyond the bamboo, some tall cypress and red pine trees from another green plane, their lower trimmed edges forming the upper part of the frame. The trees are then a link between the mountain and the middle ground of the garden and it is through their trunks that one views the breath-taking scenery. In the shoin of the Shoden-ji Temple (early 17th century), the linearity of a low white wall accentuates seven clusters of pruned shrubs against a foreground of raked sand and a background of Mt. Hiei. (fig. 3.6).[5] At Nanzen-ji (circa 1605), a composition of white sand with three large rocks and three small rocks is laid out close to the garden wall from east to west and are interspersed with two pine trees and evergreen shrubs, all viewed as a composition against the backdrop of the Daiorichi-san mountain.

The experience of such shoin gardens are in many ways parallel to the perception of Japanese landscape paintings. With no ground line to position the composing elements, distinct successive perceptual planes become the composing parameters forming foregrounds, middle-grounds and far walls, the viewer's eye leaping from one plane to another across space or void. As such the most significant architectural element of these gardens is its enclosing wall, fence, or hedge, defining the extent of the pictoral composition, filtering out visual unnecessities, creating the backdrop for the foreground, and delineating that which is near from that which is beyond. What this suggests is the importance of personal participation, in reading patiently step by step, the numerous details and visual offerings of the landscape. From a design standpoint, the technique of shakkei attests among other things to the meticulous site planning of the shoins. Building locations were determined not only per the terrain, but also per their relationship with distant features, natural or man-made, and most of these decisions must have been made directly on site.

SYMBOLIC LANDMARKS

There is more to the inclusion of a distant natural landscape in a shoin garden than its pure visual value. There are mythic and symbolic connotations that are far less comprehensible to non-Zen adherents. Many Zen temples are made up of a number of symbolic elements known variously as *jikyo* or *kochi* (liter-ally "ten stages"). They are landmarks impregnated with meaning and inherent components of a culturally appointed environment without which Zen temples and monasteries would not be a reality.

Tenryu-ji is the oldest Zen garden in Japan, designed by the Zen priest Muso Kokushi in 1339 on the premises of the former Kameyama palace. It has a two-tiered dry waterfall composed of imposing rocks, seen against the luxurious foliage of the opposite bank of the pond from the *daihojo* (abbot's living quarter) verandah. It is said to have had real water falling into the pond, but it is more reasonable to think that the waterfall was made dry from the beginning because the sounds of the Oi River running in Arashiyama, beyond the Kameyama Hills, could be heard in the garden in those days.[6] The point is that the backdrop to the stretch of white sand between the large daihojo and the Sogen-chi pond were the hills of Kameya-ma and Arashiyama, borrowed into the garden composition, without which its comprehension was incomplete (fig. 3.7).[7]

Of the ten such landmarks at Tenryu-ji, five are natural features. Of these, two are directly in the surrounding mountains: Nengerei (Mount Arashiyama's summit) and Banshodo (the pine forest on the Arashiyama's southern slopes), their names imparting a specific meaning to these environmental elements.[8] For instance, Mount Arashiyama was called Nengerei (literally "peak of the picked flower,") the name derived from the fable wherein the Buddha used a single flower as his teaching (discussed earlier).[9] It is claimed therefore that apart from the Sutras and Buddhist dogmas, the role played by jikyo as unwritten and unexplained teachings on the essence of Buddhism cannot be underestimated. This double coding of the surrounding natural landscape as symbols of esoteric teachings remains a consistent theme of many Zen temples–such as the *jikkei* (literally "ten scenes") of the Kennin-ji and the Sokoku-ji Temples, or the *fukei* (literally "landscapes") of Myoshin-ji. The

Figure 3.7 Top and bottom: Tenryu-ji Temple, Kyoto. Zen garden with Mount Arashiyama as backdrop.

garden and their mountains here are an integrated macrocosm, the very foundations upon which a Zen temple stands, both as establishments of Zen teaching and
academic learning.

Where mountains and valleys are not part of their natural surroundings, shoin
gardens have built artificial mountains within their confines by arranging rocks and
shrubs on a natural hillside. The garden of Tofuku-ji Temple's Fumon-in (early 17th
century) is an example of a *tsukiyama* (artificial hill) garden, wherein elements of the
dry landscape coexist with a profusion of shrubbery (fig. 3.8). In front of the Fumon-in building is a wide expanse of sand with a simple checkerboard pattern that
varies depending on the interweaving of the raked and unraked sand bands. To the
rear of the sand is a rising tsukiyama of manicured shrubs creating the effect of a
high mountain against the backdrop of trees. Typical of tsukiyama gardens, there is
a small, narrow pond at the foot of the artificial hill with a two-slab *yatsuhashi* bridge
and another single-slab stone bridge. The Chishaku-in Temple (late 17th century) is
also known for its re-fined tsukiyama with manicured shrubs and angular rocks rising high and close to its shoin, creating the impression of high mountains (fig. 3.9).
At the foot of the waterfall dissolving into the oblong pond along the foot of the
hill stands a *mizu-wakeishi* (stone that divides the water into two) this natural three-
slab stone bridge surrounded by an intricate configuration of shrubs and rocks.

GARDEN AS NARRATIVE

In contrast to the static perception of the shoin garden – where it was largely
about a frozen frontal view with a fixed line of sight – some gardens required the
viewer to read their composition as a sequence of events—like the unfolding of a
picture scroll. Here the summation of the various individual vignettes was as important as the autonomous parts, thereby bringing in a sense of motion into the
entire experience.

At the Daisen-in at Daitoku-ji Temple (1509), the significance of the karesansui
is not in its abstract com-position of rocks but in its symbolic narrative of nature.

Figure 3.8 Top: Tsukiyama (artificial hill) garden at Tofuku-ji Temple.

Figure 3.9 Middle and bottom: Tsukiyama (artificial hill) garden at Chishaku-in Temple.

Figure 3.10 Daisen-in dry gardens, Daitoku-si Temple, Kyoto.

Here, more than twenty rocks of various sizes, shapes and textures are packed in a small garden of less than 100 square meters to depict a landscape of mountains, a waterfall and a river (fig. 3.10). The water (represented by the white sand) starts deep in the mountains in the far distance (represented by camellia shrubs in the rear), making a waterfall in the valley to form rapids that wind and dash against the rocks. Two gigantic crags tower before the camellia shrubs, representing cliffs or mountains in the foreground. After passing a slab stone bridge, the rapids become deep water, emerging as a wide, serene river that passes under a corridor (the corridor represents an artistic abbreviation to depict the water all the way from its start to its eventual journey to the ocean). After safely traversing the stormy rapids and emerging into the open, tranquil sea, there is a large rock in the shape of a boat, called a *funa-ishi* headed for the ocean with a full load of treasures. Here rocks play the role of the hero symbolizing the austere, strong will of the seeker of truth, who resists and rejects things worldly and human.

In the Sakuteiki, the author considers man-made natural landscapes superior to natural ones. The rationale behind this intriguing statement is that man-made Japanese landscapes emulate only the best parts of nature weeding out all redundancies and distractions, and doing away with "meaningless stones and features."[10] In his book "Secret Teachings in the Art of Japanese Gardens," David A. Slawson has offered detailed elaborations on these techniques, stemming from his personal experiences as an apprentice in Japan. With meticulous diagrams that analyze the rock compositions of famous places, from Daisen-in to Nishi Hongan-ji, Slawson reveals how what appears to the common eye as relatively natural landscapes, is in fact exactly the opposite: a careful exercise in planar recession, depth and perspective.[11]

CONTRADICTION & DUALITY

There are shoin gardens that resist the idea of compositional narration and are dominated instead by two (or more) completely contrasting scenes meant to be viewed from two different angles from within the shoin interior. This perception in every sense devalues the impression of the garden as a continuous mural surrounding the shoin, and creates two autonomous vistas that if attempted to be viewed through the corner, created a perceptual tension.

Figure 3.11 Top: Hosen-in shoin
garden, Sanzen-in Temple, Kyoto.
Combined view of entire garden.

Figure 3.12 Right and bottom:
Autonomous views of the garden
through two walls of the shoin.

In his essay "Frontal Perception in Japanese Architectural Space", Gorge Ferras has elaborated on the shoin at the Hosen-in at the Sanzen-in Temple.[12] Two right angled walls of this shoin open into two contrasting views (fig. 3.11). Looking through the first wall, one sees a pine tree suggesting qualities of masculinity and strength. Looking through the other, one sees a grove of bamboo suggesting qualities of femininity and grace. Looking at the corner and viewing both together it is difficult to comprehend any garden-to-garden continuity. And since the walls of the shoin themselves are different in their composing elements, any attempt to view this garden as a continuous mural accentuates the tension. The landscape can either be perceived as autonomous views when one sits frontally towards a single wall and enjoys them one at a time, or as a conscious conflict, but never as a single continuous narrative surrounding the building (fig. 3.12).

Considering the meticulous attention Zen garden makers gave to their creations, it is not far-fetched to argue to that such contradictory compositions were conscious devices to enhance Zen meditation. Their inherent visual paradox is analogous to a Zen *koan*, a terse statement that defies rational explanation often given to Zen novices to meditate upon. The idea of accepting a paradox as the ultimate reality forms part of Zen philosophy, embracing the notion that if something appears true, it is only seemingly so, with its antipode also part of a larger reality.[13]

FROM SITTING ZEN TO WALKING ZEN – A VIEW FROM THE ROJI

The shoin gardens were Japan's first radical landscape design departures from its Chinese predecessors. The succeeding gardens of the Tea Ceremony were the second. In the Momoyama Era (1570-1616 CE), the need to keep Zen novices awake in monasteries during meditation sessions, among other things, brought in tea-drinking. This gradually evolved into an elaborate ritual called the Cha-no-yu, the Tea Ceremony, a spiritual art form that involved a host preparing tea for a guest, and that physically included a *roji* (tea garden) and a *chashitsu* (tea-room).[14] The Cha-no-yu thus offers an instructive comparative optic to further reflect on Zen gardens as well as understand the evolution of Zen spatial concepts in Japan.

Figure 3.13 Bottom: Kennin-ji Tea Garden and Hut, Kyoto.

Figure 3.14 Opposite page: Koto-in Tea Hut, Kyoto. Left: Detail of Lattice. Right: Interior.

Numerous books have elaborated in the architecture of the Tea Ceremony, which in itself bears an elaborate history.[15] To focus on the intention of this chapter, I will refrain from these specifics and describe the concepts broadly. It must be mentioned however that from Sen-no-Rikyu, to Kobori Enshu, the story of Tea Ceremony architecture, from its beginnings at the Todai-ji temple, to the various tea-room layouts, based for instance exclusively on the location of the hearth, testifies to the richness of this subject.[16] What I describe below is the larger themes than run through this diverse architecture; the threads that connect the traditional spatial conceptions of this ritual across Japanese history.

Quintessentially, the roji is a gathering of rocks, random stones, dewy ground, trickling water and moss covered stone lanterns, all surrounding the chashitsu. The garden is divided by a *chumon* (inner gate) or a *nakakaguri* (low gate) into two parts, a waiting area and the inner garden of the Tea Hut. Bending over through this low gate makes the transition into the world of tea. A fence usually encloses the entire precinct beyond which trees filter out the secular world and also shield the Tea Hut from direct view. As one advances in the roji, the space progressively becomes smaller sanctifying and preparing the visitor for the intimacy of the innermost space of the tea hut. (fig. 3.13).

The Tea Hut reveals the underlying theme of rusticity and refinement involving an inveterate use of natural materials to bring out their inherent aesthetic qualities. This theme is mainly summarized through two modes of expression, *sabi* and *wabi*. Sabi refers to individual objects and an environment generating a rustic imperfection. However when used in the context of Zen, sabi implies a state of total annihilation or absolute emptiness. To achieve this state of absolute void is the aim of every Zen Buddhist. The Tea Ceremony strives to cultivate this. On the other hand, Wabi implies quietness and tranquility, referring to a way of life associated with simplicity and minimalism. In the context of the Tea Ceremony, the approach to the hut is imperative to abet a wabi state of mind, when both host and guest must cast away all that is mundane and redundant so that the atmosphere of tea may be absorbed. This conscious notion of rustic simplicity is expressed in the architecture of the Tea Hut. For example, the lattices on the shoji windows are made not of wood but of split bamboo. The rice-paper panels making up the *shoji* may be pro-

EXPERIENTIAL SEQUENCE OF THE CHA-NO-YU

Outer Gate   Random Stones

tected on the exterior either by vertical bamboo grills, or by the wattle of the wall interior, all left exposed to enhance the rustic visual effect. The wooden baseboard of the decorative alcove may be carefully chosen for its knots, elevating the rusticity of the space. Then there is the preference for monochromes to bright colors not only in the walls but also the coarse pottery of the tea utensils, rather dull in color and imperfect in form (fig 3.14).

However, as Kisho Kurokawa has pointed out, this seemingly dull theme "is not a rejection of color"[17] and the aesthetic stereotype of the tea room, and by extension the quintessential Japanese aesthetic, is not one of a supposedly Zen minimalism. "The hidden lesson here is that only those who are already well acquainted with the splendor of cherry blossoms and crimson-tinted maples can truly appreciate the wabi of a stark weather-beaten thatched hut."[18] In this sense, the tea master Sen-no-Rikyu in fact conceived of the rustic tea hut as the "ideal place in which to express the beauty of a single flower..."[19]

One might say then that the architecture of the Tea Ceremony is an experiential compound unlike an architecture that is more objectively perceived through form and shape. The roji, the chashitsu, the various appurtenances and the physical and spiritual parts of the ceremony manifest a ritualistic architecture of progressive purification, involving the sloughing of all that is material to retain only that which is the bare essential. As a Zen master once explained, the essence of the Tea Ceremony is that "by seeing the *kakemono* (scroll) in the tokonoma alcove, one's sense of sight is cleansed; by smelling the fragrance of the incense and the flower in the vase, one's sense of smell is cleansed; by listening to the boiling water in the kettle, one's sense of hearing is cleansed; by gently handling the tea utensils, one's sense of touch is cleansed; by tasting the quaint bitter tea, one's sense of taste is cleansed; and thus when all the senses are cleansed, the mind itself is cleansed of all defilements."[20] (fig. 3.15).

The roji and the shoin gardens taken together are a study of contrasting overlaps. They are both about human interrelationships between a room and a garden. The shoin garden embodies the idea of "sitting Zen", in that one alights within a space to view a garden as the ultimate experience. The Tea Ceremony in turn embodies the idea of "walking Zen" in that one walks through a garden to arrive

Trees

Privy

Tea-Hut

Lantern

Machiai

Stone Bagin

THE FOUR PRINCIPLES OF THE CHA-NO-YO

'WA' (Harmony)

'SEI' (Purity)

'KEI' (Reverence)

'JAKU' (Tranquility)

SPIRITUAL ESSENCE OF THE CHA-NO-YU

By seeing the kakemono one's sight is cleansed

By smelling the fragrant incense one's sense of smell is cleansed

By listening to the water boiling one's ears are cleansed

By handling the tea utensils, one's sense of touch is cleansed

By tasting the tea one's sense of taste is cleansed

Figure 3.15 Cha-no-yu concepts. Top: Diagrammatic sequence of key events from roji to chashitsu. Middle: The philosophical principles of the Tea Ceremony. Bottom: The experience of the Tea Ceremony.

Figure 3.16 Huntington Gardens, Pasadena, California. Top: Dry Zen garden. Opposite page: Pond Garden

in a room as the final experience. In the shoin gardens, one views an abstract or miniaturized natural scene. During the Tea Ceremony in turn one emulates a walk through a forest to reach a hermit's hut.[21]

The chashitsu, as an architectural space, emerged from the shoin, evolving over time, and through various tea masters, its own aesthetics and spatial concepts. If one traces the origins of the tea ceremony in Japan, one reaches the thirteenth century, when Nambo Chomei, the founder of the Sufiki-ji temple in Chikuzen, went to Sung in 1259, studied Buddhism under the Kyodo of the Keizan-ji, and returned in 1286 with a *daisu* (stand for tea utensils). This daisu was taken to the Daitoku-ji temple, and given to Muso, the founder of Tenryu-ji temple. Muso began Cha-no-yo with this daisu and set down the formalities for its use.[22] In other words, before Sen-no-Rikyu and other famous tea masters began conceiving an architecture for a tea hut, the ceremony was part of a monastic shoin, adapted for this new use.

In both the shoin and tea gardens then, the aesthetic focus is as much about objects and forms, as the thoughts and feelings aroused by them in the participant. In both, the room and the garden are agents enabling participants to sense, experience and actively engage in the creation of beauty in every-day life. Both experiences demand conscious personalization and participation. Both use refined metaphors and mythic associations. Both emerge through, and by extension, manifest tenets of Zen.

THE POST-WAR "ZEN" GARDEN

Following World War II, new Zen-inspired garden prototypes began to emerge both through the social background of its patrons as well as a different mindset of its designers. In his 1960s article "The Secret of the Rock," architect Kenzo Tange noted unabashedly that he "liked the carved rock, because it reflects the will of the carver."[23] In 1989, celebrated sculptor Isamu Noguchi in an interview stated that "Man's hands are hidden by ....many effects of nature, moss and so forth....I don't want to be hidden. I want to show, therefore, I am modern. I am not a traditional Ueki-ya, tree trimmer."[24] As Nitschke points out, such attitudes surfaced as "dualism between man and nature previously unknown in Japanese garden architecture, and the desire to impose upon nature the supposed distinct will of man."[25]

The settings for these new gardens were the courtyards, entrances of major buildings or even public plazas. The cultural tread tying them back to their Zen predecessors was the presence of the rock as the main compositional element as well as the search for beauty through random form. But they were different from their ancestors in many ways. First, they were not emulations of any natural scenes, rather abstracted original compositions created by the minds of their artists. Second, they were not necessarily created as meditative compounds, but more as aesthetic moments that contrasted with their surroundings. And third, they were not tied to any canons or evolved wisdoms, rather free to be interpreted by the will of their creators.

Nitschke calls out a number of cases to delineate the differences: In 1958, Kenzo Tange designed a pond garden to the south of his Kanagawa Prefecture Government Office building. For the first time, it introduced hewn rocks into sculptural forms, as seen in the garden's 10 x 40 yards water basin. In 1961, sculptor Masuyuki Nagare, in one of his gardens for the Palace Hotel in Tokyo, placed a rectangular-carved waterfall into a rectangular water basin. In the 70s, Hiroshi Murai created a "Cool Garden" in a marble-clad courtyard in the Longchamp Textile Company building in Kyoto. The white marble floor recalled the austere snow-laden raked sand bed, with two dried leafless trees placed with their roots directly atop the marble. In 1975, Mirei Shigemorei created a garden for the Hotel Sheraton Grande with raked pebble pat-terns and a spiral stone motif juxtaposed with natural forms of rock clusters. And in 1989, Itsuko Haseg-awa created a winding garden stream, lined with abstract metal trees in the Shonandai Cultural Center in Hasegawa.[26]

These new attitudes can be read as representative of both the increasing ambivalence towards a past, as well as a new-found excitement to modern aesthetics and tendencies. What is significant however is the effort in these gardens to not outright obliterate or negate history, but seek conceptual and aesthetic threads that keep alive the memory of a tradition—however thin or forced they may appear to be. One might argue that projects such as the ones mentioned above trivialize the profound essence of the Zen garden as an artistic commodity. But on the other hand, in an age and time when Japan along with much of the world was on a high of discovering modernity in all its guises, the fact that architects and artists sought to hold on to historic concepts or even their fragments is laudable and in some ways responsible for celebrating and keeping alive the idea of the Zen garden within post-industrial Japan.

CONCLUSION

The multitude of shoin gardens discussed above, and in turn the evolution of the tea gardens, affirm the Zen emphasis on constant experimentation and spontaneity. The differences between the abstract dryness of Ryoan-ji and the clipped shrubs of Entsu-ji , are in fact differences in personalizing mediums to reach a common eventual goal. It is important to note here that many of these landscapes emerged from practical constraints. For instance, in the war-filled Kamakura and Muromachi eras, it was becoming increasingly difficult for monasteries to economically sustain large ponds and water bodies, and the aesthetic of emulating water through other materials was in fact a response to this limitation. The importance of this landscape tradition, however, is not only in its aesthetic value, not only the meaning it holds for the exhibitor, but also the mental attitude through which they are made. Where these gardens stand out is in the way gardeners or tea masters created and maintained them with meticulous detail, be it the raking of dry sand or the shaping of trees and shrubs to elicit the exact natural effect. These gardens teach us that ordinary objects and events become beautiful when one wholeheartedly invests in them without any pretention of past or future. This is analogous to the tea ceremony, or to Zen calligraphy. This is the Zen of the Japanese garden.

This attitude however, has significant bearings at both the micro and macro scale. As discussed before, many of these gardens have sensitive relationships with their macro-environment that demand an equally important investment. Today many new high-rise buildings block the traditional views from such gardens. One such threatened shakkei garden is at the Entsu-ji Temple that borrows the Hiei mountain as an integral part of its garden lay-out. New construction projects planned in this part of the town represent an immediate threat, and one insensitively placed and over-scaled building is enough to make irreparable damage. Construction activity also endangers environments of great symbolic value such as the historic urban landscape around the Yasaka pagoda in the Higashiyama area of Kyoto. The verdure that surrounds the city and the moods of the changing seasons and climate have always been an essential part of the cultural experience of these Zen gardens in a way that might be unsurpassed compared to other landscapes across the world.

In his book "Japanese Gardens," Gunter Nitschke has summarized the evolution of the Japanese land-scape across history as a transformation from "prototype to type and stereotype."[27] In this light, there are at least four guises Zen gardens enjoy today. The first is as original monastic landscapes. They continue to be preserved and maintained with many adaptations, but without losing their core values, ideas and processes. Ironically, many of the most famous of these are now tourist attractions, hardly used for meditation. The second is as themed emulations of Japanese Zen landscapes, all over the world. While scholars of Japanese gardening criticize these tendencies as shallow and thin, the fact is, these landscape set-designs, do succeed in creating the catchy allure of the familiar Japanese exotic of rocks, raked sand and clipped trees and shrubs. They cater to a specific audience, and for a specific purpose that is significantly different from their original intentions (fig. 3.16). The third presence of Zen gardens continues through the works of contemporary masters and apprentices that pass on the authentic canons and principles of Japanese garden design as it has been done over generations. Here, the more one delves into dissecting the secrets of Japanese gardens from manuals and can-ons, the more one realizes that their central message is to "not copy existing gardens, but rather…. reflect selected qualities of the natural environment so as to nurture the hopes and needs of the client,"[28] be it monks, abbots, emperors or ordinary citizens. And the fourth is the idea of the Zen Garden as an aesthetic reference interpreted through modern materials and methods, as described in the previous section.

"In absolute quietness, the voice of the cicada is absorbed into the rocks" the poet Basho once wrote in a whiff of Zen epiphany. Whether he was walking through a forest path, or sitting in a shoin, is not the point. The point is that he had discovered that ultimately, Zen teaches us another comprehension of time and space. Time, instead of being a linear onward-moving concept, can exist in many simultaneous dimensions. Instead of being a homogeneously shaped, perfect and unchanging thing, time can be seen as separate fragments of a larger reality. None of them tell the complete truth. But all of them exist. This eventually is what Japanese Zen Gardens tell us. It is not their authenticity that matters as much. What matters far more is our attitude to perceiving them, internalizing them, and therein experiencing other states of mind. As Fosco Mariani observes, they negate any faith in intellect. "Salvation and illumination come suddenly, they explode in intuition. The garden is therefore one of the most delightful points where the I and the not-I can dissolve and sublimate, like the mixing of the waters of the river and ocean. The garden is more important than treatises, syllogisms, or ancient writings. It is the song of things."[29]

One day, my father pulled out a delicate Japanese reed scroll from his stash of hidden collections. He had bought it from a Portuguese man in Goa, knowing it was damaged. For a week, each evening, he meticulously joined the broken reeds and touched it up to perfection. Then he hung it in our living room. There she was—a beautiful Japanese lady posing gracefully by a brook with a fan in her hand.

As a boy of seven, I think I fell in love with her, because I was obsessed with giving her a three-dimensional form. I used an egg shell for her face, some black cotton for her hair and some colored thread and pins for her ornaments. My mother made her a kimono, which we stuffed with paper. I remember being frustrated that she looked better in the scroll than my personalized version.

In time, I got over the doll, but not the lady in the scroll. Since my first trip to Japan, I have been on the lookout for her twin or kin, but so far, she has been one of a kind. A few years ago, my parents finally gifted me the scroll and now my Japanese lady has a special place in my living room.

When I look at the scroll, I think of many things: A collector's wit in recognizing the potential of a damaged masterwork and his perseverance in restoring it. A mother's dedication to fulfilling the whims of her child. And an innocent mind's natural drive to dissolve the line between fact and fiction.

Kimono-clad ladies on the path to Kiyomizu Temple.

Nanzen-ji Shiro shoin wall.

Chapter 4
The Mondrian in the Japanese Room

In 1960, photographer Yasuhiro Ishimoto, in collaboration with architect Kenzo Tange, published a book titled "Katsura: Tradition and Creation in Japanese Architecture" with a foreword by the eminent Modern architect Walter Gropius.[1] In presenting the by-then celebrated Katsura Villa as an iconic Japanese paradigm, the authors had omitted the aristocratic retreat's architectural dynamism, virtually abstracting its buildings and gardens into black and white planar patterns, as if to deconstruct its architecture into monochromatic photographic expressions. While many photos captured the shoin's facades, they were intentionally cropped, erasing the elegant cambered roofs and trees integral to the language of the building. Every non-linear element that connoted access was intentionally excluded; any feature with rich formal implications was left out. The camera focused only on the surfaces that defined architectural space: *tatami*, *shoji*, *byobu*, ceilings of *kasa-buchi* (long split boards) – all planar elements that were articulated by linear motifs such as pillars, crossbeams and *nageshi* (lintel joints).

Ishimoto's and Tange's abstractions of Katsura blatantly resembled the planar compositions of De Stijl paintings, created here by the lines of the shoji, and the supports and beams apparent in the facades beneath the elevated floors.[2] Like experiencing paintings by Theo Van Doesburg and Piet Mondrian, one could observe in their abstractions, a search for the laws of equilibrium and harmony applicable to both art and life. In their apparent quest for an expression of clarity and order, Ishimoto and Tange had, just like their Modernist Dutch counterparts eliminated all components of representational realism, reducing the compositions to their most basic elements: straight lines, plane surfaces and rectangles.

This deconstruction of the Katsura Villa was a significant polemic for its time. It received significant attention from the authors' Modernist peers, but it was also criticized as self-indulgent. "This is a visual record of the living Katsura as it exists in the mind of an architect and a photographer" Tange wrote in the book.[3] "We who made the record may conceivably be accused of dismembering Katsura, and those who come to know the place from pictures given here may well be disappointed to find upon actually visiting it that it is different from what they had expected."[4] Since the authors had not elaborated on the broader intentions of this presentation, it is difficult to verify what they had hoped to achieve, but it is hard to believe that someone of their knowledge and intelligence would not have had a deeper idea.

Figure 4.1 Shoin and Tea Hut walls, ceilings, and floors as Mondrian-like compositions.

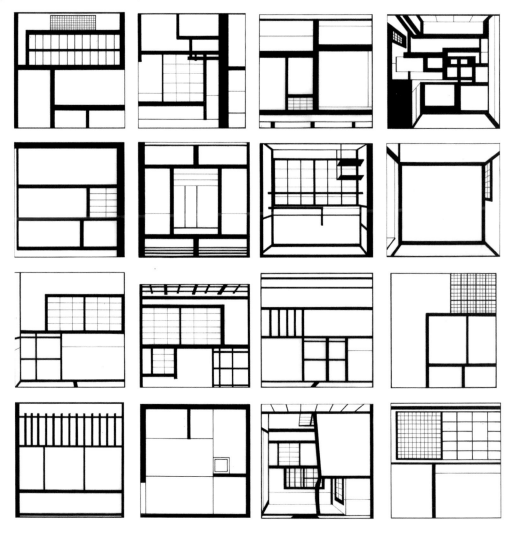

Ironically, while the book may well have been a biased Modernist perspective of the retreat, it is in many ways closer to the visual goals of traditional Japan than those of modern art. While Ishimoto and Tange's polemic on Katsura may affirm their Modernist tendencies, it also makes an obvious connection to Japan's own visual traditions of frontality, linearity and abstraction. It is not too difficult for anyone familiar with traditional Japanese architecture to see how Japanese rooms, particularly shoins and tea-rooms can engender through one's subjective mental fantasies, the reduction of their austere and rectilinear modular compositions to their simplest harmonies. One can mentally transform the physical built form of the room into an abstract compound transcending conventional visual regimes. The walls of the room can become autonomous compositions, and through the dissociation of these frontal elements, one can enjoy a new ocular perception of reality, comprehending space not through size, shape and scale, but through immateriality, abstraction and metaphor. Re-reading a typical traditional Japanese room can result in the most unconventional experience – one can see the biggest Mondrian painting one could ever dream of (fig. 4.1, 4.2).

KINESIS

In traditional Western architecture, a wall is an element of resistance shutting out light, heat and noise, and, simultaneously protecting the occupants from intruders. In Japan, the functions traditionally associated with a wall have been rather ambiguous. With sliding shoji, *fusuma* and *amado* panels separating rooms, the idea of a transient, movable infill replaced the conventional wall as a static barrier. A traditional Japanese room could inflate itself by opening its elastic walls. Space extended through a horizontal additive process, with walls as mere interruptions that could be taken away. Traditional Japanese space–like an organic void–had no beginning, middle and end.

To separate one room from another you would slide an opaque fusuma wall or bring in a *byobu*, a portable folding wall with decorative paintings to express a particular occasion. In the early Nara period, such opaque boards used as room dividers began to get increasingly translucent to bring in light, and evolved into the

Figure 4.2 Frontal wall compositions. Top: Detail of shelf wall, Shugaku-in shoin, Kyoto. Bottom: Shokin-tei tea hut interior, Kyoto.

Figure 4.3 Opposite page: Nomura Tea House tokonoma, Kanazawa. Frontal versus angular view.

latticed shoji, where two or more layers would slide within a single sill with the push of a finger. And binding all these flexible walls along the outer boundary were the opaque wooden amado panels that could be closed to protect the interior from rain.

Japanese walls were flexible because they were free from structural constraints. In stone construction, with walls carrying the roof weight, there were structural limits to the room size and the number of rooms determined the size of the house. But in Japan, the roof was always erected first during the construction process and the space beneath articulated later. The Japanese word for partition, *majikiri*, clarified this tradition, *ma* referring to the intervals between the supporting posts as well as the space under the roof, and *jikiri* or *shikiri* implying the subjective division of this space freed from structural obligations. And so contrary to most cultures where the house began from a single room, in traditional Japanese architecture the house evolved into a single room by virtue of such transient walls.

FRONTALITY

Photographing a traditional Japanese room like a Zen shoin is difficult. In other cultures, the image of a room showing two walls and a corner is far more interesting than the frontal photo of a single wall. The furniture and objects of art that adorn a room are best seen in their three-dimensional complexity when viewed at an angle. A room is a spatial experience of volume rather than surface. The walls serve as backdrops to define the spatial boundaries within which one associates with free-standing objects, shaping space between and around them. By contrast, a traditional Japanese room is visually far more pleasing when viewed frontally.

In comparing frontal versus angular photos, it is apparent that the visual calm and stability of a wall in the Japanese room is lost when one attempts to capture the corner. The *tokonoma* (alcove), the only delineated ornamental space of a traditional shoin interior appears most pleasing when one sees it head on, reading the scroll and the objects on the baseboard as a unified framed composition. The paintings on the fusuma panels are best read when one sits perpendicular to them. The garden composition that may capture a distant mountain as part of the frame can only be perceived when one views it frontally through the opened shoji (fig. 4.3, 4.4).

Figure 4.4 Top: Ryogen-in Tea Hut interior. Frontal versus angular view.

Figure 4.5 Opposite page: Daikaku-ji shoin interior, Kyoto.

This contrast in spatial perception is no coincidence. Many Japanese rooms were designed through the process of *Okosheizu*.[5] Each wall was conceived as an independent two-dimensional composition that was then 'tilted' up under the already erected roof to make an enclosure much like a paper carton. Further, Japanese rooms were never entered at an angle, and there is no plan in traditional Japanese architecture that entertained a diagonal entry into an interior space. A room was entered at right angles to a wall, and every entry into any adjacent room also occurred in the same manner. With no fixed furniture to imply any definite seating pattern, and no field of objects to walk through, it was the tatami pattern of the floor with its right-angled colored edges that became the structural organizer of the interior. It carried the implicit order for seating in relation to specific elements such as a tokonoma, as well as its wall compositions. As Arthur Drexler observed, "If the floor is imagined as an abstract picture composed of rectangles, it will be seen that the divisions on the frame enclosing the picture – the walls of the room – are affected by the floor pattern itself. The black lines dividing the floor surface not only suggest to the architect the placement of columns and those intervals of shoji which will best relate a room to its garden, but also tie together wall and floor in a harmony as varied as it is consistent."[6]

Traditional Japanese space was frontal space. Unlike its European counterpart, with no furniture on the floors and no objects on the walls, it was more about surface than volume, more about ambiguity than arrangement. The built-form of the room, though physically measurable through length, breadth and height was spatially experienced as an empty void. There was nothing to associate with and nothing to imply a sense of scale. The only constants were the surfaces that enclosed it. The Japanese room began and ended with its walls.

FLATNESS

Traditionally, Japanese walls were perpetually flat. No curve ever entered the interior. No acute or obtuse angle ever broke their strictly perpendicular relationships with each other. Even with the walls freed from structural constraints, the same Japanese that insisted on curves in their roofs seemed averse to any kind of curvilinear surface within their rooms.

So great was this affinity to the flat surface that openings within walls with shoji and fusuma were also always sliding. Unlike the Western door and window that opened ajar, thereby introducing a vanishing point and hence a perception of depth into the visual frame, the flat composition of the Japanese wall was never disturbed. The sliding panels ensured that there was never a vanishing point to disturb the dominance of the frontal surface (fig. 4.5, 4.6).

The Japanese room could thus be likened to a paper box, each of its six faces representing a fold in the sheet glued together to form a cube. Seen this way, the consistent flatness of its composing surfaces is easily apparent as an overall theme. The flat expanse of the tatami floor was typically accompanied by flat ceilings. They were typically made of a lattice of lightwood strips about 18 inches apart fastened to the wall by a ledge called *mawaribuchi*. They were held aloft by poles hung from the rafters, with 1/8-inch thick boards nailed on top to making the finished ceiling a lattice of parallel lines.[7] Enclosing this flat top and bottom were the main composing elements of the room, the walls.

RIGHT ANGLE

These walls consistently favored the right angle. Their compositions were made up strictly of horizontals and verticals. No diagonal ever disturbed this rectilinear order. Structural braces and ties were not always horizontal, and though it is known that traditional Japanese buildings occasionally used diagonal bracing, they were invariably concealed within the thickness of a plaster wall, never bringing a diagonal into the visual composition.[8] The vertical elements of the wall were the supporting columns of the structural timber cage. They had fixed and conspicuous locations, and stood in tandem with horizontal structural counterparts.

It was indeed these horizontal members that established the scale of Japanese interior. Approximately 1 ken (6 feet) above the floor was a beam called *nageshi*. It served as the structural brace to tie the columns together and held the tracks for sliding shoji or fusuma panels. The portion of the wall above the nageshi ranged from 18 inches to 3 feet in height.[9] It was filled in with white plaster or a shoji when along an exterior wall, or an ornate wood lattice called *ramma* when between interior

rooms to help in air circulation. The nageshi was always revealed on both sides of a wall, even in cases where it did not support sliding panels. In all cases, this tie beam remained the dominant horizontal member of the wall composition (fig. 4.7).

So pronounced was this persistence for horizontals that Japanese carpenter-architects in some cases introduced superfluous horizontal elements as part of the structural cage. For instance, at the intersection of the wall and ceiling was a horizontal member called *tengo-nageshi*, often appearing like a major structural element. Yet ramma when plastered typically detracted the visual strength of this horizontal, making the ceiling to appear weakly supported. To remedy this effect, a strip of white plaster 6–8 inches high was inserted just below the ceiling, making it appear to hover above the room, as seen in the Ninomaru at the Nijo Castle. The tengo-nageshi did not have any structural function and remained a purely decorative line in an overall composition.[10]

Similarly, the nageshi was visually scaled beyond its practical requirements, and a thin grooved plank flanked by two boards was made to appear like a solid beam. When it spanned 3 or more ken (18 feet) – typically between rooms under a fusuma wall–it was divided into two lengths, caught at the center by a post hung from the beam above. This post was smaller in its dimensions than a normal column, giving the nageshi as much visual prominence as the columns. Even at the cost of redundancy, Japanese walls were thus compositions of exclusively horizontals and verticals. There is no rationale to explain why the Japanese never hesitated to shroud anything that would visually disturb the strict order of the right-angle.

Figure 4.6 Opposite page: Myoman-ji shoin interior, Kyoto

Figure 4.7 Top: Nageshi as part of larger wall composition. top left: Kodai-ji Temple shoin interior, Kyoto. Note the different compositions of the two walls; top right: Sekisui-in shoin interior, Kozan-ji Temple, Kyoto. Note the raised height of the member above the tokonoma.

AUTONOMOUS COMPOSITIONS

The walls of a traditional Japanese such as a shoin were also often conceived as autonomous compositions. Nothing could be more antithetical to the corner of a traditional shoin than a glazed Modern corner-window that blurs the meeting line of two walls. In the Japanese tradition despite the walls having no structural value, the corner of two walls was never anything more or less than a structural post. Even in rooms facing gardens, when the in-fills were completely removed, the corner of the rectangular plan was never left as an open space between two posts.

That is not to say that the Japanese did not entertain the concept of wall-to-wall continuity. The fusuma paintings that adorn the walls were often conceived as a single gigantic mural surrounding the space. When the scene reached a corner, it simply slid behind the post and jumped onto the next perpendicular wall continuing the depiction. Landscape themes were typically the main subject of shoin interiors and when one looks through the composing members of a wall, it seems as if one is viewing a surreal garden surrounding the room (fig. 4.8).

But in looking at such paintings, one realizes that this perception of wall to wall continuity does not last too long. It is difficult to read the room as a continuous composition not so much due to the corner post, but rather the distinction between the adjacent wall compositions themselves, particularly above the nageshi. This too is apparent at the Ninomaru at the Nijo Castle. In many cases, no two walls in a Japanese room were ever the same, almost seeming like they were composed independent of each other. On two meeting walls, the nageshi were in many cases at slightly

Figure 4.8 Top and bottom:
Frontal view, Daikaku-ji Temple
shoin wall paintings, Kyoto.

Figure 4.9 Opposite page: Wall to
Wall conditions.
Clockwise from top left:
Shinnyo-do shoin interior, Kyoto,
showing fusuma with implicitly
continuous landscape painting;
Daikaku-ji shoin interior, Kyoto,
showing fusuma with autonomous
landscape painting; Daitoku-ji
Zuiho-in shoin interior showing
fusuma with literally continuous
landscape painting; Keishun-in Tea
Hut interior with autonomnous
wall compositions.

different heights, from one half to two or three times the depth of the nageshi itself, as if the plane of the wall continued into the space beyond the room. The consequent difference in the rammas above the nageshi reinforced the non-continuity of the two horizontals. In many rooms, like Zen shoins, it is easier to read the walls one at a time as autonomous compositions enclosing a physical space (fig. 4.9).

Thus, as Gorge Ferras has noted, if one were to abstain from perceiving a Japanese room in the three-dimensional sense, and quietly alight in front of a wall, one would undergo an entirely new spatial experience.[11] The wall would be perceived as an abstract compound suggesting calm and repose. One would encounter a wondrous assemblage of squares, rectangles, right angles and lines. Perhaps one would see the infinite expanse of the horizon, or an outstretched grassland, or an urban grid, or the intangible force fields of a tree. Or perhaps, one would see the biggest Mondrian painting ever (fig. 4.10).

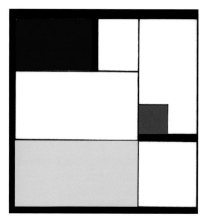
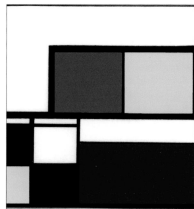

Figure 4.10 Top and opposite page: Shoin wall compositions as Mondrian-like paintings.

LOCATING JAPANESE VISUALITY

The traditional Japanese notion of additive horizontality can be said to be analogous to Mondrian's (and other De Stijl artists') tendency of overlapping space.[12] Arthur Drexler has noted that traditional Japanese rooms were arranged like boxes of various sizes packed unevenly in a carton, his observation exemplified through paintings showing several rooms in a Japanese house without any vanishing point, extending into infinity – like a series of Mondrian rectangles juxtaposed on a canvas.[13] With the consistent absence of perspective and a distant vanishing point, spatial depth was achieved through planar succession with one's eye leaping from a lower to a higher plane across a misty void. The Mondrian canvas, like Japanese space, with its abstract language of ordered geometry, clarity and ethical force, has no perceptual beginning, middle or end.

Another parallel is the directness of the point of vision, particularly as seen in the traditional Zen technique of meditation known as Zazen. During Zazen, one sits motionless directly facing a wall, dissociating oneself with the rest of the room. In appreciating a Japanese wall frontally, one likewise mentally segregates this frontal element from the rest of the space – a tendency evident in the work of Japanese film maker Yasujiro Ozu. As the 1940s came to an end, Ozu began to fuse his early American influences with an overriding desire to reduce his framing techniques. In his later films, he reduced all camera movement (pans, dollying, and crabbing) to nil, and replaced traditional shots and reverse shot techniques with a system whereby each character looks straight into the camera when speaking to someone else.[14] This had the unusual effect of placing the viewer directly in the centre of conversations—as if being talked to—instead of the Hollywood convention of alternately peering over characters' shoulders during such sequences. Furthermore, Ozu decided to reduce his choice of transition effect. There were no fades, wipes, dissolves. They were all replaced with the straight cut. Reducing his techniques in this way, reduced distraction and focused all attention on his characters. In addition to being motionless in his later work, Ozu's camera, from early in his career, was often placed at a very low level, as if the viewers were sitting cross-legged, at the same level one sits on tatami for a tea ceremony or in a Japanese home, or while meditating. This

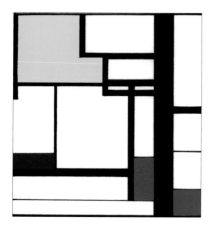

was all a celebration of one of Japan's most distinctive spatial perceptions, one that very few architects recognized during Japan's wooing of Modernism. In this light, Tange and Ishimoto's deconstruction of the Katsura too is a celebration of the visual and spatial tendencies of traditional Japan.

There is no direct evidence to tie Tange and Ishimoto's Katsura compositions, Mondrian's art and traditional Japanese visuality. Perhaps their most profound nexus ultimately lies in their eventual goal–one that transcends realism to manifest the power of subjective visual perception as a guide to humanity. The Buddha's claim that "All material shape should be seen by perfect intuitive wisdom as it really is" suggests the pluralism of the physical world, ordinary knowledge being only relatively true.[15] This distinction resembles Mondrian's notion that "the emotion of beauty is always obscured by the appearance of the object. Therefore the object must be eliminated from the picture" affirming his complete rejection of artistic objectivism.[16] When in 1920, he dedicated his booklet "Le Neo-plasticisme" to what he called "future men", he encouraged the substitution of the conventional and literal facts of appearance with a new harmonious cogitation of life; an attempt to understand "a true vision of reality."[17] Here, space not as an empirical object, but as a transcendental ideal, a key to a higher world of knowledge. There is nothing in the present which was not in the past, nothing in the future that is not in the present. Like in the cosmos, one stage follows upon another until it becomes void. Then a new cycle begins, just like the stages, in a timeless, endless succession. Like the Universe it is timeless, it is without boundaries, it is infinite.

My first destination in Japan was the 140-meter-tall Gurando Purinsu Hoteru, the Grand Prince Hotel Akasaka, designed by none other than Kenzo Tange. My first memories are of its white marble lobby, then my hotel room, and shortly thereafter, looking down at the Tokyo night from the rooftop lounge.

In March 2011, the hotel closed for demolition. When I drove by earlier this year, it was much shorter than the one I remember twenty years ago. Demolition workers have started at the top, working their way down. They have inserted temporary supports and reinforced the top floor with steel beams to create a sort of adjustable lid. After an electric-powered crane removes all the material from each floor, the top floor and roof are lowered using massive jacks. From outside, it appears like nothing is going on, but in fact the hotel is quietly shrinking from the inside, some six meters every ten days.

By the end of 2013, "my" Grand Prince Hotel, will have quietly disappeared, like a cherry blossom. When I visit Chiyoda next, there will only be a memory of my first memory in Japan.

Cherry Blossoms in bloom at Ueno Park.

Kinkaku-ji (Golden Pavilion), Kyoto.

Chapter 5
Space-Time and Japanese Architecture

To equate the Western architectural duality of space and time in the traditional Japanese sense, one has to splice the two words to make them read space-time. The hyphen captures effectively the Japanese idea of space and time as one inseparable continuum – in that it is difficult to experience architectural space without perceiving some sense of time. In experiencing traditional Japanese architecture, it seems as if its affinity to empty spaces, to the concept of cyclical renewal, its seemingly endless garden paths, meticulously celebrated seasonal rituals, love for age and patina, and most evidently its traditional choice of wood as building material, point rather assertively to contemplations of transience and change and therein a consciousness of time. Japan's spatial and formal concepts seem better understood through this lens of ephemera, for the Japanese have had architectural priorities other than those of the strictly Euclidian trinity of length, breadth and height. It is as if traditional Western architecture used time to experience space, while traditional Japanese architecture created space to celebrate time.

It is not that Western architecture has not engaged in perceptions of time. Monks in the Middle Ages for instance, divided each day into eight ceremonial periods corresponding to the liturgical phases of monastic life, from *Matins* (the darkness of early morning), to *Compline* (the late evening twilight) appropriating actions universally prescribed for each period. Their elaborate rituals conjured elaborate perceptions of change and relatedness, and therein, of the passage of time. Yet one could argue that from the ancient Greek preoccupation with exterior form to the Roman attention to interior space, and from Gothic structuralism to the Renaissance obsession with spatial depth, Western architecture was, in fact, less about perceiving time and more about exploring the formal complexities of space.[1] From the Renaissance to the first decade of the twentieth century, perspective remained one of the most important constituents of spatial representation, and the four-century-old habit of seeing the world in a Renaissance manner – that is in terms of three dimensions – had rooted itself so deeply in the Western mind that no other form of perception seemed imaginable.

Not until the early twentieth century did Western architecture see for the first time an inclusive attitude towards notions of time. It began with Hermann Minkowski's (1908) proclamation–"space alone or time alone is doomed to fade into mere

Figure 5.1 Top and opposite page: Mountain shrines at Nanzen-ji Temple, Kyoto.

shadow; only a kind of union of both will preserve their existence."[2] With modern physics conceiving space, not as Newton's absolute, static entity but as relative to a moving point of reference, Modern art for the first time since the Renaissance saw new conceptions of space through Cubism and Futurism. The Cubist tendency to view objects not from a single point, but simultaneously from all sides, ushered new notions of 'superimposition', 'interpenetration', 'simultaneity' and 'hovering' as seen in Picasso's 1914 "Still Life" and Ozefant's and Malewitsch's Cubist rationalizations. And simultaneously the poet Marinetti's (1909) claim–"the splendor of the world has been enriched by a new beauty: the beauty of speed"–affirmed his Futurist discovery of time through objects in motion and distortion.[3] It was this concept that the painter Marcel Duchamp expressed in his 1912 "Nude Descending the Staircase," and Picasso in his 1937 "Guernica" through 'elasticity' and 'movement'. And thus to the three dimensions of the Renaissance which had held good for so many centuries, there was added a fourth one – time.[4]

SPACE, TIME & THE JAPANESE MIND

It is against this backdrop that one must understand the traditional Japanese sense of time – one that may seem as ambiguous to the Western mind as the traditional Japanese sense of space, largely because it lacks a formal means as the key to its understanding. In fact prior to the influx of Western ideas in the Meiji era that began in 1868, there was no Japanese word to describe the idea of architectural space as an entity in itself.[5] A new word–*kukan*–had to be created to communicate the idea of Japanese space three-dimensionally for the Western mind to associate with. Evidently, Japanese architecture had traditionally been experienced less through the lens of formality and more through the Japanese sense of transience – not as an object of permanence, but as a series of events that had to change from time to time. Japanese architecture in this sense was a different experience altogether.

The early Shinto traditions of Japan help authenticate these concepts. Shinto Japanese were keenly aware of unusual natural phenomena such as large trees and unusually shaped rocks as modes for *kami* (spirits) to emerge into this world. These *shintai* (literally "spirit bodies") were revered not just for their formal attributes, but also for their perceived super-natural association. But the kami did not dwell in these

objects perpetually; they occupied them intermittently, and through this cyclical possession brought about a constant flux in the perceived nature of the place. The frame of time between the kami's coming and going from the object was overtly expressed in the term ma[6] – implying in its original sense not necessarily something positive, but rather a non-eventful gap, a temporal moment between two different phenomena, two contradictory elements or two dimensions of varying natures. This sense of space and place through time was fundamentally different from the idea of three-dimensional geometric space (fig. 5.1).

The idea of the world as a sequence of discrete events and non-events separated by intervals became the undertone of Japanese life. For instance ma was an important feature of Japanese music, whether traditional folk or imperial courtly: in the moments between beats, a musician or singer was free to embroider an original melody per his own specific mode of expression, acknowledging the time frame of the interval. Likewise rooms within the Japanese interior were given the suffix ma primarily in recognition of their existence as empty intervals between distinct physical events in the form of columns and partitions. This perception of the momentary in-between represented the first Japanese notion of space-time.

Buddhism entered Japan in 538 CE with its central doctrine of transience.[7] In emphasizing evanescence as the spiritual foundation of all existence, it reinforced the Shinto emphasis on the interval between events with a simultaneous awareness of the fleeting nature of the event itself. The idea of *mujo* (literally "impermanence") now began to elevate all things quotidian as transitory parts of a larger continuum. Buddhism imparted another layer to the Japanese space-time concept contemplating the fleeting nature of life through the predictable natural cycles of birth, decay and regeneration. Buddhism found in Japan one its most profound forms in Zen. As mentioned in Chapter 3, along with its rejection of scriptural authority, Zen emphasized the concept of *satori* (enlightenment), not as the eventual goal of a long spiritual journey, but as an instantaneous intuitive flash of revelation that could happen anywhere, anytime.[8] It surfaced therein yet another layer within the extant Buddhist perception of time through evanescence – that of the unpredictable sliver of the spontaneous moment wherein space and time became one.

Ingrained within the Japanese mind are these simultaneous perceptions of space-time. There is the idea of ma as recurring intervals between sequential events

Figure 5.2 Top: Ise Geku, Mie – tutelary shrine. The empty space next to the shrine is where the new shrine is constructed every twenty years.

Figure 5.3 Opposite page: Seasonal changes at Kiyomizu Temple Pagoda, Kyoto.

and non-events. There is the perception of gradual predictable changes, and there is on the other hand, the capture of an unpredictable momentary flash – all of which are embodied in architecture and the built environment.

CYCLES, RHYTHMS & RENEWALS

In 1989, the death of Emperor Hirohito concluded the sixty-four-year Showa Era (era of "enlightenment and peace"), and a new era titled Heisei ("achievement of peace") was instantly announced. As Gunter Nitschke has noted, "tens of millions of calendars were discarded and replaced as the nation literally went back to year one. Time (had) been renewed."[9] This idea of measuring time through cycles came to Japan from imperial China in 645 CE with the Taika Reform, and in 1867, it was decided that a *nengo* (new time-period marker) could begin only with the reign of a new emperor.[10] The only other official renewal rite associated with a ruler was the *sento*, that is, the rebuilding of a new capital with the enthronement of a new emperor. The sento changed over the ages: In prehistoric times, it was centered on replacing the imperial palace. In the Asuka and Nara periods (552 – 794 CE), it was focused on the rebuilding of a whole capital on a new site. Following the building of Kyoto, only the place was renewed symbolically, and eventually that too was discontinued.[11]

"It has clearly been a cultural choice of the Japanese to make dwellings from living rather than dead materials, from trees rather than stones, and to rely on structures which because of their impermanent materials will have to be replaced every 50 to 100 years," notes Nitschke.[12] As mentioned in earlier chapters, the buildings of the Ise shrine are presently being replaced for the sixty-second time in a ritual called the *shikinen sengu*, the periodic renewal of the shrines embodies the ancient belief of renewing the impermanent man-made homes where the spirits dwell.[13] The sengu rituals start on a day in May in the morning, and end in October eight years later with the *sengyo*, wherein the deity is transferred from the old shrine to the new one. In structure, the shikinen sengu "imitates the ritual agricultural year."[14] As noted in Chapter 2, such practices are not unique to Ise. The Izumo shrine is renewed once every 60 years. At the Suwa shrines in Nagano Prefecture, every six years, the sixteen *ombashira* (pillars) of the two double shrines are replaced with new

ones, made from trees cut from their respective sacred mountains. Practices such as these are still prevalent within the Japanese countryside, where the replications of huts, mountains and pillars that house the *yashiki-gami* (estate-deities) are renewed at harvest time. Whether a pragmatic response to the susceptibility of wood, or a mythic linkage to ancient Shintoism, cyclical renewal as a Japanese cultural pattern is also a renewal of one's consciousness of time (fig. 5.2).

So too is it with Japan's starkly visible seasons, and the myriad rituals that have evolved to acknowledge their changes (fig. 5.3). For what is a *soan* (Tea Hut) but a temporary setting to harmonize with seasonal time, true to the rigorous meditative spirit of the Cha-no-yu (Tea Ceremony)?[15] Every element within is carefully select-ed: a *kimono* perhaps displaying maple leaf patterns in autumn and cherry blossoms in spring; the utensils, the *kakemono* (hanging scroll) and the solitary flower at its baseboard scrupulously chosen to expresses the spirit of the season outside. And so it is with the crowds that contemplate *hanami* (cherry blossom viewing festival), acknowledging the fleeting beauty of the blooming and falling flowers and their display of universal transience.[16]

The most predictable words in Japanese aesthetics, *wabi-sabi*, have, tellingly, no direct equivalent in any Western language; perhaps "rustic" might come as a rather incomplete compromise.[17] This Zen ideal on the immateriality and uncontrollability of nature is more visibly a description of the richness of degradation, the glory of transience, the beauty of patina and age, and thereby an acknowledgement of fleeting time. It explains Zen's aesthetic preferences of rustic monochromes and un-hewn posts for tea rooms, imperfect shapes for tea bowls and mossy drapes for garden rocks.

In this sense, the emptiness of the traditional Japanese tatami room is also an embodiment of transience and renewal. The portable furniture–*byobu* (folding screens), desks, cushions–arranged for a specific activity are constantly emptied, and renewed with those for another occasion. The Japanese idea of a room (also called *ma*) is thus defined less by its sliding *shoji* and *fusuma* panels and the boundaries of its interior, and more by the transient activity happening within. The room is a sort of metaphysical anti-matter, constantly beating to the pulse of ma–the gap between its temporary events and its nothingness.

THE INSTANT

A lightning flash:
between the forest trees
I have seen water.

HAIKU BY SHIKI MASAOKA (1867-1902)

In the Noh theater[18], there are moments called *senuhi-ma* when the music stops and the performer arrests all perceptible movement. These instantaneous pauses emphasize the spirit of his particular act in much the same manner as a conscious emphatic pause during a conversation. Like the Zen brush stroke or the haiku verse, senuhi-ma thus revels in the spontaneous, unpredictable sliver of the moment, embodying the idea of ma as a short gap of silent fullness and profound meaning.

Thus the legend of a Zen master (some speculate the great tea master Sen-no-Rikyu), who builds his hut along a spectacular ocean view, then erects a large wall to block it completely out of sight, save a tiny vertical slit that accords but a glimpse of the horizon as one walks past. The singular instant intensifies the view a thousand times keeping it alive forever. This sensibility that finds the glimpse far more meaningful than a gaping view explains the meticulous Japanese attention to the smallest of things: why the rare glimpse of the underside of a kimono, seems far more sensual than a scantily clad lady, or why the inside of a soup-bowl lid is more decorative that its outside. It translates into the care the Japanese carpenter-builder has traditionally paid to the underside of the timber roof, its intricate patterns and its subtle curve turning upward ever so slightly to accord a teasing glimpse of this intricacy from a distance. It explains the ambiguous, even perverse sense of Japanese privacy–where even under the most sensitive circumstances such as public baths, simple curtains rather than doors separate gender-specific rooms from each other, their inadequacies often according glimpses into places conventionally unthinkable. This is *chirari* (literally "glimpse"), the beauty of instantaneous voyeurism, strangely parallel to the Zen idea of satori (enlightenment)–in their common acknowledgment of a fleeting sliver of but a passing moment.[19]

RELATIVE VISION & ENDLESS JOURNEYS

The Japanese idea of viewing fixed entities sequentially from various vantage points is similar to Cubist notions of juxtaposition and superimposition – both negating the idea of an objective reality. In an eighteenth-century illustration of the Tokaido, the road from Kyoto to Edo for instance, the road meanders in a serpentine form from left to right depicting various significant sights along the way, one of them – Mount Fuji – appears twice in the drawing, as seen from two different places.[20]

Likewise the grounds of the Katsura Villa are laid out as a succession of views to be appreciated while strolling, views that provide frame after frame of the garden and the structures while never allowing a view of the entire garden or main building all at once. They reject a fixed single perspective, breaking down space into a series of visual space-time vistas each one distinct, unpredictable and lasting a few paused moments before traversing along the path again.

The reading of a Japanese picture scroll is a similar space-time kinesthetic, in that one comprehends – like a Futurist painting – an ordered sequence of spatial (or formal) parts 'extruded in time'. At the Daisen-in in the Daitoku-ji Temple, this idea translates into a *karesansui* (dry garden) narrative on the metaphor of Life (elaborated in Chapter 3), read with one's eyes moving from east to west to interpret every individual element in sequence. The point is that some form of kinesis or motion remains central to the experience, imparting through a perceptive relativism, a time-value to an otherwise static event (fig. 5.4).

The idea that process must take dominion over the destination is akin to the Buddhist doctrine of space-time—implying that purification requires movement, and that it progresses from stage to stage in an incremental process. Little wonder that the Japanese shrine path has always had a greater significance than the visual impact of the complex as a whole. It seems designed to delay the visitor, never revealing the entire picture, constantly evoking anticipation along what seems like an endless journey. Thus, though at first glance, the hilltop layouts of both the Kiyomizu Temple and the Acropolis appear equally amorphous, the difference is clear: The Acropolis is sited to be seen from a distance, while Kiyomizu is shrouded within its forest setting never revealing its overall image. Further, at the Acrop-

Figure 5.4 Daisen-in dry garden, Daitoku-ji Temple, Kyoto. Opposite page: Katsura Villa. View of Tea House from one of the villa's rooms.

Figure 5.5 Kiyomizu Temple, Kyoto. Top: Diagrammatic plan of temple complex. Note the amorphous arrangement of the various buildings on the hilly terrain. Bottom: The complex is experienced as a series of sequential vistas and places, without ever seeing the entire complex as a whole.

Figure 5.6 Opposite page: Path to Ise Naiku. The forest setting is humanized by a series of elements such as bridges and gates, heightening one's anticipation of the destination.

olis, one would walk up the steep processional ramps and through the Propylea to encounter the visual vista of the overall complex – the Parthenon to the right, the Erechtheum to the left and the statue of Athena straight on the visual axis. By contrast at Kiyomizu, one undergoes an experience of autonomous parts– bridges, steps, gates, lanterns, statuettes–never encountering a single vista of the overall complex (fig. 5.5).

In the Zen architecture of the Cha-no-yu (Tea Ceremony), the *roji* (tea garden) is enclosed by an outer fence with trees filtering out the secular world while shielding the tea hut from direct view. As elaborated in Chapter 3, a *chumon* (inner gate) and *nakakaguri* (low gate) layers the confined precinct into two parts: the outer waiting area and the inner area of the tea hut. This double layer, mandating entry into the tea hut through two approaches heightens the perceived distance of the journey. With each advance the space progressively shrinks, sanctifying and preparing the visitor for the intimacy of the hidden innermost space.[21]

This affinity to hiding the destination seems rooted in Japan's ancient Shinto traditions. In the Shinto sense, enclosure is less about containment and more about wrapping–like a gift-paper. In other words, it is more implicit and less protective – like the four concentric fences surrounding the Ise honden (main shrine) that suggest sacredness without the idea of a fortified wall. The fences while low enough to afford glimpses of the shrine roofs are also high enough so as never to allow glimpses of the sacred core. In this centrifugal configuration each layer elevates one's consciousness of depth within a space-time journey (fig. 5.6).

SPACE, TIME & ARCHITECTURE

In the 1950s, long after the Meiji era had already embraced the introduction of Western ideas, the increasing Japanese curiosity with Modernism was fuelled even more with the publication of Siegfried Giedion's book "Space, Time and Architecture" in Japan in 1955.[22] The Harvard art historian's architectural rhetoric had little to do with time in the transient sense, even as he passionately elaborated on the theoretical underpinnings of Cubism and Futurism as path-breaking directions in Western art, showcasing their influence on the most prolific Modern architecture

Figure 5.7 Top: Nakagin Capsule Tower designed by Kisho Kurokawa, Tokyo.

Figure 5.8 Opposite page: Building signage, Shinjuku, Tokyo. Note the steel cages that carry the sign boards.

of the time. For Japan, this Western duality of space and time was a cultural tension, one perhaps best exemplified in many early modern Japanese houses that look entirely Western save the one or two rooms that consciously retained their tatami interior. In this juxtaposition of the lonely, traditional empty room, with the otherwise object-filled Western dwelling was the imposing collision between Western permanence and Japanese ephemera.

Predictably, this tension was also the catalyst for newer Japanese architectural manifestations of time. The most evident of these came in the 1960s with the Metabolism movement, when a group of young architects applied biological analogies of "metabolism" and "metamorphosis" to re-conceive Modern Japanese cities as utopian capsular mega-structures capable of modular growth and change.[23] Attracting significant Western attention for its technical bravura, these mostly un-built proposals were to represent a distinctly Japanese attempt in architecturally amalgamating their traditional sensitivity to time with the Modernist obsession with form. As seen in Kisho Kurokawa's Nakagin Capsule Tower with its Lego-like assemblage of pre-cast cubic rooms, to the Cubist idea of superimposition, and the Futurist preoccupation with motion, the Japanese Modernist had conceived a new formalism for time through the visual metaphor of change, growth and incompleteness (fig. 5.7).[24]

This theme of ephemera has been expressed more recently in another way in architect Shigeru Ban's design for the Curtain House (1995). Here, a curtain hangs the length of two stories, framing an indoor loggia-type space when drawn, and reveals a picturesque outdoor patio when the curtain is pulled back. Behind the curtain, a set of sliding glass wall panels works with the curtain to create a completely insulated and private interior. The curtain as architectural element refers back to traditional Japanese design elements such as shoji and *sudare* (horizontal-reed screens), and fusuma doors common within the traditional Japanese house, and serves as a moving, engaging element that encourages natural air flow and ventilation. The interior and exterior can be merged into one comfortable space for the inhabitants, giving rise to experiences within the dwelling that are very difficult to achieve within a city as large and populous as the Japanese capital. Ban is most famous now for his innovative work with ephemeral materials such as paper and cardboard tubing.

To this Japanese neo-expressionism of ephemera, one must today add the commercial nodes of Ginza, Shinjuku and Akihabara. Their identities seem more

like high-tech reincarnations of decadent, frivolous Edo period *ukiyo* ('Floating World') themes.[25] Primarily embodied through Las Vegas-like simulacrums of larger-than-life neon and post-neon signage, these fluorescent skins are recurrently shed and continually updated to keep up with Japan's post-industrial whims of psychedelic consumerism. And true to Toyo Ito's observation, "If the Western city is a museum, then the Japanese city is a theater." In observing Japan today, it occurs that it is not just signage but the buildings themselves that are designed, not with the expectation of standing the test of time, but to be torn down sooner rather than later and replaced by a new backdrop appropriate to the economic and technological spirit of the times[26] (fig. 5.8).

In his essay "What Goes Up Must Come Down", Botond Bognar has noted numerous instances of this bewildering phenomenon.[27] In 1997, when he wrote the piece, the annual degree of change within Tokyo's densely built urban zones was about 30% (encompassing façade improvements to entire new structures). The average life-span of a building was around 26 years. Virtually any building had a zero value after about three years, even if built of reinforced concrete, the true value of the property lying in the ground alone. Throughout its history, Japan has always had land scarcity, explaining their tendency for spatial compaction, from mountain terracing for paddy fields to capsule buildings. As Nitshke has observed, "the tendency is to expand space by increasing experiential time through the reduction of speed and the obstruction of movement. Space is created by "killing" (slowing down) time."[28]

It is not difficult then to understand why the Japanese still await hanami and change the kakemonos in their tokonomas, why Ise's shikinen sengu lives on, and why beneath all the seemingly high-tech deliria of the Japanese metropolis, the sensitivity to the constancy of change lives on. The traditional Japanese consciousness of time endures and thrives as a cultural blueprint within its post-industrial milieu. To engage in Japanese architecture, even today, is to learn to appreciate beauty in a manner counterintuitive to how the Western world has learnt to see it, to puncture the conventional myths of permanence, and thrill in the joy of change and uncertainty.

Nothing prepared me for the 3000 lights at the Kasuga Taisha. Some 2000 stone lanterns line the shrine path and 1000 metal lamps adorn the sanctuary eaves and interiors. They have been accumulating for over eight hundred years as donations from the faithful. Years ago, they were lit by Shinto priests every day. Even now, on the two days they are lit each year, a calm luminosity drapes the entire mountain terrain.

Nothing prepared me for the 1300 red torii at Fushimi Inari Taisha. At the back of the shrine's main grounds is the entrance to a sacred tunnel with arrays of torii winding up the hill, like a harmonic chant in physical form. They too are donations by devotees, and you can find their names if you look for them. As you pass through that rhythmic trail, space and time can no longer be distinguished.

Nothing prepared me for the 8,000 weathered stone Buddhas at Adashino Nenbutsu-ji. They sit on a hill overlooking the city in absolute silence, to honor the souls of the departed. They occupy the space where the dead were left to nature during the Heian period in desperate times of war, epidemic and famine, and where relatives returned to remember their loved ones. When you stand there, words have no meaning.

Nothing prepared me for the 1001 aureate Kannons in Sanjusangendo. The central eleven-foot high seated Kannon has his golden hands folded together in front of his golden chest, and on each side are 500 other life-size Kannons also covered in gold-leaf. They each have a thousand arms—the 40 that you can count each have the power to save 25 worlds. When you stand in their soft radiance, you can hide nothing.

Adashino Nenbutsu-ji, Kyoto.

Paper lanters and neon signs, Tokyo.

Chapter 6

Deliberate Dusk: Darkness and the Experience of Japanese Architectural Space

In 1933, Japanese novelist Junichiro Tanizaki wrote an essay "In ei raisan," lamenting his nation's cultural erosion through Westernization. He used the metaphor of light and darkness to contrast the two worlds: The Western zeal for progress was presented as the persistent search for brighter light; the subtleties of Japanese tradition, as an appreciation of shadows and darkness. Since its English translation "In Praise of Shadows" by Thomas Harper and Edward Seidensticker in the 1970s, it has been hailed as a seminal literary work on Japanese culture.[1] Tanizaki's essay appeared in the Japanese newspaper Keisai Orai about three decades after Sir Arthur Conan Doyle's "The Hound of the Baskervilles" had been serialized in the Strand Magazine in London in 1902, wherein he pitted the infamous detective Sherlock Holmes with a murderous hound against a dark, macabre setting of the Dartmoor marshes of Devon. Both written well after Thomas Alva Edison's 1870's advent of the incandescent bulb had diametrically opposite allusions to darkness: Doyle's sombre, diabolical backdrop versus Tanizaki's ethereal, surreal realm of meditative reverie.

If Thomas Edison's incandescent bulb could be said to radiate the brilliance of the Sun, then traditional Japanese illumination could be said to abet the tranquility of the moon. Indeed, part of the aura of traditional Japanese space lay in its soft, subdued light, its dim shadowy world that complimented the soft textures of the *tatami* and *shoji*. This seeming aversion to light, this sensitivity to darkness and gloom remains one of the most distinguishing characteristics separating traditional Japanese architecture from the larger Western world. In fact, before the introduction of kerosene oil in Japan, the light emitted from tiny wicks, or an unsteady vegetable-wax candle flame was all the more feeble when filtered through a paper lantern. It seemed like something of a boon then, when kerosene oil entered Japan among the many things brought in by the West.[2]

Circa 1870, one of these new imports was the incandescent bulb. Though fairly innocuous by today's standards, it would within decades, erode the ancient Japanese affinity to darkness and shadows and the various esoteric rituals that had formed part of their daily life. Of course the West too had known times without electricity, gas or petroleum. But from candle and oil-lamp to gas-light, the quest for a brighter light had never ceased.[3] The Japanese by contrast had gradually developed a cul-

Figure 6.1 Below: Senso-ji Temple at night, Tokyo.

Figure 6.2 Opposite page: Changing expressions of a Noh mask under different lighting conditions.

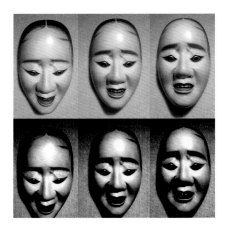

tural propensity to dark spaces. But all this was fast changing in the thirties when gold-flecked lacquer-ware was being rendered garish by electric light, and flood-lamps were turning Kabuki into a "world of sham."[4] It was this larger cultural in-undation that Tanizaki lamented through the metaphor of Japan's vanishing affinity to darkness and gloom.[5] In this chapter, I pay an architectural tribute to Tanizaki's rhetoric by tracing the origins, meanings and manifestations of this tradition of darkness and eventually its shifts within an increasingly Westernizing Japan.

DARKNESS

The concept of *yami* (darkness) had stemmed from ancient Shinto mythology, im-plying a mysterious feeling of something hidden in space. Darkness was believed to be the abode of the *kami* (spirit) and was revered as sacred space. At a Shinto shrine one therefore progressed from light to darkness shutting out all worldly distractions to enter the kami world. Even today at the Ise shrine, for instance, one of the most important rituals, the Shin *no mihashira hoken*–when the shrine's pillars are installed in the ground–is held at night in keeping with ancient Shinto concepts of conceal-ment. The Sengyo, Ise's most solemn ritual wherein the *kami shintai* (spirit deity) is carried from the old shrine to the new, is celebrated in darkness, with only a few torches lighting the procession.[6] In his fourteenth century essays Tsure-Zure Gusa, when the Zen monk Yoshida Kenko emphasized that "night is the best time also to go to worship at the Shinto and Buddhist temples, especially on those occasions when others do not go", he was affirming this ancient reverence for darkness and its idea of purification, embodied in the dark path to the sacred realm (fig. 6.1).[7]

Numerous themes of darkness pervade Japanese architectural history. In the Zen *roji* (tea garden) trees are carefully planted to create the impression of walking through a dark forest. There are no lanterns hanging from branches. All stone lamps are placed on the ground to reinforce a dark above. The dark path to the Tea Hut is a meticulously designed world to elicit self-purification.[8] In the traditional Noh theater, darkness becomes the backdrop to express the actors' emotions through the changing shadows on their masks (fig. 6.2). Traditional Japanese architectural space was experienced as much through darkness as light. It was less about reading size,

geometry and form, like the Western reading of space, and more about the perceptual experience of minimal light playing in a void. Junichiro Tanizaki was right when he compared the Japanese room to "an ink wash painting, the paper-paneled shoji being the expanse where the ink is thinnest, and the alcove where it is darkest."[9]

GLOOM

"The little sunlight from the garden that manage(d) to make its way beneath the eaves and through the corridors.....lost its power to illuminate seem(ing) drained of the complexion of life," wrote Tanizaki.[10] He was not lamenting, but eulogizing the Japanese genius that layer by layer, cut down the glare of sunlight and brought it in as a subdued gloom.

Consider for instance the manner in which the Japanese traditionally made their living places. One can begin with the myth of Susanoo-no-Mikoto, the brother of the Sun Goddess Amaterasu attributed as the first person in Japanese mythology to build a temple. He is said to have composed the song: "Many clouds appeared; And clouds covered my house like many fences; Having my wife surrounded by the clouds making the fences; Many many fences were made." Susanoo-no-Mikoto's rhetoric is implicitly similar to what Tanizaki noted many centuries later: "In making for ourselves a place to live, we first spread a parasol to throw a shadow on the earth, and in the pale light of the shadow we put together a house."[11]

Indeed, from modest dwellings to colossal temples, the first act of building was the erection of the roof supported on wooden columns. The most conspicuous feature of a traditional Japanese building was this dominant sweeping parasol made of thatch or tile, covering a space engulfed in gloom. Sunlight, blocked by the eaves, entered the room only after being reflected off the surrounding *engawa* (verandah). As it traveled upward, it became less bright eventually filtering through the *washi* (rice paper panels) of the *shoji* (lattice screens). Even during the brightest outdoors, one could not transcend the gloom of the Japanese interior that rendered the columns and appurtenances hardly visible to the eye (fig. 6.3).

Thus, contrary to the presence of light for the formal comprehension of Western architectural space, Japanese space was an *in-ei* space – a "mystical, sensual world

in which literature and logic were viewed in a shadowy light."[12] And this non-formal spatial comprehension was evoked through emotional attitudes of beauty: For instance, one of the great themes of Heian era aesthetics was the concept of *mono-no-aware*. It implied an emotional sensitivity to all things animate and inanimate, unified by a sense of impermanence. The concept expanded to acquire an undercurrent of melancholy within the subdued gloom of a space.

With the advent of Zen Buddhism, the notion of austerity was heightened through two moods of expression, *wabi* and *sabi* (discussed in Chapter 5). Wabi implied humility and an abstinence from fashionable society to cultivate an intrinsic spiritual value transcending social status. Architecturally, the dark forest like approach to a *soan* (Tea Hut) was said to prepare in the visitor a sense of progressing solitude or a wabi state of mind. Sabi in turn, celebrated age and patina, referring to individual objects and environments with a rustic unpretentiousness or an archaic imperfection, extending to the aesthetics of minimalism as suggested in Chapter 3. The rusticity of the Tea Hut suggested sabi through the emulation of a dark, rustic hermit's hut deep within the mountains.

Thus, from the time he came to serve as tea master to the diamyo Toyotomi Hideyoshi, the tea-master Sen-no-Rikyu's (1522-1591) distaste for garish color achieved widespread following with his advocacy for wabi austerity. Through his instruction, the color gray enjoyed great popularity and this ash-dyed neutral hue came to be known as "Rikyu gray."[13] In the latter part of the Edo period, gray was much favored by aesthetes, their tastes ranging from silver, indigo, scarlet-tinged, dove and plain grays, thereby permitting subtle variations in color balance. As the Japanese architect Kisho Kurokawa observed in the rustic metaphor of Rikyu gray, "its contradictory elements collide with and neutralize each other, producing a state of continuity and discontinuity, a contrapuntal coexistence that disallows sensual appreciation."[14] There is thus another quality to traditional Japanese space than the purely formal. In their gloom is a fullness of spiritual import that is quite overpowering. As the American architect Ralph Adams Cram noted, Japanese spaces "breathe mysticism and abstraction, they are dreamlike and visionary. Under their shadows alone (can) one understand a little of Buddhism."[15]

DIFFUSION

The soft daylight diffusing through the rice-paper paneled shoji is the quintessential traditional Japanese illumination. The shoji represents for Japan what glass does for the West. As noted in Chapter 2, the evolution of shoji began in the early Nara period (720 – 780 CE) when boards were used as room dividers. With the addition of thick opaque paper, these boards evolved into the opaque fusuma panels. According to Japanese architect Atsushi Ueda, with the samurai houses of the Kamakura (1190 – 1340 CE) and Muromachi (1340–1570 CE) periods liberating architecture from the previous Chinese influences, this paper began to get increasingly translucent and evolved into the light akara shoji with rice paper stretched across a grid of wooden pieces (fig. 6.4). Neither transparent nor opaque, this unique membrane took the light in, enveloped it and brought it in "like a soft surface of a first snowfall."[16]

The epitome of such diffused lighting was the Tea Hut that housed the Tea Ceremony. Here, window placement was calculated not only for ventilation and visual effects on the walls, but also to create just the right contemplative ambience when the ritual was performed. Sen-no-Rikyu and his school used *fukuro-bari* panels in the tea-room. These were fusuma boards papered in a shoji-like manner with white paper pasted on both sides instead of one. "A tea-room should neither be too bright nor too dark inside. A room that is too bright is not suitable for concentration, for the mind is likely to be disturbed, but on the other hand if it is not lit enough a sense of gloom and melancholy may be felt, which is worse. The outer windows and overhung shutters must be arranged according to the position of the sun so that a happy medium can be obtained," Rikyu noted.[17] Some tea huts had windows that could be propped open at various angles to vary the quality of seasonal light and therein the interior ambience. The Yuin Tea Hut in Kyoto for instance has a hatch on its eaves to let in starlight for the same purpose.

The Japanese affinity to diffused lighting then represents the antithesis of the Western preference of bathing space in light. Like a *haiku* (short poem) where words are at best to be felt, not rationalized, Japanese shadowy space was a "metaphysical" realm to be evoked in time, not rationalized through the parameters of form and shape. As Tanizaki explained, though the ancient Japanese knew perfectly well it

Figure 6.4 The aesthetic of shoji screens. Top: Sesshu-ji funda-in, Kyoto. Bottom: Koto-in, Kyoto.

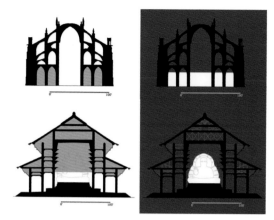

was mere shadow, they were overcome with the feeling that in that small corner of the atmosphere there reigned complete and utter silence; and there in the darkness immutable tranquility held sway.[18]

CONTRAST

The original *daibutsuden* (Buddha staute) of the Todai-ji Temple in Nara (discussed in Chapter 1 & 2) was one of the largest wooden structures in the world. Rebuilt today to half its original size, its towering interior spans a length of 188 feet, width of 166 feet and height of 157 feet. It houses a colossal 53-feet-high statue of the Buddha. Yet on the inside there is nothing to celebrate this voluminous space. There are no windows high within the walls, no light pouring down from above (fig. 6.5). The Western cathedral where the openings were perched at soaring heights to let light flood its towering verticality may have an awe-inspiring majesty, but Japanese space shutting the light from above has its own dusky splendor.

But then spatial qualities can be transformed by differences in the natural light of the day and artificial lighting used at night. In the Hagia Sofia in Constantinople for instance, during the day, light descends from openings around edges of the dome and from the windows high in the walls. The vertical space is perceived in all its grandeur. At night, the spatial impression of the Hagia Sofia is quite different: the suspended lamp fittings from the high ceiling are brought into play and hang only a few feet above the ground, defining a low space closed off by the darkness above. In Japan, however, their colossal temple interiors or the intimate domestic rooms always maintained a horizontal profile. The intricate wooden network of a towering roof was perpetually wrapped in darkness. The spatial configuration of a traditional Japanese edifice was hopelessly consistent, day or night (fig. 6.6).

From a Modernist perspective, nothing could be more antithetical to traditional Japanese lighting than the Chapel of Notre Dame du Haut at Ronchamp. Here Le Corbusier uses light as a means of accentuating the various spatial realms: the characteristics of the main spaces were underlined by small openings cut in the massive south-facing wall with clear and colored glass. The side chapels by contrast are illuminated from above, with light descending through the openings high within

Figure 6.5 Opposite page: Daibutsu at Todai-ji Temple, Nara.

Figure 6.6 Top: Comparative lighting studies by day and night. Top: Chatres Cathedral, Paris. Bottom: Todai-ji Daibutsuden, Nara.

Figure 6.7 Buddha statues in temple altars. Left to right: Horyu-ji Temple, Nara; Sennyu-ji Temple, Kyoto, Kaiko-ji Temple, Yamagata Prefecture, Hasedera Temple, Kamakura.

the towers. Corbusier differentiates the side chapels from the main space not only in terms of form, but also by the nature of their lighting. Moreover, he uses light to distinguish elements of the building from each other separating the shell shaped roof from the wall by a narrow horizontal light strip.

The Japanese seemed averse to such spatial hierarchy. As noted in Chapter 4, in a typical shoin interior, the *tokonoma* (scroll alcove), is by far the most important part of a room. But though it may be sometimes placed closer to an exterior wall, it is never accentuated in terms of lighting. It is always part of a uniform illumination enveloping the entire room. At night the darkness of a room is broken by domestic lighting devices that are placed on the floor, this low illumination complimenting the traditional Japanese custom of sitting on the floor with tables and other appurtenances also horizontally proportioned. The concept of spatial accentuation through light never quite found its way in traditional Japan.

GLINT

Gold has a peculiar relationship with darkness. It never loses its gloss like silver and other metals. It always retains its brilliance absorbing every available photon and draping it like a ghostly veil to create an illusion of depth. The glint of gold lacquer in a gloomy interior is as distinct a Japanese trait as the subdued light filtering through a shoji.

There is evidence to suggest that lacquer was used in Japan from the Stone Age, 6000 years ago, as an adhesive to attach the arrowhead to the arrow. From about 4000 years ago, vermillion and black lacquer were being coated on tableware, utensils as well as weapons and accessories. About 100 years ago, a guild specializing in lacquer art called *urushi-be* was known to have been established.[19] The point is that among Japan's traditional arts, while dyeing and hand-made paper came through the influence of China, lacquerware was born and nurtured within the climate of Japan itself. The splendor of lacquer begins with Japan's early Buddhist architecture. The oldest surviving lacquered object in Japan is the *tamamushi-no-zushi* of the Horyu-ji Temple (built 607 CE), a miniature shrine modeled after a wooden palace towards the end of the sixth century.

By the Heian period (789-1190 CE), lacquer was being used to clad colossal wooden statues in Japan's Buddhist temples. At Todai-ji, the colossal sitting bronze and gold Buddha (smaller than the two original ones), is adorned with a magnificent gold canopy of smaller Buddhas that surround him. At the Byodo-in, the colossal 25 feet tall wooden Buddha is adorned with gold leaf and lacquer with its 40 feet high canopy inlaid with mother-of-pearl. These lacquered giants sit in the dark, "their florid patterns reced(ing) into darkness," conjuring an inexpressible aura of depth and mystery.[20] "The sheen of the lacquer, set out in the night, reflects the wavering candlelight.... luring one into a state of reverie,"[21] (fig. 6.7).

The Konjikido Hall of the Chuson-ji Temple (built in 1124 CE) stands out for its use of glittering gold both inside and outside. A gorgeous altar and eleven gold Buddhist statues arranged in a row occupy this space embellished with gold leaf and lacquer adorning its pillars and dais. Nothing could be more contradictory to the monochrome rustic Japanese interior, than the dazzle of the Konjikido, reflecting the desire for eternal glory by three generations of Fujiwara rulers.

But arguably the most extraordinary experience of Japanese glint is the Sanju-sangendo Hall (literally "hall with 33 bays")[22] of the Rengeo-in Temple (originally built in 1164, rebuilt in 1266). As discussed in Chapter 1, its 33 bays stretching some 400 feet in length make not only the longest wooden hall in Japan, but also one of the most visually stunning interiors of any Japanese temple. 1,001 statues of Kannon-Bosatsu, each 5 1/2 feet tall, carved out of Japanese cypress and leafed in gold surround the central eleven-feet-tall Kannon in 10 rows and 50 columns.

The golden exterior of Kinkaku-ji is an exception in Japanese architecture, but the regal appeal of gold's luminescence did not fail to find its way into the interiors of Japanese villas. The paper used on the opaque fusuma panels separating rooms was often embossed with small gold or silver designs. At the Audience Hall in the Ninomaru of Nijo Castle, the unique quality of the interior is determined by the careful juxtaposition of wood, color and gold. Color is applied to the ceilings, but not the structural frame. Gold is applied to the ornamental nail-coverings and other hardware, providing the structure with a unifying background tone illuminated by highlights. And incorporating all these aspects are paintings used in concert with the horizontal and vertical structural grid.[23] Attributed to Kano Tannyu, they have

Figure 6.8 Gilded interior details.
Higashi Hongan-ji Temple
founder's hall, Kyoto.

gold leaf rubbed with white for their background, along with brown, copper green, cobalt blue and black India ink dominating the specifics. In the gloom of the interior, the effect with these golden walls is one of subdued luminescence, creating an illusion of depth as the gold absorbs the light from the space around it. As Drexler notes, "In the great sixteenth-century efflorescence of palace and temple building fusuma carried a weight of mural painting in black ink, or in color on a gold or silver ground, that may be said to surpass in its subtlety and its invention the greatest achievements of architectural decoration in the Italian Renaissance."[24] (fig. 6.8).

Thus, Tanizaki concluded that lacquerware decorated in gold is not something to be seen in bright light. It was to be left in the dark and picked up in a faint light. "Indeed the thin, impalpable, faltering light, picked up as though little rivers were running through the room, collecting little pools here and there, lacquer(ing) a pattern on the surface of night itself," he noted.[25]

The traditional Japanese affinity to darkness has no definite rationale, yet it seemed to be everywhere. Perhaps it stemmed from the religious influences of Shinto and Buddhism, or conversely, the subconscious influence of the dense and misty natural surroundings on a culture's psyche. Whatever the case, it must seem endearing to the West that their dominant spatial associations with darkness and gloom — from a Bergmanesque grimness to an eerie macabre–have nurtured other qualities in Japan. These notions are non-existent within the English linguistic palette, but that has hardly stopped the Western mind from trying to describe them.

NEON

Half a century after it had discovered the incandescent bulb between 1869 and 1882, Japan stumbled upon the neon. In around 1926, the first Japanese neon signs were made public at Hibiya Park in Tokyo, about two decades after their perfection by the French scientist George Claude was first presented to the public at the Paris International Exposition.[26] The colored light bulb as the prevalent illumination device was little match for the glitz of neon now ushering a revolution in light sources for outdoor advertising. Thus the 1964 Tokyo Olympics–not just an event, but a symbol of high economic growth in Japan–was dominated by visuals of this newfound "neonism".

Figure 6.9 Nocturnal signage.
Right: Shinjuku streetscape.
Bottom: Detail of Neon signage of
a Shinjuku game parlor. Opposite
page: Ginza streetscape.

In December 1979, Japan held its first examination for neon sign installation engineers. In April 1992, the formation of the Association of Qualified Neon Sign Engineers was formed. In June 1998, a series of events to celebrate the thirtieth anniversary of the All Japan Neon Association included the "Ginza Neon Light Extinguishing Performance" and the "1st Neon Art Competition."[27] This was post-incandescent Japan, where *pachinko* (pin-ball) parlors reigned supreme and where neon displays became part of a bright, zesty nightscape unapologetically contradicting the delicately diffused lanterns of the few surviving traditional streetscapes.

Thus emerged Ginza, Shinjuku and Shibuya. These new nodes are the antithesis of the dim narrow alleys of Pontocho. In the daytime they are little more than a skeleton for what they become at night. The contorted, poker-like irons that form the frames of the winding neon signs are disheveled in the day, but come sundown and they transform into a riot of electro-urbanism. Here neon, far from being an eyesore, is as much an essential ingredient of Japan's overwhelming consumerism, as a mutated offspring of its nocturnal fetishism (fig. 6.9).

More than a century has passed since Japan adopted the incandescent bulb, more than eight decades since it fell for the neon. The light bulb may have overlaid the traditional paper lantern but it was little match for the glitz of neon that ushered a revolution in lighting tastes. With the increasing demand for outdoor advertising and complex forms of communication, neon has been Japan's new means to express its development for a new time. As Tanizaki concluded "I am aware of and most grateful for the benefits of the age. No matter what complaints we may have, Japan has chosen to follow the West, and there is nothing for her to do but move bravely ahead and leave us old ones behind."[28] But then one is reminded of Mrs. Tanizaki's story of when her husband decided to build a new house. When the architect proudly claimed to have read "In Praise of Shadows" and to know exactly what his client wanted, Tanizaki replied "But no, I could never live in a house like that."[29] There was as much nostalgia as skepticism in that response – one that might best describe Japan's continuing emotional roller coaster between darkness and light.

One mid-August evening, Kyoto was in a rush. Everyone was running around trying to find a place in the city, particularly around the Kamo River. I in turn dashed south on Teramachi until I saw the shop for roasted chestnuts, and then squeezed through a tiny alley until I hit the dead-end. In this tiny eatery, a special lady has decided to bring Buddhist wisdom to ordinary people through *shoujin ryori*, or organic vegetarian Zen cuisine, otherwise available only in a few of the city's Zen temples. She too was in a rush. After she brought me the last meal of the day, she hustled to grab a milk bottle for her crying kitten, and we dashed out together into the anxious city.

At 7.59 p.m. Kyoto came to a standstill. Everyone had somehow found a place. Everyone was looking north into pitch darkness. A minute later, when a tiny glow of fire broke the black background, there was a cheer. Then another glow followed, and another. Within minutes the Chinese character *Dai* was floating in black space. Within half an hour, four other fiery apparitions appeared and slowly melted back into the darkness.

The annual Gozan no Okuribi ritual culminates the O-Bon festival, when the spirits of ancestors revisit their household altars; when people return to ancestral family places and visit and clean their ancestors' graves. The five giant *Okuribi* (send-off-fires) lit on the northern mountains of the city are received with awe as well as tears, because the spirits are returning back to their world.

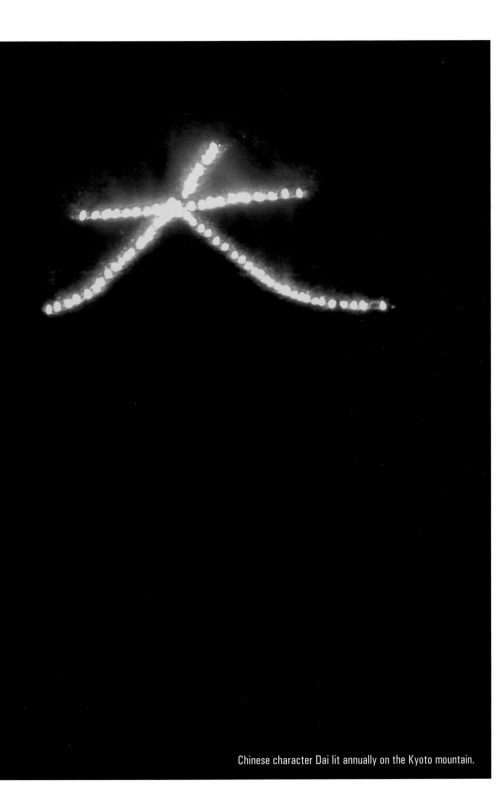

Chinese character Dai lit annually on the Kyoto mountain.

View of Kyoto cityscape from Kiyomizu Temple.

Chapter 7
Kyoto: A View from Rome

Kyoto is undoubtedly the greatest city in Japanese history. Tokyo's dramatic transformation from a feudal castle-town to a global megalopolis in half a century cannot be undermined, but Kyoto's cultural legacy and heritage is incomparable. When one thinks of Kyoto in the Japanese context, one thinks of the imperial epoch of Japan's capital for fully half of the nation's recorded history, a tangible urban testament that for more than a thousand turbulent years witnessed the emergence of a vital and independent new civilization that could be ranked among the most elegant and refined in the world.

In this chapter, I glorify Kyoto by tracing its parallel evolution with the cultural epoch of Rome. But why Rome of all places? Some might find this comparison strained or far-fetched. After all, the histories and evolutionary trajectories of these two places could not be more different: Kyoto's founding in Enryaku 19, the nineteenth full year in the reign of Emperor Kammu – by Western count 800 CE – the year of Charlemagne's coronation can hardly be compared to Rome's ancient aqueducts, viaducts and paved roads, and its foundation stones quarried from the Etruscan and the Hellenic cultures. Rome's evolution from Cloaca to Forum to Bath to its first great arenas – the Circus Flaminius built in 221 BCE; to the fifth century "when the hands that had once grasped an empire could no longer keep any part of it securely in their hold"; to the renouncing of the pagan world and the founding of the Heavenly City, all happened before Kyoto was even conceived.[1]

But that said, even as Kyoto was born, Rome deep in the waters of urban decay, was also being re-born – sprouting the politico-religious seeds of Papacy that would incept a new link between the classical and medieval city, and eventually usher it into the glory of the Renaissance. And it is here from the fifteenth century on that Rome and Kyoto finally face each other as contemporaneous models of philosophical thought, art and life, though not much would bear resemblance between them, and though neither perhaps even knew of the others' existence. Few know for instance that the Zen rock garden of Ryoan-ji, and Michelangelo's marble sculpture, the Pieta, were created exactly at the same time (in 1499). Looking at Kyoto from Rome in this sense can serve to enrich and deepen our understandings of both worlds.

But that is not why I have chosen Rome as Kyoto's discussion counterpart. I have done so because Rome remains the undisputed historic epicenter of the Euro-

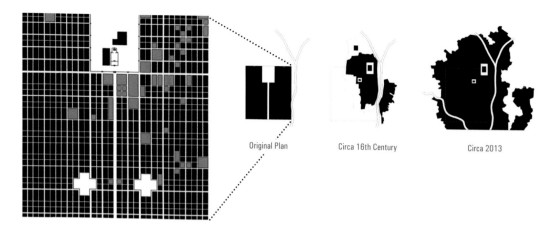

Original Plan   Circa 16th Century   Circa 2013

Figure 7.1 Top left: Diagrammatic layout of Kyoto as originally planned. Right: Evolution of Kyoto.

Figure 7.2 Opposite page left: Kyoto within its mountain surroundings.

Figure 7.3 Opposite page right: Model of Kyoto looking north. The Suzakumon is in the center ending in the palace complex.

pean cultural context – with a riveting story of rise, fall, and new beginnings, and an unprecedented span of influence reaching all the way to modern nations. My choice of Rome is more symbolic than analytical, because my comparison is not so much a historian's extractive examination of two cities, but rather a poetic celebration of what I consider to be modern Japan's cultural epicenter. By unabashedly viewing Kyoto from its greatest European counterpart, my narrative is an epistemological provocation on how and why the cultural splendor of Kyoto has remained undermined by a global audience inundated by Western dominated scholarship. By using Rome's re-known architectural and urban epochs as springing points to re-read Kyoto – my intention is to call a reader to notice the glory of Japan's greatest city and celebrate it.

URBAN ORDER

But that is not to undermine the apparent formal parallels of ancient Rome and early Kyoto. For instance, the Roman city was oriented to harmonize with cosmic order through its two principal intersecting streets – the cardo and decumanus running north-south and east-west – the Romans having apparently imbibed this urban form from fortresses built on islands or banks of the Nile during the Twelfth Dynasty.[2] Unlike the Greek city where the wall was often an afterthought, the Roman city began with such a wall, and the city, partly for religious, partly for utilitarian reasons, took the form of a rectangle. Tracing this Roman imprint on a whole series of towns from Naples and Ostia to Verona and Florence, all of them were designed as units, with blocks around 250-feet-square, their open spaces and public buildings carefully sited in relation to the main thoroughfares.

If Rome had its cardo-decumanus, then Kyoto had its Suzakumon, a principal central avenue that established its fundamental urban order. Tracing back to the considerably larger precedent of Changan, the Chinese capital under the Sui and Tang dynasties from 583 CE to 904 CE, and its eighth century Japanese predecessor Heijo-Kyo (Nara), this central urban spine ran straight from the southern gate, terminating due north in the Imperial Palace and bisecting the city into two symmetrical halves (fig. 7.1). It was the most conspicuous element in Kyoto's 3.3 x 2.8 mile

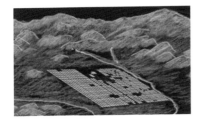

planned parallelogram form enclosing two large temple precincts, with blocks of 400-feet-square called *cho*, four of them making a *ho* or square, four ho making a *bo* or division. But unlike its Chinese precedent (and its Roman counterpart), Kyoto's original plan did away with the city wall, replacing it with an embankment and ditch and thereby leaving the city edge open to the surrounding mountains.[3]

Kyoto was enclosed by three mountains, Higashiyama, Kitayama and Nishi-yama. Mount Heie, the highest peak was on the far side of the Devil's Gate in the north-east and the entire city opened to the south onto a broad flat plain. At the center of Chinese geomancy lay the search for an ideal site upon which to build an ancestral burial vault, a house or town in harmony with existing nature. The Chinese visualized such locations as an armchair, its back being a mountain and its armrests the hills. It was this idea of the *xue* (lair) and its protective function with mountains or buildings on the three remaining sides that guided the siting of Kyoto (fig. 7.2). But there was more to these mountains than their geomantic dimensions; they were also the sacred grounds of Kyoto's greatest temples such as Kiyomizudera built in 798 CE on Higashiyama. Kyoto's seemingly relentless grid dissolved into these elevated sacred domains extending the city into the dramatic natural geography.

Of course, much before, Rome's famous seven hills had albeit differently staged an acropolis town formed out of an accretion of mountain villages. These seven hills were in fact crests between a series of blind valleys along the Tiber, and like the Etruscans who used them as tombs and cellars, they too constituted like Kyoto's hills, the truly local component of Rome's character. Rome was situated between two worlds: the western volcanic world of the *forre*, and the eastern classical landscape.[4] Kyoto on the other hand was nestled within its mountainous armchair, open and sloping towards the south. Its central north-south Suzakumon was aligned to look directly south from atop Mount Funaoka. Standing on its pinnacle one could see with absolute clarity the ordered nature of its urban grid and roofscape (fig. 7.3).

CHRISTIANOPOLIS & ZENOPOLIS

By the fifth century, after the fall of the Roman Empire, its one powerful and universal association was the Church. Rome found a new prototype in the Heavenly

Figure 7.4 Top: Tenryu-ji Temple.

Figure 7.5 Opposite page top: Panorama of Rome cityscape.

Figure 7.6 Opposite page bottom: Panorama of Ginkaku-ji garden.

City and cathedral, church, monastery and shrine spires were the first symbols of urbanity. Ancient Roman building types such as the theater, arena and bath were now easy converts into places for Christian congregation. By the twelfth century (the era of the first crusade), Rome was revered by the Latins as the metropolis of the world, the throne of the pope and emperor, who from the eternal city derived the right of temporal dominion.

The eight to the twelfth centuries when Kyoto was incepted are unthinkable without their three new sects of Buddhism. As discussed in Chapter 1, what the Tendai and Shingon sects – with Enryaku-ji on Mount Hiei, Kongobu-ji on Mount Koya, Kyoo Gokoku-ji (now called Toji), Ninna-ji, Muro-ji and the Kiyomizudera – did for the first half of the Heian era, the Amida sect did for the second: It sought a new temple prototype to express its central idea of Amida Buddhism's concept of Pure Land Paradise.[5] But Kyoto, unlike Rome, never saw the religious zeal of forced conversion. No temple of Antoninus and Faustina became the Church of St. Lorenzo; no Senate House became the Church of St. Adriano. Like Rome however, religion and faith remained a dominant force behind new and larger civic architecture. The Byodo-in temple in Uji or the Zen monastery of Tenryu-ji were former mansions of the Fujiwara lords that were readily given to religious conversion (fig. 7.4).

As mentioned in Chapter 1, the late twelfth century saw the introduction of other Buddhist sects – Ji, Shin, Nichiren, Jodo and Yuzu Nembutsu – but with its increasing adoption by the dominant military class in these war-filled times, it was Zen that would emerge as the most influential one. Its axial monastic model – from Nanzen-ji and Daitoku-ji, to Kennin-ji and Manju-ji – became the dominant prototype of the times. What Christianity did for Rome, Zen did for Kyoto: it became the dominant philosophical conscience of the culture, the economic and intellectual catalyst for its most progressive developments. By the fourteenth century even as nearly half of Rome's thousand odd pagan destinations were being absorbed into Christendom, Kyoto was witnessing the ever-increasing popularity of Zen in both its regal and military class. In both Rome – the "Christianopolis" and Kyoto – the "Zenopolis", the link between their past and future now lay within the monasteries, where new intellectual thought would bear the seeds of a renaissance (fig. 7.5, 7.6).

Figure 7.7 Top: Michelangelo's Pieta. Opposite page: Close-up of Ryoan-ji garden.

FROM RUINS TO RENAISSANCE

In the Middle Ages, Rome had been abandoned and reduced to ruins due to the papal transfer to Avignon in France. It was not until after 1418, when Pope Martin V re-established the Papal seat, that the city began its resurrection towards a great capital again. Meanwhile in Kyoto, the Onin War[6] had assumed serious proportions and razed the city's northern parts to ruins. By 1477, a decade after the fighting, Kyoto was nothing more than a place for mobs to loot what had been left. But amidst this political fragmentation, the rise of the samurai class and their affinity to Zen, along with the commingling of the imperial family with courtiers, daimyo, samurai and Zen priests, ushered a new renaissance in art of all kinds.

By the late fifteenth century, both Rome and Kyoto were flourishing again. Even as the magnificent Piazza Farnese and St. Peter's basilica were emerging in Rome, from *Noh* (drama), to *Cha-no-yu* (Tea Ceremony), the clamor of war could not drown the arts of peace in Muromachi era Kyoto. Even as Michelangelo was painting the ceiling of the Sistine Chapel, Soami was creating the Zen garden of Ryoan-ji – the former colorful and figural, the latter an austere and abstract narrative on the idea of creation and life. The creation of Ryoan-ji's garden of fifteen rocks in a bed of raked sand is speculated to be 1499. This places it as an exact contemporary of one of Michelangelo's most finished sculptures, the Pieta.

The 174-centimeter-high Pieta, a superb embodiment of Michelangelo's masterful understanding of both stone and human proportion, is carved out of a single rock of marble. The Virgin Mary cradling Christ after the Crucifixion is not abstract, but life-like down to every drape, as if balancing the Renaissance ideals of classical beauty with innate naturalism. The 248-square-meter Ryoan-ji garden in turn has fifteen carefully selected rocks grouped in proportional balance to embody everything Zen stands for. Here, each rock is meant to be admired not for their man-made augmentations but their original natural embellishments. The Pieta seeks divinity in human form: the Holy Virgin depicted as a young, ageless, serene mother, even as she holds an adult, tortured Christ. Ryoan-ji seeks the absolute through conscious abstraction negating all conventional human association and intellect. In these two masterworks, we see the quintessential artistic tendencies of Rome and Kyoto's respective sixteenth century worlds (fig. 7.7).

SIXTUS VERSUS HIDEYOSHI: THE CULT OF MONUMENTALITY

While Rome's reawakening from its Middle Age lethargy may well have been "as much a historic marvel as the rest of its destiny," its physical transformation could be largely attributed to the energetic impulse of Pope Sixtus V (Felice Peretti, 1585–1590).[7] Despite its religious centers and venerable ruins, the city's haphazard street system while impeding circulation had also diminished the visitor's vantage on its monuments. To remedy this situation, Sixtus V envisioned "Roma in forma sideris" – Rome in the shape of a star. He engaged Domenico Fontana (1543–1607) and other planners to lay out processional avenues linking the seven main churches and shrines that had to be visited by the faithful during the course of a day's pilgrimage. Thus the Strada Felice (1585-86), sloped down the hill from the obelisk before Santa Maria Maggiore, then climbed up to the summit of Pincio and the church of Santa Trinita dei Monti. It was intended (but never completed) to lead downwards again to the obelisk in the Piazza del Popolo; while continuing on the far side of Santa Maria Maggiore in a straight line to the church of Santa Croce in Gerusalemme. "Like a man with a divining rod" Sixtus V had transformed the Roman labyrinth into a visionary spectacle of monumental power.[8]

Meanwhile the crushing blow Kyoto had suffered through the Civil Wars of Onin and Bunmei – which lasted eleven years in the latter part of the 15th century – despite a quarter century of attempted recovery, could not resurrect its glorious past. There were fields and gardens extending for miles between the Kamigyo and Shimogyo regions, as if splitting the once integrated center into two. Kyoto was not an integrated city anymore. This remained for about a century until Toyotomi Hideyoshi ordered its complete rebuilding. He filled up the space between Kamigyo and Shimogyo to promote urbanization, enclosed the new city with an earthen embankment called the *odoi*, and reconstructed the Gosho (Imperial Palace) in the center of the city (fig. 7.8).

The visionary Toyotomi Hideyoshi was not a pontiff, but a warrior who not unlike Sixtus V, had risen from the lowest social stratas to a position of power through personal prowess. Upon his return to Kyoto after the battle of Yamazaki, though he first built a castle on the remains of the Myoken-ji Temple in 1584, an

Figure 7.8 Right: A rare 1696
Japanese woodblock map of
Kyoto, made in the early Edo
period during the 9th year of
the Genroku Era (1688-1704). It
shows the reconstructed city by
Toyotomi Hideyoshi. The Gosho
(Imperial Palace) is the white
rectangle in the middle of the left
edge of the city.

Figure 7.9 Opposite page left:
Diagram of Sixtus' Plan for
Rome. The circles indicate the
key monuments connected by the
new avenues. Right: Diagram of
Hideyoshi's monuments in Kyoto.
The top red square indicates
the approximate location of
the Jurakudai. The bottom red
square represents the original
Hongan-ji Temple. The red square
to its right across the river is the
Hoko-ji Temple. The white dotted
rectangle shows the profile of the
original planned city.

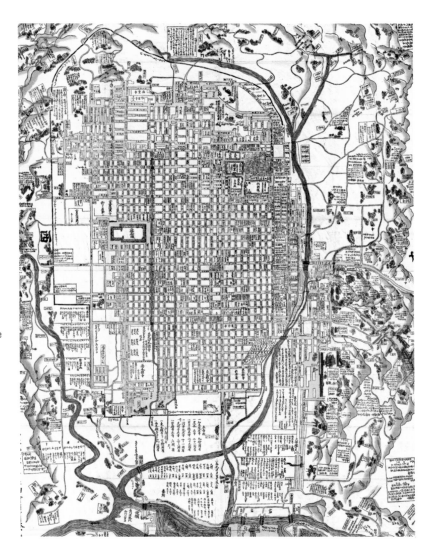

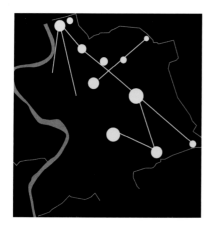
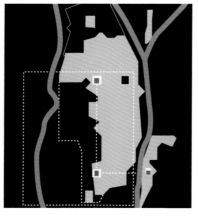

even larger castle was to follow two years later. The Jurakudai was a vast "stone-walled mountain" with 43,000 steps had iron turrets, copper doors and magnificent rooflines with "tigers roaring to the wind and dragons singing to the clouds."[9] Simultaneously in 1587 Hideyoshi commissioned the construction of the Hokoji Daibutsuden, modeled after the Great Buddha Hall at Todai-ji, calling for the making of a Buddha effigy that was covered with lacquer made from 10,000 bags of powdered oyster shell to exceed its precedent at Nara. This was to be followed in 1591 with the move of the Honganji Temple (the head temple of the Jodo-shinshu ["True Pure Land"] sect of Buddhism back to Kyoto, after the destruction of the former head temple, the Ishiyama Hongan-ji in Osaka.[10]

Hideyoshi located the Jurakudai to the city's north, just west of the ancient Heian palace, their east-west axes positioned to be roughly the same. Likewise the two new temples were placed in the city's southern half, Hoko-ji to the east of the Kamo River and facing west to overlook the Kyoto townscape below Mount Higashiyama, and the Hongan-ji to the west of the river its main building facing east. In so doing, Hideyoshi established a new visual east-west axis with the Hoko-ji Daibutsuden now visible in the distance from around Hongan-ji at a time when there was nothing but low townhouses to obstruct the view. And looking north from Hongan-ji, one saw the overpowering tower of the Jurakudai, the three edifices establishing a new visual framework for the city (fig. 7.9). A few years later, Tokugawa Ieyasu decided to split the Jodo-shin sect that had amassed colossal fortune and power into two branches to weaken its influence. The original Hongan-ji was renamed Nishi (or "West") Hongan-ji. A new temple was founded in 1602 as the "rival" branch of the Nishi Hongan-ji and named Higashi (or "East") Hongan-ji.[11] Hideysohi's megalomania thus transformed the sixteenth century Kyoto cityscape in much the same manner as Sixtus' vision had Rome. In these new monumental gestures – Hideyoshi's landmark edifices versus Sixtus' avenues and obelisks – both cities were to find an imposed yet reassured gravitas, a re-establishment of their grandiose status quo as the dominant urban centers of their worlds (fig. 7.9).

Figure 7.10 Top: One of the Ryakuchu-ryakugai screens of Kyoto showing the Shimogyo section of the city, circa seventeenth century, looking east. The Kiyomizu Temple can be seen at the top center in the far distance. The Sanjo Bridge and Gojo Bridge are depicted to the left and right respectively. Just north of the Gojo Bridge is the Hoko-ji Daibutsuden. The Higashi Hongan-ji Temple is at the lower right. The screen also shows the Gion festival parade with Yamaboko floats moving in the streets.

Figure 7.11 Right: Fragment of the Plan of Rome by Giambattista Nolli, completed circa 1748.

NOLLI & THE RYAKUCHU RYAKUGAI: THE CITY AS FORM & PLACE

Around 1728, when the Italian architect and surveyer Giambattista Nolli began work on his New Map of Rome for Pope Benedict XIV, a different sort of urban mapping was continuing in the city of Kyoto. Called the Ryakuchu Ryakugai Zu ("scenes inside and outside the Capital"), these painted screens like Nolli's visual rhetoric of Rome, depicted Heian Kyoto as a center of culture and power.[12]

Just as Nolli transformed the image of Rome from the center of Papal power and prestige to a system of grey blocks, white streets and piazzas, the Ryakuchu Ryakugai transformed the image of Kyoto from a non-egalitarian grid of square blocks and linear streets to a complex labyrinth of rich urban life. Just as Nolli had captured Rome at its crucial century-long flurry of building activity, of large triumphal spaces and significant landmarks – Piazza Navona, Piazza San Pietro, Michaelangelo's Campidoglio, Borromini's Sant' Ivo – equating the old and new, rich and poor into a single continuum of inhabited space; the Ryakuchu Ryakugai captured Kyoto at crucial junctures of the Heian, Muromachi, Momoyama and Edo periods, documenting its evolution from an early modest Heian townscape to its jubilance as a monumental castle town.[13] And just as Nolli had understood the Roman world as an urbanized extension of its surrounding marshes and campagnia, Kyoto's painted screens depicted the urban world within the persistent backdrop of its mountains (fig. 7.10, 7.11).

From the beginning, Kyoto's screens were always axonometric paintings perceived less like maps and more like stage sets. Some were composed as pairs of

six-folded screens meant to be placed together on either side of a room, negating therein the static frontal perception of a conventional visual frame. Like Rome's successive plans, they too captured Kyoto's urban evolution, often depicting only selective portions of the city as seen from selective vantage points. The Machida Ryakuchu Ryakugai Zue for instance depicted an impression of a relatively sparse and modest Heian cityscape in the first half of the 16th century. The Funaki Ryakuchu Ryakugai zue captured the early 17th century Kyoto townscape from the south looking north with the Hokoji Daibutsuden, Nijojo and the Hongan-ji temples standing out as urban monuments. And the Ikeda Ryakuchu Ryakugai Zue meant to be placed on opposite sides of the room showed Kamigyo in its left section and Shimogyo, Nijojo and the Daibutsuden in its right.

Yet unlike Nolli's clear and precise black & white, cartographic mapping of urban form, these Ryakuchu Ryakugai were colorful, pictoral, ambiguous depictions of urban place. They replaced the empty fluid white of Rome's meticulous indoor-outdoor analysis with an almost impressionist filigree of spontaneous urban activity shrouded by golden clouds. The idea of Rome as a city of piazzas and great public rooms was countered by the ambiguity of Kyoto's labyrinthine street space as an amoebic void sustaining an equally charged communal life. Rome's complex evolving palimpsest of layered history had been successively frozen as an urban artifact in time, even as the Ryakuchu Ryakugai had successively unraveled Kyoto as a fleeting slice of urban space-time, surfacing less its form, and more its people, seasons, rituals and festivals as the tangibles of its urbanity.

PIAZZA VERSUS PARK

By the eighteenth century, Rome was a city of piazzas, each wall and surface, rich, dignified and poignant, together making an urban container for great public life. No such thing can be said of Kyoto. Its numerous temple gardens did serve as gathering places, but they belonged to private institutions. Nothing like a piazza, that egalitarian figural space for communion never found a place in its glorious history. As we will discuss in the following chapter, it was its tenuous maze of streets that came to serve as the settings for publicness.

But Kyoto did have a large public space, in-fact larger than any of Rome's piazzas. It was not within but outside its planned city boundaries. The hills that enveloped the gridded polis were in fact a giant garden, its spatial expansion reaching vast distances only as much as Rome's piazzas sought perpetual social containment. Just as Piazza Novona represents Rome's most dramatic narrative on the transformative evolution of social space -from a circus to a plaza- in Kyoto's mega-garden, one finds clues to socio-cultural attitudes of Japanese splendor, refinement and recreation (fig 7.12).

Kyoto's exterior macro-garden was situated outside the odoi, the defensive barrier constructed by Toyotomi Hideyoshi at the end of the sixteenth century, clearly delineating the boundary between the central part of the city and its immediate surroundings. One would cross this three-meter-high barrier to engage in site-seeing tours and leisurely excursions within the surrounding hills. As such the Miyako Meisho Zue was considered a best-seller of its day, introducing the various areas and places of historic interest and scenic beauty. But perhaps the one most relevant to this discussion is the Keijo Shoran written by Kaibara Ekiken, and published in 1718, even though its introduction is dated back to 1706. It recommended site-seeing routes to be covered by foot within the span of a day – to the Kurama and Ohara hills to the city's north, to Kiyomizu-dera and Daigo-ji around the Yamashina hills in the east and south-east, to Fushimi and Yoshiminedera in the south, and to Horino-ji and Tenryu-ji around Mount Arashiyama as well as Takao to the west and north-west. It was possible then for Kyoto citizens to enjoy the tracks of natural landscape surrounding the city, consciously cultivated for both their sustenance and leisure. The historical ryakuchu area of the city thus had its own ryakugai garden.

Figure 7.12 Top: Diagram showing walking tour routes from Kyoto into destinations (shown in black dots) within surrounding mountains as depicted in the guidebook Kiejo Shoran by Kaibara Ekiken, circa 1718. Opposite page: Daimon-ji mountain seen from the city.

CONCLUSION – THE WEIGHT OF HERITAGE

Kyoto's story, like Rome, is one of ruin and resurrection. Recovery from its three major disasters: the fires of Hoei (1704-1710), Tenmei (1781-1788) and Genji (1864) took nothing short of major political movements leading to the Meiji Restoration (1868), when it regained its capital status only to have Japan's political situation call for Tokyo to be the center once again.[14] Citizen demonstrations bore

Figure 7.13 Top left: Typical collision and contrast between historic fabric and new development in Kyoto. Top Right: Kyoto cityscape viewed from the roof of Kyoto Station.

Figure 7.14 Opposite page: Kyoto Station.

little success, and eventually the Emperor moved to Tokyo in 1873 with former nobles and influential citizens following him. Kyoto's population plummeted from 510,000 to 240,000, but by 1932 Kyoto climbed back to a million residents, in part due to Japan's rapid urbanization. Following its celebration of 1100 years as the capital, an ambitious plan of the comprehensive "Three Great Works" was initiated. This undertook a second large-scale aqueduct project at Lake Biwa, modernized city waterworks, and upgraded transportation with streetcar facilities and improved roads, taking about 10 years to execute and requiring tremendous financial backing. In World War II, Kyoto was on the American list of targets for the atomic bomb. In the end, however, Henry L. Stimson, Secretary of War in the Roosevelt and Truman administrations – who had spent his honeymoon there – insisted the city be removed from the list of targets and replaced by Nagasaki. Kyoto was largely spared from conventional bombing, even though small-scale air raids did result in casualties. In 1964, Kyoto Tower was built as the tallest structure in the city with an observation deck at 100 meters (328 ft) and a spire at 131 meters (430 ft). Money poured from Tokyo and Osaka into speculative construction efforts, and by the 80s economic bubble, land prices soared along with inheritance taxes, forcing owners to relinquish many of their old homes (fig. 7.13). The city celebrated its 1200 anniversary in 1994.

Kyoto Station opened in 1998. 70 meters high, 470 meters long from east to west, and with a total floor area of 238,000 square meters, it is Japan's second-largest station building (after Nagoya Station) and one of the country's largest buildings incorporating a shopping mall, hotel, movie theater, department store, and several local government facilities under a single fifteen-story roof. The large spaces of the mega-building were on the one hand received as a welcome addition, particularly by the younger generation, who saw in it a setting for newer spontaneous forms of public life not available in the rest of the city. But on the other hand, many Kyotoites were largely reluctant to accept such a mega-structure, and there was much criticism about architect Hiroshi Hara's design, particularly since it also incentivized a wave of new high-rise developments such as the twenty-story Kyocera Building (fig 7.14).

Even before the opening of Kyoto Station, there were those that argued that the creation of Tokyo, in a sense, had come at Kyoto's expense, and they were not entirely incorrect."[15] The city appears confounded by conflicting desires – to be completely traditional on the one hand, while completely up-to-date on the other.

Figure 7.15 Between heritage and modernity. Top left: Kyoto cityscape with Nishi Hongan-ji Temple complex in forground. Top right: Kyoto streetscape at night with temple gate in background. Opposite page: Philosopher's Walk.

One of the more creative critiques was a manga series by Toshifumi Shimizu that appeared in Kyoto Journal # 27 (1994) "The Death and Resurrection of Kyoto," a special issue to commemorate the city's 1200th anniversary. The *manga* begins with Emperor Kammu (Kyoto's founder) summoning his magical powers to destroy the modern city and create a new one in its place. Four spirits of Kyoto's past: Okuni (originator of *Kabuki*), Fudo-myo (Buddhist slayer of evil), Michizane Sugawara (patron saint of learning), and Kannon (deity of compassion) dissolve the city of land speculators and construction cranes, and magically replace it with traditional streetscapes of two-story dwellings and tree-lined streets set against the backdrop of Kyoto's hills, where there are no cars, and where everyone only walks or bikes.[16] In that same issue, sixty new "Alternatives" were proposed towards "making Kyoto a better place to live," ranging from tax incentives and "shakkei" (borrowed scenery) restorations to creating curbside recycling stations. The one that stood out for me was called "Reclaim the Moon."[17] It proposed that on four full moon nights of the year, all traffic would be banned from 5 p.m. to 5 a.m., to let citizens wander through the city to visit friends, attend outdoor concerts, partake in tea ceremonies, and take in the opened temple gardens all night.

Heritage conservation remains the dominant intellectual rubric surrounding Kyoto's present and future, and because the city was spared by the destruction of the Second World War, the preservation of its traditional cityscape has taken on a special historical significance. The city was given the right to register cultural properties in 1981, and by 1987, 384 buildings were officially preserved by national, prefectural and municipal laws. Five years later in 1992, municipal laws preserved 277 assets altogether, and simultaneously, the exceptional scenic areas in the city's surrounding mountains were also designated as conservation areas.[18] But even so, concurrent planning regulations dealing with height constraints, floor-area ratios and light angles have failed to garner any significant positive transformation. With the past and future in perpetual conflict in Japan's ultimate cultural repository, heritage management remains Kyoto's biggest dilemma (fig. 7.15).

Meanwhile, Rome has its own dilemmas. On the one hand, from the Renaissance to the Ecole des Beaux-Arts, Rome had inspired a pedagogy that recognized the built form of the historic city as critical to the solution of contemporary

problems. While the Bauhaus rejected this idea, it is this recognition that inspires students, architects and conservationists to continue to talk about Rome for important pedagogical reasons. Predicated in the idea that precedent comes not from the history of events or styles, but rather from the history of ideas abstracted from events – a return to Rome has constantly been reconstituted in the Western intellectual circles. On the other hand, the fate of preservation and heritage conservation in Rome looms large as funding for the maintenance of the country's archaeological riches has been slashed by 20% since 2010.[19] In 2008, archaeologists announced the discovery of the tomb of Marcus Nonius Macrinus, the final resting place for the Roman general who served as inspiration for the movie Gladiator. But in December 2012, Italy's cash-strapped ministry of culture declared it was unable to find the several million Euros required to protect the ruins and turn them into a tourist attraction, and the Gladiator's Tomb may likely have to be buried once again.

Kyoto's issues are somewhat different from Rome, among other things, in the fragility of the wooden town heritage that cannot be evaluated using the same criteria as towns built in stone or brick. Change, and more importantly in-authenticity will have to be tolerated and accepted, if any of this heritage is to be saved. The good news is that, looking at ongoing efforts, Kyoto does recognize that its heritage is more than its buildings: it includes its festivals, rituals, and ultimately its people. If that is so, then this cultural wealth should be the shared responsibility of its property owners and users, local public, concerned activists, and finally the Japanese national community, all working towards a larger goal. For all the intentions of a few concerned citizens, the consequences and eventual manifestations of urban change always emerge from a city's specific power structures, and the degrees to which voices and visions, whether top-down or bottom-up are effectively heard and acted upon. Kyoto's future too will emerge from the complex negotiations between its desires to hold on to a rich past and its aspirations for a post-industrial future, and ultimately, from the degree of its resolve to be recognized as the quintessential Japanese city.

In Shibuya, hundreds of Japanese walk across a colossal intersection every few minutes manipulated by Tokyo's relentless metropolitan thrall. But in its narrow backstreets and alleys, this roar dissolves into a mysterious calm. It was in one such backstreet that I chanced by Ishizawa. He was rolling home his daily collection of beer cans.

Ishizawa's home is a space under the Japan Railway tracks, where he spends his nights and stores his daily keep for sale each Thursday. He is not the only one that has refused the government's stipend for the homeless, and chosen instead to start his own business of gathering beer cans, to make about a third of that stipend each month. Each day, his friends and he take a prescribed route through the charged streets of Shibuya, and return to their blue tents and stick shelters to drink, cook and eat together. That day, Ishizawa invited me to his home. He introduced me to his friends. He told me his story. With moist eyes he confessed that they would rather die under the train tracks than accept money from the government.

In Shibuya's seductive terrain of eros, pleasure and fashion that seems to have possessed everyone with a raw ecstasy and an obsession to hide from the world, Ishizawa and his friends are the last samurais alive.

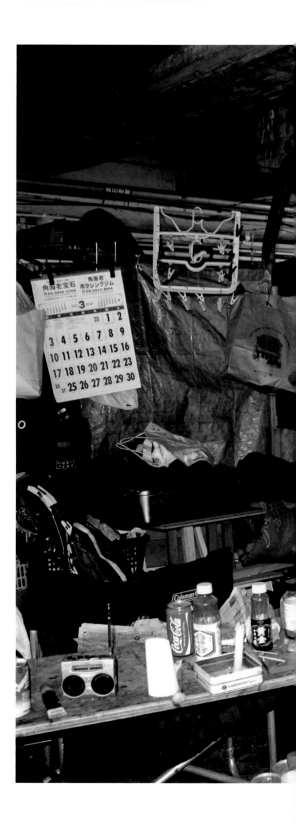

Ishizawa's Home.

Gion Festival annual parade.

Chapter 8
The Japanese Street in Space and Time

In traditional Japan, it was the labyrinthine, tenuous street and not the square that was the center of civic life. Unlike the medieval Western fabric where squares overlaid the network of urban streets, in Japan squares were non-existent. Anything resembling one existed only as semi-private shrine grounds or palace courts. In a stratified social structure with the emperor at its head, there was no communion in any democratic sense. Looking at plans of traditional Japanese capital cities like Heijo-kyo (Nara) or Heian-kyo (Kyoto), there is no conscious expression of formal community space. The only prominent definition was the main avenue running through the middle of the city and ending in the palace complex (fig. 8.1). The rest of the fabric was a grid of streets punctuated by temples and mansions.[1] What were the formal and social characteristics of the traditional Japanese street? How did they change with Japan's industrialization? And what is their place in Japan today where increasing globalization is bringing other desires and expectations of public life?

STREET & TOWN FORM

In the eighth century capital of Heian-kyo for instance, the main central avenue called Suzakumon was 28 *jo* (280 feet) wide with other east-west and north-south streets varying from 4 jo (40 feet) and 8 jo (80 feet) to 12 jo (120 feet) and 17 jo (170 feet) in width. There were two distinct areas officially set aside for the East and West Markets, one in either half of the city.[2] But with the city's economic decline and the Hogen and Heiji rebellions in the 1150s, the markets gradually died as places of commerce. Buying and selling concurrently expanded into the city itself. It began booming around intersections of various thoroughfares such as Machi Street (modern Shimmachi Street), which ran north-south near the middle of the Left Capital. These trading streets with shops on either side prospered with the decline of government control over the markets with craftsmen establishing guilds to organize private trade for their own products. By the war plagued years of the fourteenth century, with difficulties in transporting goods to and from the capital, the street as a place of work, buying and selling and as the scene for secular and sacred ceremonies was the fundamental element of a variety of habitats such as market villages, port towns, shrine towns and castle towns.

Figure 8.1 Painting showing the city of Nara in the Showa Era, circa 1926. This is a view from the east, looking west. Note the original rectilinear city plan and continuous street grid. The Todai-ji Temple is the center of the image. The Horyu-ji Temple is at the bottom left corner.

With no distinguished urban commons or city center, even capitals like Kyoto were polycentric cities of multiple linear cores. In the sixteenth century amidst the many changes he initiated in the urban structure, Toyotomi Hideyoshi (1536-1598) restructured the local divisions within the urban grid. The existing *machi* (city districts) that had been bounded by streets, were now quartered into core quadrant neighborhoods called *cho* which in turn were reassembled in fours around intersecting streets to form new districts again termed machi. In this new urban structure, these linear seams were not mere boundaries, but in fact the meeting grounds of the various surrounding communities. As incorporated places of enhanced social interaction, they encouraged an architecture that unified the two faces of the communal spine into a single cohesive compound.

Not all Japanese urban habitants were rectilinear grids. Towns like Tsumago, in present day Nagano Prefecture were never planned and developed organically through trial and error, but with a consistency of dwelling design with occasional flourishes. The town has changed little over the years, and ongoing restoration programs have enhanced the streetscape by moving telephone poles behind the homes. By contrast *jokamachi* (castle towns) like Hikone were based on plans, with a web of concentric and meshed grids, all surrounding a central castle.[3] The castes were plastered in white and in some atypical cases such as Odawara, this aesthetic spread throughout the townscape, houses often plastering their lower levels if not their entire surfaces in white (fig. 8.2).

The planning of Edo, which became the capital of Japan in 1603, reveals another pattern of streets and urban form. Edo was built with great consideration

to the views of the mountains from the lowlands. The basic position of its major thoroughfares was designed to provide views of the city's scenic spots including Mount Fuji, the Masashino Plain, the Sumida River, Mount Tsukuba, Mount Kanda, the Yushima and Hongo Plateaus, Shinobugaoka (Ueno), the Main Enclosure and Nagatacho Plateaus, Mount Atago, Shiba-Zojoji Urayama, Shiba Maruyama and many others. For instance, Honcho Avenue was laid out on the route connecting Mount Fuji with the Tokiwabashi area, and the road from Kyobashi to Nihonbashi was laid out in the direction of Mount Tsukuba. Thus standing on Honcho Avenue and looking southwest, one could see Mount Fuji further away; from Kyobashi, one could glimpse Mount Tsukuba to the northeast.[4] It was believed that the God Kunitokotache lived on Mount Fujiyama, and that the spirit of the mountain protected the people. Fujiyama thus remained a significant sacred and secular reference with woodblock artists like Kiyonaga, Hokusai and Hiroshige frequently using it as a backdrop to their street scenes.

STREET COMMUNITY & RHYTHM

Typically, streets were lined with *nagaya* or *machiya* (townhouses) abutting each other with little or no individuality in design save the arrangement of openings and treatments along the façade.[5] In fact at the end of the Tokugawa period, every townhouse was based on a unified dimensioning. Heino Engel has written on this Japanese building standardization system: the size of the rooms was counted according to the number of *tatami* mats and all the structural members of the house

Figure 8.2 Opposite page: Painting of the castle town of Tsuyama, circa 1700. The castle is the beige shape in the center of the image. The castle moat is the grey form circling it. Note the change in street grids within and outside the castle moat.

Figure 8.3 Preserved traditional streetscapes. Below: Town around Ise Naiku, Mie Prefecture. Bottom: Imaicho.

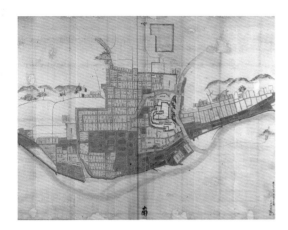

were calculated on the dimensions of the tatami.[6] All building elements in the house such as sliding doors, window slats and mats were consequently interchangeable with any other house in the town.

But this seemingly simple frontage of timber architecture, with posts set into the ground and the wall spaces filled with flexible woodwork also incorporated a number of technical innovations to mediate the street and dwelling: architectural details such as *koshi* (wooden window slatting), *agedana* (hinged and folding exterior benches, and *komayose* (low fencing to keep horses at bay.) And though each cho or neighborhood unit comprised a distinct number of streets, they were only as vaguely delineated as stated in obscure everyday terminologies such as *kai-wai* (literally "around that area"). The entire ensemble of streets thus came to connect the private areas to the city at large, renouncing the expansive grandeur of the plaza, and embracing the qualities of ambiguity, spontaneity and diversified urban space (fig. 8.3).

Over time, these streets would develop organized concentrations and nomenclatures based on various trading activities. In the seventeenth century castle town of Nagaoka for instance, streets were named according to the specific role of their residents: Okachi-machi (infantrymen's street), Doshin-machi (policemen street), or the occupations of their inhabitants: Bancho-machi (carpenter's street), Oga-machi (timber-cutter's street), or according to their trades: Cha-machi (tea merchant street), Uo-machi (fishmonger's street).

Most residences along these streets nurtured a life of minimal privacy where the sounds of a neighbor's household activity could easily be heard through the poorly insulated timber walls that separated one from another. But the accepted norms of such communities hardly encouraged delineations for privacy and publicness. Individual houses displayed a translucency, allowing the interiors to interpenetrate the street through an elastic boundary. Unlike the stasis of the Western street wall, the Japanese one was flexible. It was composed of translucent *shoji* (paper paneled lattice screens) and opaque *amado* (rain shutters) that in the absence of any permanent physical attachments like hinges, could be slid or completely removed.[7] The street edge was malleable to sustain the diurnal and seasonal rhythms of life.

During the day, the street was the hub of the community. The shoji that defined the street were slid open to allow the street space to interpenetrate the pri-

Figure 8.4 Top: Malleable street edge.

Figure 8.5 Opposite page: Street space and transformation.

vate space of the households. The threshold that otherwise suggested the transition from the street to the house, diffused domestic and commercial space as part of an activity pattern from inside to out. By night the street transformed. The amado were brought up and shut for a secure, private, interior night life. The street, now a silent spine would hold the community together till the next morning when it would change again (fig. 8.4).

This diurnal beat formed part of larger seasonal patterns. In summer, the shoji remained open. This spatial interpenetration worked wonders not just as a comfort generator, facilitating cross ventilation for the homes, but also as a display tool for the various trades by providing glimpses into the machiya interiors. During the day a curtain or *noren* would hang in the machiya entrance. It marked the shop boundary and bore the family crest mark. It was these curtains varying in size and color that distinguished one shop from another, marketed its trade and simultaneously added a soft kinetic element to the otherwise dry streetscape. Such ambiguous delineations between in and out enhanced the affinity for street life. Adults came outdoors to meet, trade and barter, children sang street songs that commemorated the seasons. Mosquito bites confirmed the peak of the hot humid summers, just as the sight of the red dragonfly signaled the coming of autumn and plum blossoms the beginning of spring. When the storms arrived the street changed again. The amado would secure the residential interiors from the harsh weather. The street would now assume a reposed, passive guise, until the weather would become benign once again.

Amidst such activity patterns, the urge for public communion was refreshed during seasonal festivals and religious gatherings. Such events were not confined to a single space. They were always kinetic, with people continuously meandering through the wide thoroughfares and narrow alleys of the community. During such events, the wooden lattices of the houses that made the street boundary were completely taken down extending the street space deep into the house interiors. The everyday private space of the household now became a semi-public viewing space, for sitting, dining and greeting the adults and children continually journeying through the streets with various floats. With paper lanterns, myriad festive fetishes hanging at every doorway, and the crowds, colors, floats and follies, the physical street gradually eroded, and became an, amorphous public field sustaining a pulsating form of com-

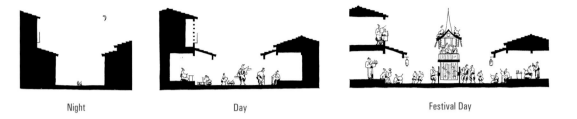

Night   Day   Festival Day

munal activity constantly changing in space and time. The street architecture, now dominant more as roofs than defining walls was merely a backdrop to a pulsating spatial entity defined only by the activity within. Then gradually, the motion would dwindle, the spell would end, the wooden walls would be brought up, and the street would become static again (fig. 8.5).

It is less the few remaining traditional streets, and more the various Japanese medieval art sources that provide valuable information in this regard. The Nenchu gyoji emaki (Picture Scroll of Annual Rites and Ceremonies) originally painted in sixty scrolls about 1173, the Ippen Shonin eden (Picture Scroll of the Monk Ippen) painted in 1299, and the pair of Rakuchu rakugai zu (Scenes in and around the Capital) dated between 1530-78, suggest two spatial and elemental readings. The first is the idea of the street as a "unified wall", the second, as an "amoebic entity", each distinguished by the specific perception of their voids and solids.

The traditional Japanese street during the private night hours represents the street as a "unified wall." Here, like a traditional Western Street, the perceptual importance resides in physical street definition. The street seems to have been generated into a purposeful figural void by the building walls that front it. The building facades belong more to the street than to the buildings, and the street is perceived as a volume carved from the mass of buildings. During the day when the street wall is opened, the perceptual importance shifts from the street space. The street does not seem to be a void consciously produced by its buildings. The street façade is perceived as a fragmented membrane, facilitating a spatial osmosis from interior to exterior.

This devaluing of the unified wall reaches its extreme on festive days when the "non-street" is born. The street façade, though porous, is now read less as a series of interpenetrations, and more as momentary chaotic spatial pulsations between inside and out, simultaneously creating and dissolving an ever-changing fluid space. It is about the differences in the fetishes, artifacts and their relative placement, all resisting one's perception of the street room as a defined spatial configuration in itself. The feeling is now of being within a larger amoebic space, than a coherent street room.

Thus, as Japanese architect Kisho Kurokawa notes "Western space is decisive while space in Japan is cohesive."[8] In the West, walls take on an extreme impor-

tance severing one interior space from another. This dualism does not arise in the
Japanese concept of space, "which rather embraces nature, bringing the outside in
and diffusing any inside outward." This plasticity of the street remains the most
distinct characteristic of the traditional Japanese civic realm. It contradicts the conventional understandings of formal civic space. It is Japan's own equivalent to the
European plaza.

TRANSITION

In 1868, the Tokugawa Era met its end in the Meiji Restoration, and Japan opened
its doors to Western influences. Ginza's evolution from the traditional wooden
street to a glitzy neon district was the first dramatic transformation in Japanese
post-war street urbanism. Established in the early 17th century, the name Ginza was
derived from the official organization of goldsmiths where Tokugawa Ieyasu had
minted his first coins in the 1600s (Ginza literally means "the place where silver is
minted"). In 1872, a zealously Westernizing Meiji government entrusted the British
architect Thomas Waters the task of replacing the fire-ravaged tinderbox maze of
wooden buildings. Waters redesigned it as a western oddity, with brick buildings
and wide tree-lined boulevards that seemed more pleasant to look at than inhabit in
the hot humid climate (fig. 8.6, 8.7). But that figment of the British urbanism too
met its end; it was leveled in the Great Kanto Earthquake of 1923, and rebuilt as a
shopping and entertainment district. It survived World War II, remaining a commercial center during the American Occupation in the 1940s, eventually transforming
into one of the most expensive places in the world during the bubble economy
of the eighties.

With the Kanto earthquake in 1923 drawing attention from the inner city to
the apparent safety of the western agricultural hinterlands, the traditional idea of
Edo's dense urban neighborhoods was overlaid by the Western recipe of British
planner Ebenezer Howard's Garden City model.[9] The Japanese countryside was the
new-found inspiration and the setting for a new village-like lifestyle. With increasing
governmental support, both for its comparative safety as well as its nostalgic reference to the bucolic garden city Edo had once been, the first of these planned devel-

Figure 8.8 Opposite page:
Preserved historic streetscapes,
Kyoto.

opments called Denenchofu (literally "garden suburb") opened in the late twenties after the completion of the Meguro-Kamata railway that connected it to Tokyo. The plan replicated Howard's garden city diagram with concentric and radial streets and became one of the most successful planned developments in Japan.[10]

Postwar democracy brought newer ideas of community and Westernization that gradually began transforming the traditional meanings of the Japanese street. High inheritance taxes discouraged the preservation of traditional houses and streetscapes. With newer concepts of home ownership, houses resisted abutting and preferred to individualize. Segregated land use, and increasing automobile dependence created exclusively residential zones. The idea of the transparent traditional row-house began to get interiorized as the concept of privacy began to get more defined. By the sixties, the street as a community place was a forgotten prototype. "Gone was the round-the-clock, bustling neighborhood activity," wrote Kisho Korukawa.[11] "Residential areas have been so thoroughly reduced to serving solely for dwelling that they have effectively sacrificed the intensely intermingled and diversified use of space that historically characterized the heart of the city. Now they are populated solely by housewives, old people, and children by day, and they revert to a lifeless, silent fringe where no one dares venture out alone at night."[12]

Today, preserved historic streetscapes like Ponto-cho in Kyoto instigate a whiff of nostalgia, representing a fragment of the past (fig. 8.8). Ponto-cho centers on one long, narrow, cobbled alley running from Shijō-dōri to Sanjō-dōri, one block west of the Kamo River. Here *sudare* (horizontal reed blinds) still flutter in the wind and noren display their crest marks in the soft light of paper lanterns. Ponto-cho stands out in comparison to most other older parts of Kyoto, like the vicinity of the Kiyomizu Temple, where one usually witnesses the stark and uncomfortable adjacencies of modern buildings and historic machiya. From 1984-94, more than 40,000 traditional machiya were destroyed in Kyoto's downtown's areas alone, forcing the relocation of more than 100,000 residents.[13] The problem with such collisions is not as much their contrast in height or style, but more so their relationship to the street. The traditional transparency is now typically replaced by an opaque nihilism that if multiplied over the entire street length, leaves nothing more than a conduit for moving vehicles.

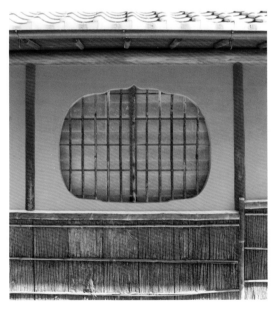

NEW IDENTITIES

Figure 8.9 Top and opposite page: Within the Senso-ji Temple complex, Asakusa, Tokyo.

That said the street is still the fundamental element of Japanese urbanism. Numerous other forms of public space and public life have emerged in post-war Japan (discussed in Chapter 10), but ultimately, street-life thrives in other forms whether in metropolitan Tokyo or historic Kyoto. Generic streets have their own Japan-ness: some streets are characterized by a consistently fine-grained lot or building width, with buildings as little as ten-feet wide and more than ten stories high, giving the street a distinctly thin vertical texture. In suburban neighborhood streets, vending machines at almost every street and alley corner have also now become a characteristic Japanese urban trait. On the whole however, the generic streets of the Japanese city are an ad hoc accumulation of modern buildings of various heights, types and frontage conditions defying any cogent classification. It is within this accumulation that one finds streets that stand out, not necessarily as designed rooms, but as places that have over time begun to display clear new identities associated with Japan's contemporary urban condition. I focus here on five such places all within the confines of Tokyo: the Asakusa district, Takeshitadori, Omotesando, Shinjuku and Shibuya.

Asakusa owed its existence and historic prominence to an accident of history. Two brothers in the 7th-century B.C.E. discovered on a nearby riverbank a diminutive statue, believed to be of Kannon (God of Mercy), around which Tokyo's most famous temple, Senso-ji, was built (fig. 8.9). Edo's Kabuki troupes, thought to be degenerate and subversive by puritanic Tokugawa authorities, were banished in 1841 to the then-hinderland of the Asakusa farm fields outside the feudal city limits. Prostitutes who had once catered to the carnal fancies of the Edoites were also banished here, and what emerged was a grid of intimate streets accumulated around the temple complex, forming a clear district of sorts. What stands out today at Asakusa, is the transformed and appropriated character of these historic streets. Surrounding the temple, one finds an entire hierarchy of street types and widths, from intimate lanes barely wide enough for a car to pass through, to former streets that have now been covered with canopies and converted into exclusively shopping walk-streets. Hardly any historic building survives around the temple, but even so, the formal pattern of the district is amply clear. This complex mesh of covered,

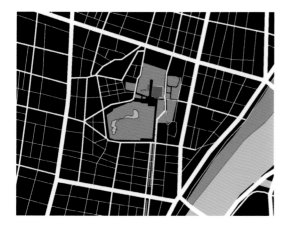

paved and unpaved streets with knick-knack shops, restaurants and pantomimes contrasts vividly with the fringes of the district now lined with opaque public housing. The rich, messy vitality of Asakusa's streets are exemplary of the uncanny richness of street character and urban life that even the best designers can only aspire to create (fig. 8.10).[14]

Two streets in Harajuku, on the Yamanote Line in the Shibuya ward of Tokyo capture the contrasting extents of new streetlife. The first is Takeshita-dōri, an intimate pedestrian-only street that caters to youth fashions selling Gothic Lolita, visual kei, rockabilly, hip-hop, and punk outfits. Its arched gated entry is situated literally across from the Harajuku station, separated only by a modest two-lane cross-street (fig. 8.11). With the street dropping down gently from the entry, the first view of a visitor is a dramatic frame of young hip shoppers crowded in an intimate two-story spine dominated by pop art. The area first became fashionable during the Tokyo Olympics in 1964 because of its proximity to the Olympic gymnasium, and the chance of meeting somebody famous in the streets began to draw large crowds. Many of the back streets too are preserved where one can pass by every conceivable type of shop for clothing and accessories, as well as a high number of beauty salons, and eventually emerge into the formal regality of Omotesando.

Omotesandō is the most formal street in Tokyo today, a Japanese avenue in the Western sense if ever there was one (fig. 8.12). Lined with mature Keyaki trees, this four-lane arterial, with ample sidewalks and street furniture is referred to not as the Suzakumon but the Champs Elysses of Japan. Omotesando means "the front approach." It was originally built in 1920, and served as the main access to the Meiji Jingu Shrine from Aoyama Street. One can still find the stone lanterns on each side of the street marking the entrance. After the 1923 Great Kanto Earthquake, the famous Dojunkai Aoyama Apartments, the first multi-housing project of its kind in Japan was built along the street in 1925. Today, Omotesando leads straight down to Kotto-Dori (Curio Street) offering luxury brands like Chanel, Gucci, Louis Vuitton, and Prada and is the setting for Japan's annual St. Patrick's Day Parade on March 17. Few streets in Asia come close to Omotesando's regal formality. However, its current transition to the shrine is a pitifully abrupt asphalted intersection, with a utilitarian pedestrian bridge that visually cuts off the shrine's entry from the pedestrian

Figure 8.10 Opposite page: Streetscapes around the Senso-ji Temple, Asakusa, Tokyo. Top: Diagram of street grid around the Senso-ji Temple. The main shrine building is in red.

Figure 8.11 Top: Takeshita dori, Tokyo.

Figure 8.12 Opposite page: Omotesando, Tokyo.

experience of the spinal space. Omotesando reminds us that streets as great formal rooms is not a Western idea; that urban design matters, and that ultimately, street design at its best is not about the street room itself, but also its transitions to and from its side streets and eventually its important adjacent destinations.[15]

Such adjacent contrasts in street form, character and scale are also present in Tokyo's other prominent districts such as Shinjuku and Shibuya. In Shinjuku for instance, one instantly moves from the grand neon spectacle of the arterial to its intimate side streets and alleys where despite the continuing riot of signage, one immediately catches the change of street scale (fig. 8.13). Finally, one ventures into the incredible intimacy of its former red-light district Gorudengai, a grid of pedestrian lanes barely wide enough for two people to walk by. Dimly lit, they are lined with continuous arrays of one-room-wide, two-story townhouses that have today been converted into mini-bars and restaurants. In Shibuya, a similar contrast is evident in the walk from the station plaza into its back roads and lanes, where a variety of smaller shops and places teem with public life and commerce. What stands out in this district however in contrast to Shinjuku or Ginza is the drama of the Shibuya Crossing. The alternating spatial pulsations of droves of pedestrians walking from one side of this colossal intersection to the other defies the conventional parameters of both street and plaza, representing instead a mutated form of Japanese public life that now dominates its contemporary frenzy (fig. 8.14).

THE JAPANESE STREET IN PROSPECT

Though the forms of Japanese streets have changed, it appears then that the traditional idea of the street as the armature of public life continues in many forms. The annual Daidogei World Cup Street Performance Competition in Shizuoka for instance, suggests Japan's globalizing dimensions.[16] For four days each November, a menagerie of pantomimes, jugglers, musicians, clowns, magicians and artists descend from the world over to perform and compete on these streets for a $ 20,000 jackpot. Performances run 11a.m. - 4 p.m. every day with impromptu night acts as well. By any measure, the Daidogei is a huge event, some 54 acts performing in 30-minute intervals at 25 locations with over 1.5 million people attending from all over Japan.

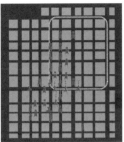

By contrast, during festivals, which form such an integral part of Japan's urbanity, the traditional parading of floats through streets continues to this day. Each year during Gion Matsuri on July 17, 32 tall wooden floats, each belonging to a different neighborhood are paraded through the streets of downtown Kyoto (fig. 8.15).[17] They are pulled by hundreds of white-clad locals, with others perched precariously on the floats themselves providing encouragement, directions and musical accompaniment. Every float represents an ancient legend, and is decorated with rugs and textiles. Armor and treasures are displayed in the windows and front rooms of the businesses and families who have lived for hundreds of years in those Muromachi and Shinmachi streets north of Shijo. The juxtaposition of these ancient, symbolically-charged constructs moving through the wide, asphalted, sealed-off thoroughfares, against the backdrop of high-tech consumer-oriented stores may look out of place, yet the age-old expression of the festival as a "moving museum" persists. Numerous such festivals – Kanda Matsuri in Tokyo, Takayama Matsuri in Takayama,

Figure 8.13 Opposite page top: Shinjuku nightscape.

Figure 8.14 Opposite page bottom: Ginza nightscape.

Figure 8.15 Top: Gion Festival parade. The inset shows the various float types and their routes within the district.

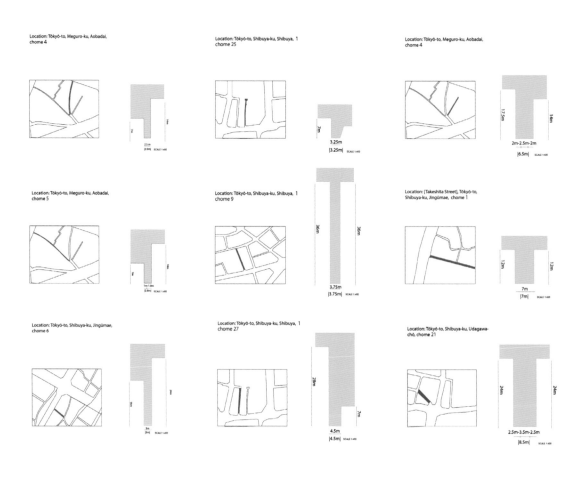

Location: Tōkyō-to, Meguro-ku, Aobadai, chome 4

Location: Tōkyō-to, Shibuya-ku, Shibuya, 1 chome 25

Location: Tōkyō-to, Meguro-ku, Aobadai, chome 4

Location: Tōkyō-to, Meguro-ku, Aobadai, chome 5

Location: Tōkyō-to, Shibuya-ku, Shibuya, 1 chome 9

Location: [Takeshita Street], Tōkyō-to, Shibuya-ku, Jingūmae, chome 1

Location: Tōkyō-to, Shibuya-ku, Jingūmae, chome 6

Location: Tōkyō-to, Shibuya-ku, Shibuya, 1 chome 27

Location: Tōkyō-to, Shibuya-ku, Udagawa-chō, chome 21

Figure 8.16 Morphological analysis of street types in the Shibuya district. Street widths range from 2.5 meters to 38 meters.

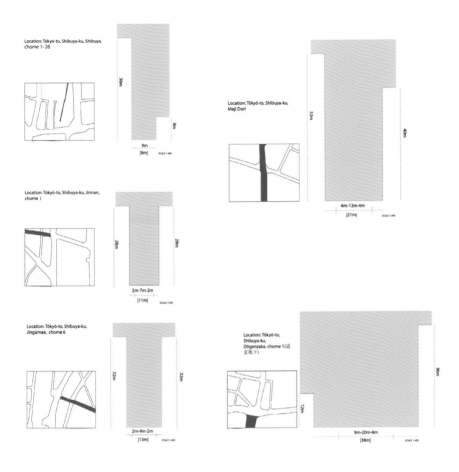

Nebuta Matsuri in Aomori city – affirm their continuing rigor of traditional street life in the contemporary Japanese consciousness.

All that said, in reflecting on the patterns of the Japanese street in time and space, one must not forget the myriad other forms of publicness that have emerged in Japan today. In this complex culture, *maiko* (traditional dancers) continue to greet traveling businessman arriving on the Shinkansen bullet train, and the Tea Ceremony continues to be performed in high-rise enclaves. In this non-feudal, post-democratic, post-Western Japan, globalization along with the ease to manifold information now has other cultural expectations. It is this truism that remains at the heart of any discussion on Japanese urbanism, along with the place its traditional urban elements and patterns will find therein. The task at hand for architects and urbanists then is to facilitate the successful mediation between the desires for these new symbols of globalization, with the evolving identities of Japan's traditional gathering spaces – as both cultural connections to its past, as well as pointers to its future (fig. 8.16).

Back in India, my father keeps a display of collectibles under the glass table-top in his office. One of them is a beautiful postcard of the colossal bronze Buddha in the Todai-ji temple in Nara. I have admired it since I was barely three feet tall. Years later, I remembered that postcard, when I stood in front of the fifty-foot, five-hundred-ton gentle giant.

As I took in the daibutsu's towering presence, I felt proud to trace it to my Indian lineage. After all, had it not been for the Indian sub-continent where the Buddha was born, there would have been no Todai-ji. But then, in that dusky temple interior, I had another epiphany: Had it not been for the Greeks, we in India would have never given the Buddha the over-sized Apollonian majesty he now bears. It was the cultural syncretism between Hellenistic culture and Buddhism, which developed between the 4th century BCE and the 5th century CE and flourished during the Kushan Empire that ushered the anthropomorphic rendition of the Buddha along with the development of Mahayana Buddhism. It was this Indo-Greek trajectory that traveled to China and from there to Japan, and the daibutsu is the teleological end of that cultural combine.

The complexity of a cultural genome opens it up to all those who want to claim it: I can claim Todai-ji's Buddha of Indian lineage, as much as the Greeks can claim his Indian sculptural ancestors as their own. The great Buddha at Todai-ji then has both Indian and Greek genes; he is a mongrel offspring of East and West.

Buddha statue in the Todai-ji Temple, Nara.

View of Tokyo Tower, Roppongi, Tokyo.

Chapter 9
The Western Genome in Japanese Architecture

The eminent American architect Robert Venturi's first trip to Japan came as late as 1990. Two and a half decades earlier, he had authored "Complexity and Contradiction in Architecture," a path-breaking volume calling out Modern architecture's nihilism to history and tradition, spelling out its cultural limitations and arguing for a far more reflective and inclusive attitude.[1] From the backdrop of this seminal contribution, more than two decades of critical observation, and more than half a century of Japan's transformation separated him from former reflections on the Far East by other Western architects such as Bruno Taut, Frank Lloyd Wright, Jorn Utzorn and Walter Gropius.

Venturi criticized his Modernist predecessors for having missed the point: They had limited their perceptions to the sublime austerity and structural clarity of traditional Japanese buildings. They had failed to notice, or at least include in their writings, the simultaneous contradiction of the vivid hues of moving *kimonos* or the myriad colors of the Japanese garden. Venturi argued that the decorative foreground was as much a part of the aesthetic comprehension of Japan as its austere backdrop of buildings; the contradiction was necessary to complete the aesthetic equation. Tokyo, the dense collage of traditional dwellings amidst corporate high-rises, old wooden streets amidst regiments of commercial signs, juxtapositions of micro and macro capitalism, of ancient shrines and zesty neons seemed to "have its act together."[2] He marveled how "taxis, always immaculate, whose roof lanterns, in a variety of forms, symbols, graphics, and colors (made) cockeyed configurations……in an urban infrastructure of straight streets and wide avenues lined with trees or regiments of commercial signs, or crooked lanes lined with utility poles draped with myriad wires."[3]

Venturi's provocative reaction was as much the result of his personal ambivalence towards Modernism, as the time in which he saw Japan for the first time. In 1990, he was witnessing the most remarkable offspring of an entire century of confluences between Japan and the West. From the time Japan opened its doors to the Western world, Japanese architecture had become the subject of a two-sided dialectic. The Western intrigue with Japan was only as strong as the Japanese zest for Western import. The not-so-long-ago self-sufficient culture became a new intellectual forum for the Western world, and this seemingly complex dialectic in turn, a

Figure 9.1 Top: Ginza, circa 1920 showing streetcars. They disappeared by 1972 with the rise of buses and taxis.

Figure 9.2 Opposite page: Early Western architectural influences. Left: Diet Building. Right: Kyoto City Hall.

newfound catalyst for emerging Japanese architects to seek new interpretations of their own traditions. In many ways, these confluences with the West remain some of the most paradigmatic and transformative junctures in Japan's history, and are therefore fundamental to a deeper understanding of its contemporary built condition. What follows is a broad survey of these exchanges, tracing how the idea of Japanese architecture morphed into the ambiguous compound that evades any cogent identity, and into the complex cross-cultural phenomenon we find today at the ocean's edge.

EARLY ENCOUNTERS

Japan's first interactions with Western culture started in the middle of the sixteenth century, when the Portuguese with trading bases in Goa and Macao established contacts with the insular archipelago. Saint Francis Xavier had arrived in Japan in 1549 and founded the first Jesuit mission, and by the early 1600s, nearly half-a-million natives had been christened. In 1615, the first Spanish ship arrived from the Mexican port of Acapulco, at the behest of King Philip III. That same year, a Japanese delegation from the city of Sendai left for Rome to meet Pope Paul V Borghese. But even as a new period of cross-cultural relations appeared to be growing, the anti-Christian Hitedada became Shogun, and suppressed Christian zeal over the next two decades through the merciless persecution of converted natives. Japan was closed to all outside influence. Only a tiny Dutch trading settlement in the port town of Nagasaki maintained an indirect tie with Europe by a ship that would arrive from Macao once a year.

Not until 1853 would Japan emerge from this self-imposed isolation. Four American "black ships" commanded by Commodore M.C. Perry had set anchor threateningly in the Edo bay. They would force Japan to embark on a new period of trade, with the first American-Japanese treaty drawn up in 1854. In 1868, the Tokugawa Era found an end in the Meiji Restoration, with the abdication of Shogun Tokugawa Keiki and his military shogunate and the restoration of Emperor Mutsuhito.[4] The capital was moved from Kyoto to Tokyo. With the new government aimed to make Japan a democratic state, the boundaries between the social classes

of the Tokugawa regime were gradually broken down. To transform the former agrarian economy into a developed industrial engine, many Japanese scholars were sent abroad to study Western science and languages, while foreign experts were brought in to teach and share their knowledge and talents.

IMPORTING THE WEST

Early Meiji architecture was initially influenced by the colonial architecture from Chinese treaty ports such as Hong Kong. In the port town of Nagasaki, the British trader Thomas Glover, for instance, built his own house in just such a colonial-influenced idiom using the skill of local carpenters. His influence helped the career of British architect Thomas Waters who had designed the Mint in 1868, in Osaka, as a long, low building in brick and stone with a central pedimented portico, as well as the Commercial Museum in Tokyo, thought to have been the city's first brick building. In 1872, Ginza, the central district where Tokugawa Ieyasu had minted his first coins in the 1600s was destroyed by a fire, and a zealously Westernizing Meiji government entrusted Waters the task of replacing the tinderbox maze of wooden buildings with fireproof materials (elaborated in Chapter 8). Waters redesigned Ginza as a western oddity, with brick buildings and wide tree-lined boulevards (fig. 9.1) and it was eventually leveled in the Great Kanto Earthquake of 1923, and rebuilt as a shopping and entertainment district. Ginza was one of Japan's first significant Western architectural imports on a grand scale.

Another such effort of significance was the Diet building (fig. 9.2). From 1886-87, two German architects, Wilhelm Böckmann and Hermann Ende were invited to Tokyo to draw up two plans for a Diet building. Böckmann's initial plan was a masonry structure with a dome and flanking wings, which would form the center of a large government ring south of the Imperial Palace. However, there was public resistance in Japan to Foreign Minister Inoue Kaoru's internationalist policies, compelling the architects to also submit a more Japanese design that introduced traditional Japanese architectural features in many parts of the building. These designs were never built, but were used for the Tokyo District Court and Ministry of Justice buildings. In 1898, Prime Minister Itō Hirobumi interviewed the American architect

Figure 9.3 Top: Early Western architectural influences. Left: Tokyo Station. Right: Daiichi Sogyo Offices.

Figure 9.4 Opposite page: National Museum, Ueno Park, Tokyo.

Ralph Adams Cram, who in turn proposed a design featuring tiled roofs and a large enclosure of walls and gates. But the Itō government fell as Cram was en route to the United States, and the project was dropped.[5] In 1910, the Finance Ministry in an attempt to take control over the new Diet building, recommended that the new building emulate an Italian Renaissance architectural style, but this was criticized as too arbitrary. The ministry subsequently sponsored a public design competition in 1918, and 118 designs were submitted for the new building. The first prize winner, Watanabe Fukuzo, produced a design similar to Ende and Böckmann's, and the Diet Building was eventually constructed with a floor plan based on Watanabe's entry. The roof and tower of the building were inspired by another entrant, third prize winner Takeuchi Shinshichi, chosen because it reflected a hybrid architecture compared to the purely European and East Asian designs proposed by other architects. Thus, contrary to what one may think from a distance, the Diet building remains a significant paradigm in the recent history of Japanese architecture, offering insights into the Japanese reluctance to fully embrace Westernization in its early stages, while allowing both Western and native architects to flirt with ideas that were essentially non-Japanese to begin with.

"The first sight of a Japanese home is disappointing….. it is unsubstantial in appearance and there is a meagerness of color," wrote Edward Sylvester Morse in his 1888 book "Japanese Homes and Their Surroundings."[6] He was noting the austere, monochromatic traditional Japanese interior as compared to its ornate Western counterpart in what would be the first Western narration on Japanese life. The marine biologist, who first visited Japan in 1877 to study brachiopods had accepted the professorship of zoology from the Japanese government in the Imperial University of Tokyo. He shared his vast knowledge of Japan with Americans in numerous public lectures, especially the 1881 Lowell lectures on collecting Japanese art and artifacts. Simultaneously, the introduction of Japanese prints in the 1862 London Exhibition and the 1867 Paris Exhibition had made an enormous impact on European Impressionist painters, including Manet and Van Gogh.[7] Intrigued by these new ideas from another land many Westerners left for Japan just before the inception of the Modern movement in their homeland.

Josiah Conder was the first European architect to enter Japan. He established a design studio in 1877 and become the avant-garde architect of the Meiji period.

He designed approximately seventy buildings that attempted to merge Eastern ideas with historic styles from his native land. His Mitsui building completed in 1894 introduced the Victorian style for the first time in Japanese history. His sensitivity to Japanese gardens also resulted in an influential book "Landscape Gardening in Japan" (1893).[8] It was arguably this book that remained the literary backdrop for the re-known American architect Frank Lloyd Wright when he was commissioned in 1916 to design the Imperial Hotel in Tokyo.

By 1922, when Wright was completing the Imperial Hotel, Japan had already dived into an era dominated by the import of Western ideas and goods. Everything Western was suddenly good and desirable; every style of Western building was dotting the Japanese landscape (fig. 9.3. 9.4). Thus Wright, himself a Japan enthusiast hardly felt the need to emphasize literal "Japan-ness." He chose instead to create a building that remained in his own words "true to the spirit of old Japan" but "was not for apologists – but for enquiries, not for fakirs busy with superficial taste and morality, but for seekers of evidence of the vital creative power of man."[9] With the Japanese looking for something American and the Americans for something Japanese, Wright's building did not escape attention. The basic axial plan of the hotel with common facilities in the center with two symmetrical bedroom wings was reminiscent of the Phoenix Hall of the famous Byodo-in Temple in Uji. One Japanese architect, Kikutaro Shimoda (1866-1931) who had also submitted a proposal for the hotel competition before Wright's involvement, claimed that Wright had plagiarized his concept, and transformed it from the proposed Japanese-style tiled roof to a flatter one on a stone and concrete building. The protest was ignored and Wright's building was constructed. But Shimoda's outrage drew attention to the prevalent trend of Japanese architecture that was being increasingly undermined.[10]

That trend was the *teikan* style. It was a "Japanese nationalist" concept that had begun in the late 1920's as a way of amalgamating Japanese and Western architecture. Sutemi Horiguchi (1895 –1984) was one of its pioneers having designed the Shien-so (House of Purple Haze) in 1926 as an Art-Deco style box with a tea hut-like thatched roof. Major competitions in the 1930s and 40s were all dominated by this trend. Even Kenzo Tange who would go on to become one of Japan's greatest Modern architects had designed the winning competition entry for the Nittai Bunka

Figure 9.5 Top: West facing facade of the Gamble House designed by Green & Green, Pasadena, California.

Figure 9.6 Opposite page: Kings Road House designed by Rudolph Schindler, Los Angeles, California.

Kaikan (Japan Cultural Center in Bangkok) in 1943 with large roofs and columns visibly inspired by the Imperial Palace in Kyoto.[11]

The 1920s also saw the emergence of another Western model of community living in Denenchofu (discussed in Chapter 8). The Kanto earthquake of 1923 had drawn attention away from Edo's dense urban neighborhoods to the safety of the Japanese countryside inspiring a new village-like lifestyle based on British town-planner Ebenezer Howard's Garden City model. Denenchofu opened in the late twenties, its plan replicating Howard's garden city diagram with concentric and radial streets with a rail station and park as its commercial center. Residential lots originally platted between 360 to 1000 square meters were gradually subdivided to accommodate more than 30,000 residents who lived in garden fronted dwellings on tree-lined streets. Despite all the historic references, it seemed more Western than anything else Japan had seen at the time.

EXPORTING JAPAN

To complete this discussion, one must not forget the concurrent genomes of Japanese architecture that found their way to the West. Here, I focus on three early influences, primarily because they suggest the breadth and nuance of this exchange, before the onslaught of the International style. The work of the brothers Charles and Henry Greene (1868-1957 and 1870-1954) in California, at the turn of the century, is one of the more obvious instances. As Kevin Nute notes, "the Greenes themselves made no secret of their admiration for Japanese art and architecture, and in some of their early designs in particular even employed several overtly Japanese motifs, including the *iriimoya* roof form."[12] Their masterworks such as the Gamble House in Pasadena suggest Japonisme through its, raw timber details, intricate joinery, extended eaves, stone lanterns and the use of the roof as a dominant formal element recalling Japan's magnificent timber buildings (fig. 9.5).

Another known example is the work of Frank Lloyd Wright, who, while freely acknowledging an important philosophical debt to Japanese art, and to the woodblock print in particular, consistently rejected suggestions that Japanese architecture had any direct impact on his work. Kevin Nute has provided the most scholarly

insight into this nexus to date. In his book "Frank Lloyd Wright and Japan: The Role of Traditional Japanese Art and Architecture in the Work of Frank Lloyd Wright," Nute excavates several parallels: The goiige-style plan form of the Nikko Taiyu-in-byo versus the Plan of Unity Temple, Oak Park, Illinois; the gongen-style plan form of the Nikko Tosho-gu, Tochigi Prefecture versus the Johnson Administration Building, Racine, Wisconsin; and the vertical section of the east pagoda of the Yakushi-ji Temple versus the vertical section of Wright's un-built St. Mark's Tower project as well as that of the Johnson Research Tower in Racine, Wisconsin.[13]

One case that has been speculated about, but not elaborated on is the Kings Road House designed by Rudolph Schindler for himself in Los Angeles in the 1920s. Shindler had never visited Japan. It was his training with Frank Lloyd Wright that had perhaps opened him to Japanese notions. The Kings Road House elicits a delicate Japonisme in a number of ways: it connotes an almost *wabi-sabi*-like aesthetic of conscious rusticity, its spaces filled with ambiguous dark, dim, shadows playing in a void recalling Tanizaki's narratives of Japanese homes. The walls are bare and the floors are naked. During its heyday, the furniture was rather minimal for a Western residential interior. The spatial experience of the house is a series of autonomous frontal planes along a sequential path, like the subtleties of walking through the additive spaces of the Katsura Villa. All rooms are low and horizontal with an abstinence from double height spaces or vertical volumes. And its pinwheel plan with three 'L' shapes spinning out from a central fireplace, pull the arms into yards bringing the garden to interface all rooms in the dwelling (fig. 9.6), making the room feel like a *shoin*.

What stands out in these three relatively contemporaneous cases is their differences in inspirational sources and subsequent interpretation. As Nute points out, most of the similarities between the work of Weight and Japanese structures tends to be "at the level of plan and section rather than in superficial details."[14] In the work of the Greens, it is traditional Japanese form more than space that frames the extent of the concepts. The Gamble House for instance is Western in plan, organized around a hierarchy of shaped rooms and furniture, influenced less by Japanese spatial notions, and more by the regional Southern California Bungalow. The Kings Road House as discussed above appears to be Japanese in space, not in form. Seen

Figure 9.7 Top: National Museum of Western Art designed by Le Corbusier, Ueno Park, Tokyo.

Figure 9.8 Opposite page: Tokyo Tower, Roppongi, Tokyo.

from the standpoint of Japanese history, these examples have escaped recognition as significant paradigms in Modern architecture, even as it was being rigorously embraced in a changing democratic Japan of the twenties. While Le Corbusier's Villa Savoye was hailed as a new paradigm, written and spoken enough to exert its imprint beyond the West to Japan, the Kings Road House for instance was suppressed and ignored amidst the stampede to stigmatize the 'machine ideology', outcast as having no place in the International style as a coherent stylistic movement, and left to a lonely exile in Los Angeles.[15]

EMBRACING MODERNISM

Returning back to Japan, we now turn to German expatriate architect Bruno Taut, who went on have significant influence on the rubric through which Japanese architecture would be understood in the West for decades to come. In 1933, when he was documenting traditional Japanese houses, he lamented on their increasing propensity towards adopting Western lifestyles. Booming Tokyo appeared to him as a "nauseating" monstrosity.[16] Favoring traditional puritanism, his influential book "Houses and People of Japan" spelt out what was to become the generic Western understanding of Japanese domestic architecture for decades.[17] But more than the book, it was his eulogy on the Ise Shrine and Katsura Villa as discussed in Chapter 1 that remained the force behind the changing scene. The rustic monochromes that had disappointed Morse particularly wooed Taut. He condemned the Toshogu Shrine at Nikko for its polychromatic ornamentations as he fell in love with the austerity and rusticity of the Katsura Villa. Taut had successfully managed to recast the impression of traditional Japanese architecture through his own Modernist bias for functional minimalism.

By the mid thirties, fueled by, yet hardly limited to Taut's influential proclaim, Modern architecture began to hold sway in a Japan ever ready for more change. The American architect Antonin Raymond who came to Japan to assist Frank Lloyd Wright on the Tokyo Imperial Hotel experimented with the idea of the Western vertical living room in his own house in 1923. His designs such as the Kawasaki Residence (1934) were dominated by this feature along with a Japanese garden on

one side and a *kura* (storage space) on the other. Raymond went on became a major force in Japanese architecture, his Readers Digest Tokyo Office (1951) showcasing how reinforced concrete construction could in fact express the same lightness as traditional Japanese buildings. By the fifties, with many young Japanese architects such as Kunio Maiekawa and Junzo Yoshimura completing their training in his office, the era of Japanese Modern architecture had begun.

The decision to invite the Swiss-French architect Le Corbusier, one of Modern architecture's foremost figures, to design the National Museum of Western Art in 1950 was not unpredictable (fig. 9.7).[18] When Corbusier arrived in Japan in 1957 to oversee the construction, he too visited the Katsura Villa and made drawings and notes. But unlike Taut, his proclamations on Japanese architecture were limited to merely how the tea hut interior seemed busy with too many lines, and how the stool-like seats in the arbor were shaped like a swastika. Whether Corbusier remained unimpressed by the non-sculptural qualities and aesthetic minimalism of Katsura or not, his tryst with Japanese architecture was amazingly evasive, brief and innocuous.

Le Corbusier was not the first Modern architectural celebrity to engage in this exchange. It was Walter Gropius, who would more than any of his peers, extend the intellectual dimension of this East-West exchange. When he visited the Katsura Villa in 1954, his awe at the building's simplicity deepened his own convictions about structural purity. Through two significant figures, Kenzo Tange, a then emerging architect, and Robin Boyd, a young Australian architectural critic, Gropius' intentional support manifested in four major texts on Japanese architecture. Tange published "Katsura: Tradition and Creation in Japan" (1960) and "Ise: Prototype of Japanese Architecture" (1965) Boyd published "Kenzo Tange" (1962), the first ever English language monograph on an oriental architect and, "New Directions In Japanese Architecture" (1968), an informative study on the current architectural development in Japan.[19] The book on Katsura was significant in many ways: First, it officially re-surfaced the rustic retreat as a Japanese architectural masterpiece reinforcing Bruno Taut's earlier proclamation. Second, it began with a foreword by none other than Gropius himself, banking on his international reputation to reassure the world of its architectural relevance. And third, it presented the Katsura Villa through exclusive photos that carefully cropped off any curve or landscape, reducing the presentation

Figure 9.9 Top and opposite page:
Yoyogi Stadium designed by
Kenzo Tange, Tokyo.

to a series of abstract Piet Mondrian-like paintings of straight lines and rectilinear shapes as elaborated in Chapter 4. The Katsura rhetoric was a well-timed tactic. Its widespread acceptance in both Japan and the West affirmed the thin line that now separated Euro-American Modernist ideals with Japan's architectural desires.

In 1958, when no building in Tokyo exceeded ten stories, the Nikken Sekkei's Tokyo Tower appeared in Shiba-Koen, one of the city's busiest areas. The 333-meter landmark was a copy of the Eiffel Tower in Paris, but slightly higher than its French original. It not only broke the existing building height barrier of ten stories, but also symbolized the increasingly blurry boundary that now separated Japanese Modernization from Westernization. Japan had embraced the West. It had provided a mirror for every major Western architect to see what he had wanted to see in its architectural traditions. The myriad seeds of Western Modern architecture were beginning to take root within Japan's seemingly open-ended ideals. Japanese Westernization and Modernization now seemed mutually indistinguishable (fig. 9.8).

This entry of Japan into the mainstream of Modern architecture had not gone unnoticed. In 1966, Harvard architectural historian Siegfried Giedion published the fifth edition of his esteemed book "Space, Time and Architecture."[20] He wrote a special page on Japan's ongoing tendencies as an important Modern regional development. He was impressed by Kenzo Tange's sports facilities for the 1964 Tokyo Olympics, with their curving tensile steel roofs referencing Japan's traditional roofscapes. Giedion saw this as a key to successfully amalgamating Western and Eastern spirits. Evidently a distinctive Japanese Modern architecture based on an aggressive use of modern technology was beginning to emerge, representing a new dialogue with Western Modernism (fig. 9.9).

REGURGITATING MODERNISM – METABOLISM & BEYOND

In this new Japan of industrial pluralism, where the emblematic question was now about finding deeper social meanings to an increasingly westernizing culture, one of the answers centered around grandiose utopia. The Metabolism Group (whose work was surprisingly close to the English Archigram) reacting to the pressures of Japanese overcrowding, proposed constantly growing and adapting plug-in me-

ga-structures where the living cells were prefabricated pods clipped on to tall vertical cores.[21] They argued that unlike the architecture of the past, contemporary architecture had to be changeable and flexible to both reflect and meet Japan's dynamic reality. The most exhibited of these proposals was the 1960 "Plan for Tokyo" by Kenzo Tange & URTEC, a visionary scheme for expanding Tokyo across the bay in a series of nine linear interlocking multi-tiered infrastructure loops, with large urban spaces under ten-story high sloping roofs, bridging off the central spine.[22] None of these grand visions came into realization, but the seeds of such ideas conceptually impregnated their smaller works such as Kisho Kurokawa's Nakagin Capsule Tower and Kenzo Tange's Yamanashi Press and Radio Center, and Fuji TV Building (fig. 9.10). At its best, the smaller Metabolist work succeeded in its own way at pointing the finger that Giedion had prophesized: In many examples it suggested the character of a modern technological mechanism whilst recalling the constructional clarity of Japan's traditional post and beam construction. But this rhetorical avant gardism, too far a cry even for Japanese optimism, met its deserving assessment as a "fuss" of "change-loving structures", a "mere anachronism, a thousand years out of date, or to say the least, not an advance of modern architecture in terms of theory and practice."[23] It eventually began its evident decline at the Osaka Expo in 1970.[24]

Ironically, the most profound critique against such futurist protocols came from one of the Metabolism's founding members, the Cranbrook and Harvard trained Fumihiko Maki. Though as part of the Metabolist coterie, his name became associated with large-scale urban designs and plans, his buildings were anything but mega-structures – a term that ironically he had invented. Deploring the separation of architecture and planning, he criticized in his 1964 essay "Some Thoughts on Collective Forms" the ongoing tendency towards "static compositions of individual buildings" that bore little semblance to the grain of the city.[25] He argued against mega-structuring and for "the vital image of group form" that was derived from "the dynamic equilibrium of generative elements and not a composition of stylized and finished objects."[26] The Hillside Terrace Complex in Tokyo started in 1969 would exemplify Maki's realization of the significance of traditional town-making methods (fig 9.11). The mixed-use project would be designed and built incrementally over the next 25 years, its flexible master plan absorbing radical changes in layout and build-

Figure 9.10 Top: Fuji TV Headquarters designed by Kenzo Tange, Minato, Tokyo.

Figure 9.11 Opposite page. Left: Hillside Terrace Complex designed by Fumihiko Maki. Right: Spiral, a multi-use building, with gallery space, multipurpose hall, cafe, restaurant and bar, salon, and shops designed by Maki, in Minato, Tokyo.

ing typologies, whilst maintaining the open character of its public space, its intimate courts and meandering passageways. Maki's emphasis on the spatial design of the public realm was a pioneering effort amidst the Japanese architectural cacophony – nothing like it had been seen in Japan's recent past.

Unfortunately priorities of those like Maki remained relatively peripheral. The succeeding work of the "Japanese New Wave" though comparatively modest in scale seemed far more accepting of the notion that one could in the Japan of the seventies and eighties, hardly hope to achieve any meaningful relationship between the single building and the urban fabric as a whole. Assuming an almost fatalistic attitude towards the megalopolis, it was Toyo Ito that clarified a new cultural notion of closed domains to counteract the disorder of Japan's "Non-Place Urban Realm". Arguing in his 1978 essay "Collage and Superficiality in Architecture", that richness in the Japanese city was perceived less through the historical accumulation of buildings, and more "out of a nostalgia for [a] lost architectural past which is indiscriminately mixed with the superficial icons of the present", he defined the goal of his architecture, not as the pursuit of that nostalgic satisfaction, but as the expressing of a certain "superficiality of expression in order to reveal the nature of the void hidden beneath."[27]

Prompted by its advancing information society, the gradual shift from an architecture of industrial "hardware" towards one of intangible "software" was hardly difficult.[28] Without renouncing the tectonic and engineering bravura of its earlier modernism, architecture was now concerned with the ephemeral, striving less for monumental permanence and more for an ambiguity in meaning. The increasing use of both lighter ordinary materials such as Teflon fabrics, perforated aluminum, wire mesh, cloth and paper, as well as the latest technologies in lighting, including lasers and computer controlled spatial simulations intended buildings as parts of the rapidly changing environment rather than permanent and deterministic forms. Tokyo, where thousands of structures and buildings got demolished and replaced every day, affirmed the fierce and fleeting reality of the emerging Japanese megalopolis.[29]

When American architect Charles Moore, one of the most audible voices against the placelessness of Modern urbanism visited Japan in 1977, he could not help but voice in his essay "Impressions of Japanese Architecture" how his con-

tinuing awe at Japan's "magic gardens of purest peace" was defiled by its "endless degrading sprawl; the bad air; the shapeless, scattered mass that connects the suburbs from the land, engulfs the real places, and dims the hopes for continuing occupancy of the planet."[30] Thus while Japanese megalopolises seemed to be as chaotic and alienating as any in the West, it was the recognition of this impoverished urban realm that saw the emergence of the introverted enclave, a critical attitude most evident in Tadao Ando's austere concrete. His tension with universal modernism and idiosyncratic tradition had prompted an essay "From Self-Enclosed Modern Architecture toward Universality" as early as 1962, distilling a methodology of "closed modern architecture" in response to a non-feudal, overpopulating, post-war Japan.[31] Lamenting the loss of its most persistent architectural tradition – the "intimate connection with nature and openness to the natural world"[32] – his small austere courtyards, such as in the Koshino House (1981) and Kidosaki (1986) House, sought through detail, light and wind, a contemplative perception that was "overlooked in (the) utilitarian affairs of everyday."[33] Ando's work represented a refreshing Modern paradigm for the contemporary Japanese metropolis while bearing enough theoretical and tectonic innovation for Western intrigue. Perhaps his Modern austerity appealed to contemporary Western architects, just as Japan's traditional austerity had to early Western Modernists (fig. 9.12).

GLOBAL STARCHITECTURE

The contemporary Japanese urban landscape is today a seemingly chaotic collage of Western and Japanese architecture at all scales – from colossal mega-structures and modestly sized yet impeccably detailed showrooms, to iconic towers (fig. 9.13). In the case of mega-structures, one effort that stands out is the Rafael Vinoly designed immense Tokyo International Forum, because it was among other things born through the first open competition ever announced in Japan in 1989, receiving nearly 400 tenders from 68 countries (fig. 9.14). Located in the Marunouchi district of Tokyo, the program includes three massive auditoriums, a large exhibition hall and a huge underground station among other facilities. It was completed in 1996, with a remarkable transparent Glass Hall, "an elongated, narrow lens whose

Figure 9.12 Top left: Church of Light designed by Tadao Ando.

Figure 9.13 Top right: Asakusa Culture and Tourist Information Center designed by Kengo Kuma.

Figure 9.14 Opposite page top left: Tokyo International Forum designed by Raphael Vinoli.

Figure 9.15 Opposite page bottom left: NTT Docomo Yoyogi Building, Shibuya designed by Kajima Design, Tokyo.

Figure 9.16 Opposite page bottom right: Tokyo Metropolitan Government Building designed by Kenzo Tange, Shinjuku, Tokyo.

planimetry is such that it 'leans' on the Japan Railway tracks, with its trains….rushing silently by"[34] creating interior views of "extraordinary effects of psychological suspension."[35] Another case is the Port Terminal in Yokohama (2002), won in an international competition by the Office of Foreign Architects, that realizes a dynamic "liquid" architecture wherein "horizontal floors bend and meet one another with no separating walls; glass sheets close the remaining openings."[36]

In turn, Japan's iconic towers range from the Norman Foster designed Century Tower in Bunkyo (1991) to Cesar Pelli's Mori Towers in Roppongi (2001). I call out two cases here because of their imagery to the Japanese skyline, not as technical marvels, but as semantic objects, implying provocative meanings and symbolisms. One is the Art-Deco-like NTT Docomo Yoyogi Building (2000), a skyscraper located in Shibuya in Tokyo, Japan (fig. 9.15). At 240 meters (790 ft) tall, it is the third tallest building in Tokyo. After the installation of a clock in 2002, it was the tallest clock tower in the world, surpassed in 2011 by the Mecca Royal Hotel Clock Tower in Saudi Arabia. The tallest and most prominent tower is Tokyo in the Metropolitan Main building No.1 (Discussed further in Chapter 10). This 48-story complex is located in Shinjuku with three levels below ground (fig. 9.16). The design of the building by architect Kenzo Tange has many symbolic touches, most notably the split at the 33rd floor which spurts twin-towers above the base and creates an iconic profile that has now given the label of Japan's "Gothic cathedral."[37]

Even modest sizes efforts such as the deconstructivist Koizumi Lighting Theater in Chiyoda-ku by Peter Eisenman (1990), and the Showroom Ambiente in Minato-ku by Aldo Rossi (1991), have offered Western architects a canvas to display signature styles associates with their international repute. Other efforts have offered both Western and Japanese architects an opportunity to generate cutting-edge buildings, experimenting with materials, spatial configurations, and programmatic organization. Renzo Piano's 15-story Hermes building is sited on one of Ginza's most crowded corners, entirely faced with specially forged glass bricks featuring "mobile, vibratile surfaces bordered with mirror silvering."[38] Along Omotesando, the formal boulevard fronting the Meiji Jingu, is the Jaques Herzog and Pierre de Meuron-designed transparent edifice for Prada, with a six-story blue-green glass facade enclosed in a continuous diagonal beehive steel mesh, as well as a number

Figure 9.17 Buildings along Omotesando. Left to right: Dior Showroom, Louis Vuitton Showroom.

Figure 9.18 Opposite page: TOD building designed by Toyo Ito.

of exceptionally detailed other high-budget buildings (fig. 9.17). On the same street is the TOD building by Toyo Ito wrapped in a skin of criss-crossed concrete braces (fig. 9.18). Light enters the building through the clear glass that fills the gaps between the braces on the north side with opaque glass towards the south, facing rows of low private houses. The concrete braces also serve as space dividers inside the building where natural materials, stone, wood and leather, reflect the quality of TOD's leather goods.

Two other small-scale efforts by Ito – who in 2013 became the fourth Japanese architect to win the prestigious Pritzker Architecture Prize, joining Kenzo Tange (1987), Fumihiko Maki (1993), and Tadao Ando (1995) – deserve particular mention.[39] The Tower of Winds, designed in 1986, captures the visual complexity of Tokyo metaphorically in terms of a never-ceasing, ever-changing wind. The tower, a light sculpture that responds to wind speed and directions, was designed years before anyone else explored the use of photo-responsive glass in the same way. Ito's Sendai Mediatheque, a library that opened in 2001 is also an exemplary proposal conceptually rooted in an idea of a "fluid" space of technology discussed in his 1997 article "Tarzan in the Media Jungle."[40] Rather than viewing media as a foreign element to nature, Ito embraces new media and computing as an integral part of the contemporary urban environment. The building is conceived as a transparent cube through which thin floor plates are suspended on seaweed-like "tubes" all linked with the Mediatheque's mission to be barrier-free.

Another Japanese architect whose work has deservedly gained global attention is Shigeru Ban. His experiments with alternative materiality, particularly paper tubing came as early as 1986 before any of his programmatic commissions. His early work focused on paper's structural integrity particularly through paper tubes used by manufacturers in textile factories. In 1994, when a magnitude 7.2 Richter scale earthquake devastated Kobe, it offered him a unique reconstruction project: Not

Figure 9.19 Opposite page:
Everyday objects: Knick-knacks,
dolls and fans.

only were his temporary shelters cheap and easy to develop, they also incorporate community participation, and offer more versatile living conditions compared to traditionally used tents. The 172-square-feet modules have paper tubing for walls with small gaps between each member to allow ventilation and can also be taped up for insulation. The roof is made up of a waterproof tenting material while the foundation consists of donated beer crates filled with sandbags. In the subsequent design of his "Paper Dome" in 1998, straight paper tube joists were connected by laminated timber joints which are independently expensive but coupled with paper tubing created an inexpensive budget.[41] Ban's work assumes particular relevance amidst the problems in finding an alternative construction material to wood, even as the use of trees for framing continues to create significant deforestation problems in Japan.

VENTURI'S JAPAN

It is against these unequivocal trends that Robert Venturi's reaction on his first visit to Japan in 1990 remains significant. He too saw in Japan, a bit of himself, and thus what had been nauseating to Taut was enchanting to him. For him western architects had isolated their views to ancient Japanese shrines and buildings, excluding the markets along the way that teemed with varieties and juxtapositions of color, pattern and scale making the simple shrines even more sublime against this complex context. He returned home not with the imprint of Japan's traditional austerity, but with an intricate collection of the colorful and spontaneous Japanese everyday (fig. 9.19). He brought back myriad little objects and fetishes from Japan's streets and flea markets – "dolls, dishes, balls, boxes-in-boxes, hairpins, statues, chopsticks, chopstick holders, comic books, and idols, made of, among other things, plaster, porcelain, paper, bamboo and lacquered wood, all skillfully crafted and colored." He displayed them at the Philadelphia Museum of Art in 1995 calling it "Skill, Care and Wit: Miscellaneous Objects from Japanese Markets."[42] Venturi had refreshed the outlook on Japan, resurfacing the colorful Japonisme of painters like Manet and Monet that lay buried in the Western mind under heaps of Modern Japanese imagery.

Figure 9.20 Japan's East-West
dialectic.

Almost half a century since its first Western perceptions, Robert Venturi had stretched the Japanese metaphor from the rustic monochrome to the hued riot, challenging the entire palette of disappointments and eulogies from Morse to Taut. Charmed as much by the culture's high-tech gadgetry as its myriad flea market fetishes, it was this complex palette of the indigenous and global, that he found an effective ensemble. Like Ruth Benedict who in her 1946 book "The Chrysanthemum and the Sword" first hinted to understanding Japan as a paradoxical culture – pacifistic yet warlike, conservative yet given to innovation – Venturi implied the Buddha Hall of Todaiji, the Katsura Villa, and the Ise shrine as necessary yet incomplete ingredients of the neo-modern Japanese consciousness.[43]

Venturi seemed determined to present the turn-of-the-century Japan as a natural outburst of paradoxical fantasy. Two decades earlier in his book "Complexity and Contradiction in Architecture," he had justified the necessary position of commonplace elements in architecture to "accommodate existing needs for variety and communication." He recognized Japan's neo-modern clichés, banality and mess as the context for its current architecture, and this new architecture in turn as a context for them. With the publication of his essay "Two Naifs in Japan" (1991) that included a sketch "Learning from Tokyo" to express what he called the "hidden order of the kimono,"[44] Venturi affirmed his assessment of the cultural realities confronting Japan as "a convincing chaos… an ambiguity without anguish."[45] Having not traveled to Japan before and spared of witnessing the panorama of Japanese modernization, he was more than many others able to perceive a complex monoculture with completely unbiased eyes. He embraced it with the same caution as he had the honky-tonk elements in the Nevada desert which he wrote about in his other influential book "Learning from Las Vegas."[46] He thus implied that what he liked in Japan might not have been acceptable to him elsewhere. Just as Rome had been his inspiration behind "Complexity and Contradiction in Architecture," Japan two decades later was his lens to revisit the East-West dialectic that was for long lying dormant in the West.

CONCLUSION

One can argue that the entry of the Western genome in Japan, its gradual embrace, subsequent establishment through Modernism, and eventual mutation through ideas such a Metabolism, in a way expands the same complex tapestry of Japan's foreign versus indigenous cultural threads for another age and time. The difference, I would argue, is that here more than any other time in Japanese history, one finds many paradigmatic moments of sudden mutations and shifts. The sheer thrust of these forces – many of them unexpected – generate, unlike Japan's historic examples, equally sudden and instant cultural reactions and reflexes that were hardly contemplated or reflected upon.

"Japan-ness moves roughly in 25-30-year cycles" notes Arata Isozaki in "Japan-ness in Architecture", his refreshing discourse on the dilemmas of Japanese architecture in an increasingly globalizing milieu.[47] It also suggests his personal struggle to marry Japanese and Western thought: "For Japanese Modernists – and I include myself – it is impossible not to begin with Western concepts. That is to say, we all begin with a modicum of alienation, but derive a curious satisfaction – as if things were finally set in order – when Western logic is dismantled and returned to ancient Japanese phonemes. After this we stop questioning."[48]

These words can be read as a Japanese metaphor for a hundred-year love affair with the West. In this affair, both Japan and the West seem to have no idea how much they really love each other. Their mutual feelings show many shades – craving, respect, awe, curiosity, and even competitiveness. They remind us of the fascinating ways in which cultures dream and fantasize about one another, and the complex modes through which opposites attract. For in a way, nothing could be more opposite than Japan and the West, nothing could be more antipodean, both in the manner these cultures have understood the world and in turn expressed it. The offspring of this long love affair are therefore unprecedented. They belong to both worlds and none. They have their own identities. They are as Japanese as they are Western depending on who is looking at them, and where from. Their only true identity drifts somewhere between Japan and the West, somewhere between Japan's own nostalgia and utopia, recurrently contradicting itself and evading any fixed recognition (fig. 9.20).

Walking uphill from Shibuya to Meiji Jingu, we passed by a farmers' market in front of the famous Yoyogi Stadium, designed by Kenzo Tange for the 1964 Tokyo Olympics. My friend, a well known architect, pulled out his camera in excitement. Then he complained that he could not get a clean shot of the architectural icon, because the tents and people were interrupting his frame.

How easily we edit the city. How conveniently we weed out evolving histories and identities. I for one find the market against the curved grey Modernist concrete far more provocative than the bare sculptural photos of the Yoyogi stadium I had seen as an architecture student. When I look back, none of those photographs had any people in them. All that mattered was the genius of form, construction and tectonic, not the realism of its evolution and appropriation.

The juxtaposition of the people's market and the architectural icon is like a pair of mirrors: one reflects the former aspirations of a born-again nation; the other reveals its post-bubble maturity.

Farmers Market in front of Yoyogi Stadium.

Nightscape, Shinjuku, Tokyo.

Chapter 10
Manifesting Democracy: Publicness and Public Space in Post-War Japan

J apan's defeat in World War II marked the end of a world. Even as the Japanese seemed ready for newer value orientations under the foreign power, the American Occupation (1945-1952) sought to insinuate not only a democratic political system, but a democratic society and culture to support and maintain it: The Emperor who had not so long embodied divinity was now reduced to a mere symbol; the armed forces were dismantled; the former Meiji constitution was completely revised and officially adopted in 1946; and the Diet was to be the Japanese parallel of Western parliaments. The American Occupation "intentionally implanted and nurtured" the first industrialized democracy in the non-Western world.[1]

If Japan represents the six-decade-long legacy of this Western democratic implant, then the Japanese city becomes the setting for examining its multifarious urban manifestations. The focus of this chapter is on examining public space, in particular tracing the intellectual and formal search for expressions of democratic space between the end of World War II to the beginning of Japan's 1980's economic Bubble, and charting their shifts, contradictions and transformations by complex post-democratic entities. The intention is to expand the rhetoric of a relatively understudied period of recent Japanese history and reflect deeper on the forces and meanings of public space as seen in the Japanese city today. Underlying this analysis is the assumption that there is such a thing a "democratic space", a public sphere distinct from the state for public debate, deliberation and consensus. Tracing its evolutions and mutations can both help reveal Japan's cultural cleavages, and affirm the reappraisal or negation of its democratic aspirations. The new forms of post-war public space and publicness in Japan can therefore be seen as the contested and negotiated terrain of socio-political renewal and cultural identity.

MEMORIALIZING PUBLIC MEMORY: THE HIROSHIMA PEACE PARK

In 1949, the site of the Hiroshima bombing was memorialized into a public space, the Hiroshima Peace Park (1949-1955). Designed by Japan's consummate modernist architect Kenzo Tange, its triangular site was structured as a radial plan centered on a large trapezoidal green between the Memorial Museum to the south and the Cenotaph to the north (fig. 10.1). The idea of a public park as a large social space was not

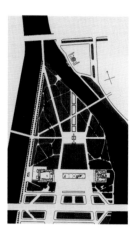

Figure 10.1 Top: Hiroshima Peace Park designed by Kenzo Tange.

new to Japan. Large semi-public gardens and parks typically associated with palaces, villas and temples were an intrinsic part of Japan's traditional social patterns for centuries. Even as recently as 1924, the Ueno Park had been established in the city of Tokyo through an imperial land grant by Emperor Taishō. But the Peace Park was a different paradigm in that it commemorated, for the first time, a narrative of public memory wherein the images and recollections of thousands of ordinary citizens would be translated into a single public setting of national importance. It was, in this sense, not only a spatial emblem of Peace, but also of Japan's new democracy.

Ironically, the Park chose to prohibit public grieving for the effects of the bombing – a mandate that would have significant social consequences. As historian John Dower noted: "Suffering was compounded not merely by the unprecedented scale of the catastrophe…but also by the fact that public struggle with this traumatic experience was not permitted…. With but rare exceptions, survivors of the bombs could not grieve publicly, could not share their experiences through the written word, could not be offered public counsel and support."[2] Further, just as certain forms of public expression were prohibited, others seemed encouraged, particularly the discourse of peace, aimed among other things towards the strategic American interest of portraying the bombing not as a catastrophe, but as the teleological end to the war.

The design of the Peace Park also sought a selective voice in the name of peace, bypassing the struggle against certain injustices. Foremost among these was the legacy of *hibakusha* or the bombing's survivors of Korean descent who had been present in Hiroshima only due to their relocation as forced labor. Following the bombing, they had been given a marginalized status with inferior treatment for both physical and psychological injuries. In 1985, the Peace Park became the setting for an outraged hibakusha gathering organized around a plan to renovate the museum to register their continued plight. It was only after considerable debate that the memorial's general narrative from bombing to peace was retained, but significantly subdued by acknowledging the lingering mistreatment of hibakusha of both Japanese and Korean descent.

As the inaugural spatial manifestation of Japanese democracy, the Hiroshima Peace Park was fraught with complexities. If it embodied patriotism and peace, it also represented the failure to understand the difficult ways in which a wronged populace attempts to communicate its trauma and loss. While peace remained its dominant message, its suppressed and manipulated forms of publicness were evidence of an infant democracy's poor cultural translation, and the conflict between a universal need for critical memory and a less sanitized display of history.

THE EUROPEAN PLAZA AS IMPORT

This idea of the Western plaza was an urbanist import alien to Japan's authentic traditions. As discussed in Chapter 8, in traditional Japan, the labyrinthine tenuous street, not the square, had been the center of civic life. Pre–war Japan had seen the making of major public spaces such as the Hibiya Park in Tokyo (1903) that had been the stage for mass protests against the treaty terms of the Russo-Japanese war, as well as the setting for the funeral of former Prime Minister Okuma Shikenobu. But the idea of the plaza as a figural public urban void had remained absent. Despite "*tsuji* (crossroads) used for posting *takafuda* (placards for government notices), and *kawara* (riverbanks as a place of asylum for various social out-casts) there was, as the research group Japanese Urban Space concluded after an extensive study of fifteenth and sixteenth century cities, "no Western style tradition of picturesque urban scenery….to be found in Japan; rather temporal or visual enclosures were set up here and there for rituals or festivals."[3]

The idea of the plaza was poignant in the Western architectural consciousness of the early 1950s. As an aftermath to the war, the rhetoric on urban cores had shifted towards political events with the plaza as the renewed setting for rallies and demonstrations. The eighth gathering of the Congrès International d'Architecture Moderne (CIAM), themed "Heart of the City: Towards the Humanization of Urban Life" called for strategies on post-war urban reconstruction.[4] Japanese architects now under the willful embrace of Western Modernism seemed charged like their European and American counterparts to recover the role of the plaza and its traditional urban functions.

Attempting to fill a void in the formerly non-democratic Japanese architectural vocabulary, emerging architects such as Kenzo Tange began developing new public

Figure 10.2 Top: Festival Plaza, Osaka Expo 1970 designed by Kenzo Tange.

Figure 10.3 Opposite page: Tsukuba Plaza designed by Arata Isozaki. Left: Plan. Right: Rendering of Tsukuba Plaza as a ruin.

space typologies. His design for the town hall complex of his home town, Imabari, completed in 1959, included an auditorium, office center, and town hall compactly arranged around a public plaza. Tange's interest in such communal spaces dated back to his university studies of the Greek *agora* as a place where a citizen moved from the private realm to establish connections with society.

Recognizing the futility of seeking anything resembling a Western plaza in their historic cities, Japanese Modernists seemed all the more compelled to create spatial parallels. The center of the 1970 Osaka Expo is a case in point. The Omatsuri Hiroba, literally "Festival Plaza," an entity that existed neither in Japan nor the West was placed at the core of the 815-acre "Future City" exhibit. The 350 x 1000 feet space was covered by the world's largest translucent roof of its time: a gigantic spaceframe, 100 feet high, sup-ported by six pillars. Its centerpiece was "The Tower of the Sun" by Japanese sculptor Taro Okamoto, a 230-feet-tall sculpture with exhibits themed around the idea of evolution.[5] If Expo 70 represented Japan's emerging modernist ambitions, its Festival Plaza as a new spatial type symbolized its new desires of nationalism, democracy and hope 25 years following the war (fig. 10.2).

THE MUTATED PLAZA

While none of these were plazas in the traditional European sense of the term, the idea of a large gathering space did see newer forms within urban settings. In 1975, Kisho Kurokawa designed the Head Offices of the Fukuoka Bank around an immense ten-story high "engawa" as an "intermediate space for new kinds of urban life."[6] This covered exterior zone with intermittent planting beds, fountains, and sparse street furniture, sought "to imbue the space with the characteristics of both interior and exterior."[7] It reflected Kurokawa's search for an "architecture of symbiosis," emphasizing his interest in the "architecture of the street" since 1962, as an alternative to the Western concept of the plaza.[8] Kurokawa was fascinated with how the Japanese residential street had served the same purpose as Western squares: how streets lined with homes, shops, and workshops were beginning to function like an architectural "engawa"; as multipurpose, semipublic space.[9] Neither plaza nor street, the Fukuoka Building was Kurokawa's attempt at generating a new prototype for Japanese post-war urbanism.

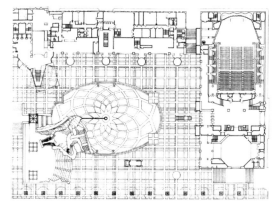

Meanwhile, the Tsukuba Academic New Town, Japan's first real post-war na-
tionally sponsored planning effort, had been envisioned as a holistic community
around a central network of pedestrian decks and a large plaza. In 1983, following
the failure of its initial phase, when Arata Isozaki was commissioned to design the
Tsukuba plaza hub, he was keenly aware of the seeming quirk within this plan. To
build an illusive city in Japan, a land where there had never been a plaza, seemed like
a "double fiction."[10] He chose to celebrate this fictitiousness consciously eschewing
"any element that appeared to be of Japanese origin."[11] He took nothing less than
Michelangelo's Campidoglio – the plaza in front of the Roman Senate, the image
of which would later become a symbol of power for so many Western cities – and
inverted it with "surroundings that appeared to collapse like Guilio Romano's work
at Palazzo del Te at Mantua," with further quotes from Borromini and Ledoux.[12]
Even as this assemblage of a concert hall, information center, hotel and shopping
mall around a sunken oval plaza provoked international debate, Isozaki published
renderings of the project's "ruins," quoting the 19th-century neo-classicist architect Sir John Soane's rendition of the Bank of England. Four decades since its
import, through this "apparition of Japan-ness.....a mere metaphor, that is to say a
rife fiction," Isozaki chose to openly proclaim his plaza as part of a series of events
and expressions that had always been directed less towards Japan, and more to the
outside world (fig. 10.3).[13]

But the evolution of the plaza in Japan affirmed its perceptual shift from an
optimistic democratic symbol into a culturally residual simulacrum. Despite its random proliferation within the Japanese city, it remained alien, failing to root itself
in a culture that seemed reticent towards it. As a metaphor of publicness, it was
never able to become the intellectual reference point in Japanese urbanism. Rather,
as early as the 1960s, the train station would to take its place as both urban center
and the chosen settings for democratic theater, evinced in the notorious Shinjuku
Station concerts.

Figure 10.4 Top: Plaza outside Shibuya Station. Opposite page: Shibuya Crossing.

PROTEST AS IDENTITY: THE TRAIN STATION AS PUBLIC SPACE

The performance of protest is not simply a mode of political expression, but also an indication of democratic success. It gives new meanings to political processes while circumventing the limitations of its institutions. Cultures of protest develop their own identities and influences independent of the state, providing important sites for contestation, redefinition and reconstruction. From the early 1960s, protest had saturated the Japanese political landscape. In 1959-60, a movement against the Japan-US Security Treaty (Anpo Toso) had claimed a life, and shockwaves throughout the nation, adding to the furor of activists seething with anti-government sentiment. In 1967, the protest at Haneda Airport with helmeted armed students trying to prevent Prime Minister Eisaku Sato's visit to Japan's Asian neighbors and the United States had resulted in some six hundred injuries. In 1968, the resident movement in Sasebo had seen thousands gathering in the small port town to protest against the entry of a nuclear powered aircraft carrier, the USS Enterprise. These were just some of the activism sites in a much wider milieu of political participation.

In the early months of 1969, 7000 anti-Vietnam War activists calling themselves the Tokyo Folk Guerilla crowded the subterranean plaza and passageways of Shinjuku Station to sing folk songs and listen to antiwar speeches. Beneath one of Tokyo's burgeoning city centers and one of the world's biggest and busiest train stations, a movement of student sects and activists were intersecting with millions of commuters from all over Japan. Hardly marginal or illicit, this implicit activism, integral to the surfacing economic prosperity of 1960s, touched the everyday life of all Japanese and beckoned them to participate in, and bring meaning to, their democratic ideals. The folk guerillas attempted to make Shinjuku Station's a public space for democratic expression. Government authorities finally broke up the protests and ended the disruption to commuters. A scene from the film shows that the authorities had replaced the sign that had previously labeled the station as "Underground Plaza."[14] They had changed the name of what was once the *hiroba* (underground plaza) to simply *tsuro* (underground passageway) in an effort to prevent people from using the space as a public gathering place.[15]

While the Shinjuku concerts represented a process of democratic political re-newal, and a search for an alternative base in the wake of the authoritarian po-litical institutions of wartime Japan, they also suggested a metaphorical twist. In their attempt to bring the people of Japan into contact with political activism, the performers had sought to excavate new sites for populist political expression. As if reinforcing the pretext used by the police to remove the Shinjuku demonstra-tions – that in Japan there were "no plaza spaces where pedestrians could legally foregather," a train station, not a plaza or park, had become the new setting for performing democracy (fig. 10.4).[16]

RETHINKING PUBLICNESS: THE DESIGN OF THE TOKYO METROPOLITAN GOVERNMENT COMPLEX

It is this contradiction that remained the intellectual subtext for the Tokyo Metro-politan Government Complex competition two decades later. The Tokyo Metro-politan Government Building (Tokyō To-chosha), also referred to as Tokyo City Hall would be located just five blocks west of the Shinjuku Station, and house the headquarters of the Tokyo Metropolitan Government, which governed not only the 23 wards, but also the cities, towns and villages that comprise Tokyo. It was a project of immense socio-political significance and its architecture had to express the post-war institutionalization of Japanese democracy.

Kenzo Tange's winning entry accommodated the City Hall in twin high-rise of-fice towers facing the Shin-juku Central Park, with a vast crescent shaped "Citizen's Plaza" fronting the lower Assembly Building to its east. In what seemed like a sum-mation of his five-decade search for democratic space, his scheme was in every way European in its formal conception recalling the idea of a great cathedral fronting a figural space (fig. 10.5). Conversely, Arata Isozaki's entry had consciously refrained from proposing anything even remotely resembling a plaza. For him the *hi* (protest-ing masses) such as those of the 1960s Shinjuku events had revealed other affinities to public space. He observed that "to the extent that workable public space could no longer be attained in an outside space, sheltered indoor spaces such as underground malls, atria, and internal circulation spaces have been created throughout the city. Hi fills up these interiors as an alternative to the plaza."[17]

Figure 10.5 Right: Tokyo Metropolitan Government Building model by Kenzo Tange.

Figure 10.6 Opposite page: Competition entry rendering of the Tokyo Metropolitan Government Building by Arata Isozaki.

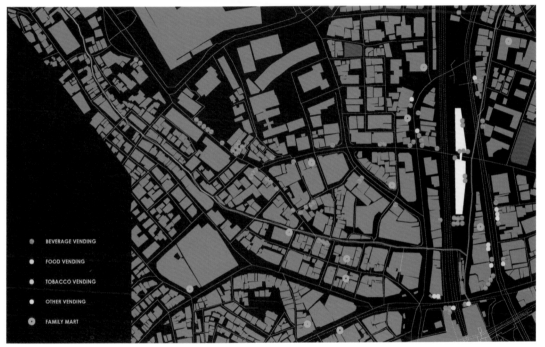

BEVERAGE VENDING

FOOD VENDING

TOBACCO VENDING

OTHER VENDING

FAMILY MART

Figure 10.10 Top and opposite
page: Nightscape, Shinjuku,
Tokyo.

Cabarello and Tsukamoto call out a number of such third spaces. The *manga kissa* for instance is an establishment with small cubicles for one or two people to relax, read comics, drink coffee, surf the internet, play video games or watch movies. The term stems from the manga comic and the kissa tea or coffee house. They are open seven days a week, twenty-four hours a day, with drinks usually free. In the early eighties, they were more like coffee shops called kissa-ten, but in the nineties, the library and internet component increased enough to change its character to more than a drinking place.[26] The karaoke box is another parallel establishment with small-size rentable rooms devoted exclusively to karaoke (singing to recorded music) events typically in half-hour increments, with food and drink service comparable to any restaurant in Tokyo. There is the *kenko* land or saunas including many types of baths, jacuzzis, game rooms, TV rooms and capsule accommodations. And there are *robu hoteru* or love hotels, devoted exclusively for consenting sexual activity (discussed further in the following chapter).

The psychedelic spectacles of the by-now notorious Japanese streets of Ginza, Shinjuku and Akihabara embody another aspect of this alternative publicness. By the seventies, with their rhetoric of neon and electro-signage beginning to mark the reemergence of previously unseen forms of publicness, it seemed as if consumerism, not democracy was the dominant force of public life in Japan. Shinjuku, hardly touched by the 1923 Great Kanto Earthquake, became an attractive businesses hub after the widespread destruction. Circa 1971, the Keio Plaza Hotel marked the opening of Japan's first skyscraper. And one of the squares, where dissident hippie gangs lived during the 1960s Shinjuku riots, became the site of an immense new department store called Studio Alta. It displayed a colossal video screen incessantly spewing out cascades of images, setting the dramatic precedent for things to come. Today, surrounding the station, there is a bustling shopping district known for among other things, its nightlife, especially in Kabuki-cho, one of Japan's most famous (and naughtiest) amusement centers. Today, Shinjuku's notorious psychedelic nightscape represents the ultimate neo-expressionism of alternative forms of Japanese publicness (fig. 10.10).

Cabarello and Tsukamoto have also analyzed how in these signage-laden streetscapes, multiple uses are often stacked atop each other creating the *zakkyo* (literally

"co-existing miscellany") building where the stairway becomes "an extension of the street," and the façade signage an advertisement for the layered uses.[27] They differ from place to place: In Shinjuku, the entire façade is covered with billboards; in Shibuya they are concentrated on the lower floors and lobbies.[28] In other words, the contents of these buildings are overtly displayed, even though they physically remain hidden behind the signage veneers. The sign-laden buildings along Yasukuni-dori in Shinjuku or those in Shibuya can thus be understood as vertical establishments of alternative spaces for publicness compared to the plazas and sidewalks of European and American cities, and equally as responses to, among other things, the limitations of land scarcity and extreme real estate prices.

What meanings underlie this spectacle of mass media and communication? If the Western plaza embodies Jurgen Habermas's advocacy for a "deliberative democracy," does the semiotic Japanese street represent Chantal Mouffe's alternative of "agonistic democracy?"[29] The former is grounded in the idea of the "public sphere" as an essential arena for populist deliberation and consensus towards the making of sound policy. Conversely, the latter believes that democracy should be designed to optimize the expression of populist disagreement. In seeking to place opponents in adversarial rather than antagonistic roles it makes democracy a process of contestation and public space the material artifact "of an evolving and messy.....process."[30]

Or does Shinjuku manifest, instead, the overwhelming of the Japanese "democratic" public realm by the spectacle of Japanese consumerism? For Shinjuku exaggerates the idea of street signage into a socio-political art. It inverts the realist viewpoint of signage reflecting society; instead, society is the mirror for the sign. It is a pretext for turning urban life into a consumerist gallery: erasing histories, inequalities and conflicts, and displacing attention from the ideologically constructed political world, urging citizens towards bemusement and obliviousness. Located within this inversion is Japan's ultimate indigenous nod towards the artistic tradition of reimagining the mundane and an affirmation that it is not democracy, but rather post-Westernization and globalization within which are nested other desires and expectations (fig. 10.11).

10.11 Building sign, Shibuya, Tokyo.

POST-DEMOCRATIC PUBLICNESS AND THE JAPANESE CITY

Sixty years since its implantation, the ideals of democracy have been embraced so enthusiastically in Japan, that the term democracy has the ability to represent one of the greatest accomplishments of post-war Japanese society. The idea of people as participants, not subjects, in political life represents a dramatic transformation within a not-so-long-ago imperial society. While certain social dimensions such as women's rights movements may not have seen dramatic advances in a society still tending towards male supremacy, the assimilation of an egalitarian democracy in Japan's remarkably homogenous and religiously tolerant society has generated relatively few minority challenges. While a broader assessment of Japan's democratic success is beyond the scope of this chapter, I believe it is safe to say that Japanese democracy compares favorably with other industrialized societies of Europe and America.

Viewing democracy through the lens of the transformation of the Japanese city affirms its inclusiveness and cultural pluralism. If democracy is but a legal text denoting its country of affiliation, then this indeed is its greatest strength. For all its political success or failure, democracy is manifested only through cultural appropriation: At the Peace Park it struggles to understand its populist dimensions. At Shinjuku, it plunges the depths of Japanese society to shape the fabric of its nascent political ideals. At Tsukuba, it morphes into an urban satire on Japan's willful Westernization. And in Shinjuku's streets, it is over-whelmed by the forces of Japanese consumerism. These shifting manifestations of post-war publicness and public space in Japan deepen the idea of democracy demanding readings and re-definitions beyond its original Western sources.

By focusing on the nexus of democracy and its public space manifestations, this chapter endeavored to re-read the evolving identity of the Japanese city amidst its ever-changing present and recent past. This identity remains both elusive and complex. It is neither wholly Japanese, nor wholly Western. Rather, Japan is a culture of imports tracing back to its ancient Chinese influences.[31] Democracy is part of this long tradition. Japan's diffusion of democratization and westernization as mutually inseparable constructs represents a cultural "problematic," the character of which, from its beginning, "has belonged to an external gaze."[32] The contemporary Japanese city must be understood, therefore, as a sixty-year-long struggle to shape a nation's democratic identity within the confines of an imposed and irrevocable East-West dialectic.

Every day, Tokyo spins faster and faster, forgetting itself. But thousands of vending machines in its unassuming streets – behind the Senso-ji temple in Asakusa, or in the neighborhoods of Harajuku – remind people that they matter. They stop them for a few seconds for a canned tea and coffee, or bottled sakura-flavored milk. And hundreds of Family Marts along ugly intersections offer onigiri, an instant snack of rice, seaweed and fish eggs that can keep you going for hours. It takes only a fast tear and pull to get it ready to eat, but it has to be done with attention. It is like a Zen brushstroke – there is no going back.

At night, Tokyo oozes with sensuality. The narrow, dark alleys, and shanty clubs and eateries of Gorudengai can hardly hide the smells of sex that pervaded Shinjuku's mid-century red-light district. In one of its micro-restaurants ten people somehow huddle together. They do not know each other. Beer smell and cigarette smoke mix with the vapor of boiling vegetables and meat, and exotic dishes emerge one after the other from behind a tiny counter. A small stairway leads to an upper floor that no one goes to anymore. A 50's poster of a half-naked woman invites attention, and the mind wanders up the dark stairs to get lost in forbidden pleasures .....until all the food is consumed.

Tokyo Night.

Tokyo cityscape.

Chapter 11
Rereading Tokyo

For most non-Japanese architects and urbanists, particularly from the West, Tokyo epitomizes the extremities of contemporary urbanism. It has been described as a "horrendous"[1] megalopolis; a "labyrinthine magma-like whole;"[2] a "frightening city, the largest and ugliest in the world;"[3] an ephemeral city where "what goes up must come down"[4] and even a city built on "compact layers of pornography."[5] In other words, like that early Western curiosity with post-Meiji Japan as the exotic other land, Tokyo has now become the global traveler's urban cynosure, albeit differently. It is a curious urban polemic that in so many ways overturns everything held believably urban, and from where one takes back tales of unabashed extremes.

Statistically speaking, compared to European and American cities, Tokyo does present some startling contrasts: The cost of living is more than 50% higher than New York. The amount of private space per capita is 66% lower. Parks constitute merely 5% of its land surface in comparison to 30% in London.[6] But despite these delirious densities, the amount of space actually occupied by its over-nine-million occupants on its 23 ku or 622-square-kilometer spread is only around 52% (though it rises up to 70% in central areas)[7] (fig. 11.1).

Compared to other Asian mega-cities such as Hong Kong, Mumbai or Shanghai, Tokyo may still standout in certain respects but it is certainly not an anomaly. And of course, none of these seemingly extreme numbers mean anything to most Tokyoites, for whom, the city is in fact a mosaic of discrete social worlds, urban neighborhoods, districts, streets, destinations, efficient trains, thousands of cafes and social places, all defined through their own cultural means and ends. In this insider's Tokyo is an elaborate and enduring framework of livability, where residents link to one another through webs of informal social, economic, and cultural ties. This side of Tokyo is less known to most casual outsiders. Were they to see it, their first impulse would perhaps be to read it as the antithesis of the major trends of modernization that associate with Japan, and therefore probably not be as excited about it.

In this final chapter, I wander around Tokyo, contemplating how to read what in many ways is the ultimate crescendo of the Japanese built environment. Where are the lines that overlap and in turn separate the outsider's and insider's impressions

Circa 1923,
Great Kanto Earthquake

Circa 1940,
Tokyo rebuilt

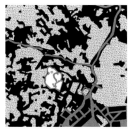

Circa 1941,
Bombing in Second World War

Circa 2013,
Tokyo grid today

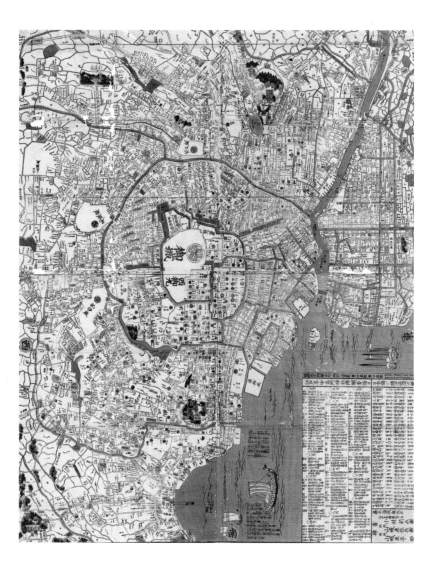

form. If Manhattan is the epitome of the flat high-rise grid, and Central Hong Kong a warped terrain of high-rises without a grid, then Tokyo is something else altogether.

With the radical increase of height limits by the government in 1963, Tokyo saw an unstoppable process of high-rise development. Starting with its earliest towers, the Sony building by Yoshinobu Ashihara (1966), and the Shizuoka Press and Broadcasting Company by Kenzo Tange (1967), both in Ginza, land pressure began to cause a dramatic upward expansion of the historically horizontal city. In the book "East-Asia Modern: Shaping the Contemporary City," Peter Rowe has identified four circumstantial patterns in this regard: The first happened through the piecemeal vertical extension of historic lots as evident in low lying areas next to the Sumida River. Here the historic bridges were filled and converted into roads, and traditional blocks were overlaid parcel by parcel with taller commercial structures along its periphery to face canals and streets, with living tucked behind and entered through gates and narrow lanes – an *anko-gawa* configuration, with a soft or low inner core and a hard or tall periphery.[16] With typical lot sizes of around 60 feet x 120 feet in blocks of around 250 feet x 400 feet, the result of this structured upward expansion is "a very sharp gradation of tall, thin pencil buildings, placed side-by-side," with an equally "sharp disjunction of moving from bustling, high-rise urbanity to quiet, small-scale traditional circumstances."[17] (fig. 11.4, 11.5).

The second happened on the eastern end of the Sumida River in the low wetland areas that had escaped the 1923 Kanto earthquake and fire. Here, the anko-gawa configuration has a more spontaneous and organic form, as can be seen in neighborhoods like Kyojima in Sumida-ku, reflecting the underlying pattern of rice fields and streams, with new streets and highways attempting to superimpose a rectilinear order. The third involved large-scale conversions of relatively open sites: The highrise fabric of Shinjuku, today one of Tokyo's densest sub-centers occurred through the impetus of rail-road and subway development. In the subsequent building boom in the seventies, relatively open height limitations produced the largest concentration of high-rise urbanity in Japan.

The fourth was the densification of Tokyo's hillsides, once the settings for the walled compounds of *diamyo* estates and monasteries. Initially thought of as ideal sites for government institutions and museums such as Ueno Park, pressures of

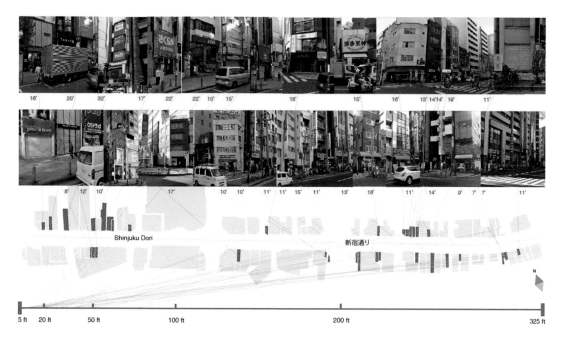

Figure 11.4 Vertical extrusion of small lots: Building-lot width analysis
of Shinjuku-dori. Note how most of the lots are between 8 to 50 feet in
width.

Top: The ango-kawa configuration, with high-rise buildings enclosing a low-rise fabric.

Figure 11.5 Right: Figure field diagram of area around Shibuya Station. The diagram shows the warping street grid that emerges in response to the terrain going up-hill towards Yoyogi Park and Meiji jingu. Opposite page below: The accompanying photo shows the dramatic grain of high and low rise development that makes up the black figure seen in the diagram.

Figure 11.6 Top and opposite
page: Toyosu urbanscape.

property values generated ad-hoc high-rise development, with developers assembling various pieces of land for large-scale structures. Particularly during the eighties Heisei Boom, when Tokyo was forced to welcome the increasing flow of (often illegal) immigrants, areas like Minato-ku and the entire western hill-belt of Yamanote became dense with high-income residents, many of them immigrants, and began looking more and more like the very American and European downtowns they had left behind.[18]

By the end of the Heisei Boom in the late nineties, Tokyo had become a transnational system "with fourteen of the fifteen largest banks in the world....and the whole Asian economic system, itself in rapid growth, linked in with it."[19] Much of original bay area city project had been developed between 1980 to 1990, and the city was now spreading towards to the southern waterfront of Toyosu. By 2001, it appeared as if the very center of Tokyo was gradually shifting to the bay. Today, Toyosu's land values continue to rise. The reclaimed land footprint is still enlarging, occupied by massive waterfront office buildings with large verdant setbacks and wide sidewalks – in other words a thoroughly planned place that is quite literally the antithesis of central Tokyo's unplanned fabric (fig. 11.6).

Italian architect Livio Sacchi, in his book "Tokyo: City and Architecture," observes how Tokyo's towers stand in "chaotic, fragmented, spurts amidst relatively miniscule buildings, on an uneven hilly terrain defying any urban logic except their location on prominent streets and their accumulation around main subway stations;"[20] and yet he argues, they endow the city with "a greater energy than San Paulo, Kuala Lumpur, Pudong in Shanghai or Chicago, and, maybe even that New York."[21] Sacchi's proclamation typifies the polemical glorification of Tokyo an intriguing antipode to the formal clarity of the European city. But it must be recognized that this dimension of Tokyo's history has had as much do with economic pressures as physical constraints. Even more significantly, all of these towers having mushroomed after the 1960's, are blatant advertisements to what many take for granted – the perpetual newness of this resilient city. We cannot dismiss the aspirations behind Tokyo's towers, and we must not necessarily accept these unequivocal extrusions as urban models to be emulated, we must simultaneously understand the complex forces that have shaped them – and therein read them for what they truly are.

RESILIENCE

It is hard for many of us to contemplate living in a city that you know will be destroyed from time to time. This is another side of Tokyo – where people measure their city's history as events between disasters. In January 2012, the Earthquake Research Institute at the University of Tokyo reported a 70% chance of a 7.0-magnitude or higher quake to strike Japan's capital by 2016. Such an event, the scientists said, could mean a death toll of up to 11,000 people and $1 trillion in damages on the world's third-largest economy.[22] Two years after a 9.0-magnitude quake and resulting tsunami devastated northeastern Japan, the country's disaster-response experts are more nervous than ever about the ground beneath their feet. Famed Japanese seismologist Katsuhiko Ishibashi has noted that because "there hasn't been a large-scale earthquake around Tokyo since 1923…..there's a high probability a violent tremor will strike the region (in the foreseeable future), stronger than the one that hit two years ago."[23]

In Tokyo, as in many other places across the country, each district has its own evacuation spot, emergency road, and temporary facilities with its own hazard maps showing the areas of possible major damage and fire. For a long time, evacuation spots in Japan were located within the local community, with public schools and local parks as the main places for temporary evacuation. Today around 200 locations are registered within Tokyo for temporary emergencies including local parks, public schools, gas stations, and convenience stores. There are also more than thirty larger designated evacuation open spaces (with a minimum area requirement of 90-square-kilometers) with hazard maps created by local communities and the city government showing the emergency route for getting to these areas safely and directly. A simple water utilization facility called *rojisan* has been set up by local residents in the Tokyo's Mukojima district, wherein rainwater is collected from the roofs of private houses for garden watering, fire-fighting and drinking water in emergencies. The rojisan also serves as a public place where community members can share their ideas towards survival during a natural disaster.

Additionally in 2012, The Tokyo Metropolitan Government announced a disaster preparation plan that uses the city's fire hydrants as water stations for shelters

Figure 11.7 Top: Diagram of Tokyo's primary mobility network. The main highways are in blue. The train network is in red. Opposite page: Shinkansen bullet train.

in the event of an earthquake or similar disaster.[24] Roughly 130,000 fire hydrants throughout the city (according to the local government's Bureau of Waterworks) will be able to provide fresh water to as many as 5,000 refugee shelters, serving nearly eight-million people who are predicted to be stranded in Tokyo in the event of a major earthquake.[25] To prepare for the fire hydrant plan, necessary supplies to turn them into water stations, like water hoses and standpipes, are being distributed to Tokyo's wards, cities, and towns. In April 2012, it was determined that as much 45% of Tokyo's water supply could be cut off in a major earthquake leaving access to water only in stockpiled bottles and water tanks at the approximate 200 emergency supply bases throughout the city.[26] The government has subsequently announced that it will also offer training programs for residents on how to supply their own water.

In February 2012, Martin Fackler reported in the New York Times that in the "darkest moments" of the 9.0 Tohoku earthquake and tsunami on March 11, 2011, Japanese leaders not knowing the actual extent of damage at the plant "secretly considered the possibility of evacuating Tokyo.[27] It did not happen, but the catastrophe has instigated impelling large-scale planning efforts centered on an entire backup city for Tokyo. The plan is titled "Urban Plan B", and calls for the construction of a new city to be called IRTBBC (Integrated Resort, Tourism, Business, and Backup City) or NEMIC (National Emergency Management International City) and to be located on the site currently occupied by the Osaka International Airport at Itami.[28] ITRBBC would be designed to take on all the functions of Tokyo in the event of a catastrophe. The centerpiece, a 650 m-high- tower alone, would house 50,000 residents and accommodate a work-day force of 200,000 people from the Osaka region.[29]

In Tokyo, disaster preparedness is at work at all scales – from modest neighborhood-centered efforts and city-wide programs to entire regional strategies – relying both on the old and the familiar, as well as the new and the innovative. And while it seems counterintuitive that an urban geography of recurring quakes, tsunamis and typhoons should be compact rather than spread-out, thereby increasing its susceptibility to disasters on a larger scale, as Vishaan Chakrabarti argues "spreading out only leads to oil dependence and further environmental degradation, which in turn

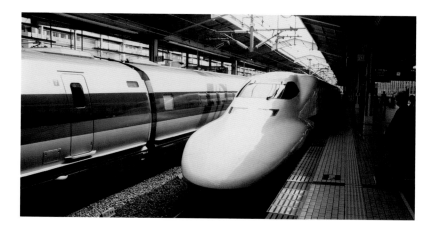

leads to sea-level rise and fiercer storm surges."[30] In its ongoing patterns of "planning for the unplanned," Tokyo compels us to reconsider the definition of disaster planning from an exception to a normative aspect of strategy and policymaking.[31]

TRAINS

In their essay "Four Hours: Orchestration of Timespace" Solomon, Morris and Dimmer call attention to a daily Tokyo pattern occurring every twenty-four hours around midnight: As train services discontinue for an approximately four hour period during the night, they observe, Tokyo "experiences a fundamental shift in its patterns of commuter circulations" – people rushing to finish their respective duties or grab a instant snack to reach the station as fast as possible to get home.[32] They argue this to be "a significant void at the heart of Japanese cities" and posit for a twenty-four hour operation of city trains as a potential impetus for urban revitalization.[33] This "void" is an intriguing aspect of Tokyo particularly if one knows that in its thirty-million-strong metropolitan area, annual urban rail ridership is approximately double that of the entire public transport industry of the United States. From subways to overhead trains, Tokyo takes its inhabitants with extreme efficiency to its limits and back.

Japan's first railway line opened in 1872. It was a mere 29 kilometers from Shimbashi to Yokohama and used British technology and rolling stock.[34] The Meiji government had initially decided to develop a state railway system, but with lack of sufficient capital, and an eager private sector ready to invest in new technology, the government permitted private businesses to build and operate railways while offering some financial assistance.[35] But circa 1907, the nationalization of major trunk lines belonging to seventeen private railway companies spurred a sudden expansion of the government railways' network at the expense of private railways.[36] By 1910, 90% of the rail was run by the government changing the destiny of Japanese mobility.[37] Following the war, the railway became one of the most important tools for urban development. With a weak planning system, and a relatively undeveloped road infrastructure, commuting by train and subway became the most effective travel means for those who lived in the suburbs and worked in the city center.

Figure 11.8 Top: View of Tokyo Skytree and cityscape from Asakura.

Figure 11.9 Opposite page: Nightscape at Shibuya Crossing.

Circa 1959, Japanese workmen finished installing the high-speed rail system in as little as five and a half years. The tracks officially opened on October 1, 1964, just in time for the Tokyo Olympics. The Shinkansen Bullet Train was the new prototype of public transit. Originally running the 320-mile-track between Tokyo and Osaka and costing 640-million dollars to build, it would grab both national and international attention for its comfort, punctuality, and 125 miles-per-hour speed (now 300 miles-per-hour), and go on to become the most popular form of transportation in modern Japan. During the Shinkansen's 48-year history with nearly seven billion passengers, no passengers have been killed in train accidents since the service began. There have been no passenger fatalities despite frequent earthquakes and typhoons with only one derailment during the Chūetsu Earthquake on 23 October 2004.[38] Today the Asama Shinkansen is a part of an endless line of Shinkansen trains running from Tokyo to Nagano with stations on all Shinkansen lines efficient enough not to steal too much space in the populated megalopolis (fig. 11.7).[39]

Tokyo's train stations have no dead spaces. They pack the utilitarian aspects of a transitional node with commerce, leisure, media, fashion and other advanced spaces for creation and innovation. Shinjuku Station for instance occupies approximately fifteen acres, and serves four light rail companies. It has two underground levels for the subway trains, and two high-rise department stores and restaurants, with drugstores, lockers, shops and boutiques at almost all levels. Multiple entrances connected to the streets extend into bus and taxi depots, shuttle pick-up to airports, and finally entire underground passages directly linked to high rise buildings. What these stations have done in effect is recalibrated the city into a series of clearly identifiable transit districts that perform at three levels: that of the street, that of the high-rises that surround them, and that of the sophisticated subterranean world connecting them.

There is then, another reading of Tokyo – as a series of train rides from district to district. Stephen Barber's book "Tokyo Vertigo" is organized precisely on this experience. It moves from district to day to night – from Shinjuku, "Tokyo's burning heart in the late 1960s,"[40] and Shibuya, where "the presiding deity is Hello Kitty,"[41] to Daiba, Tokyo's massive reclaimed annex, to finally the Imperial Palace – evoking a bewildering series of urban sensations and images (fig. 11.8, 11.9). During such

rides, and between these districts, the train window is literally a lens on Tokyo's history, showing frame by frame, the innumerable moments of an compact accumulation of modest plaster buildings and neighborhoods, urban grids, back alleys, train-tracks, old canals, and spurts of commerce and retail all mangled in a rich frenzy of Japanese signage (fig. 11.10, 11.11, 11.12).

All this ends near midnight. It is when the taxis take over, with their immaculate roof lights, clean interiors and soft-spoken drivers. And when one takes to the road one begins to comprehend another reading of Tokyo: there are no axes or landmarks to add any kind of navigable structure. On the one hand are streets retaining characteristics of their old feudal framework, originally conceived to slow down enemies by multiple dead-ends and closes.[42] On the other are the massive expressways, pedestrian bridges, and rail-tracks slashing through the fabric. This double suspended network is built without any figural intention or hierarchy, even though it is created to reduce traffic at intersections. It ultimately results in a labyrinthine form, whose comprehension seems best through speed and mobility, as if moving through a contorted grid placed on a perpetually fluctuating terrain. Tokyo's mobility infrastructure is arguably the most visually conspicuous dimension of its urbanism. It is what enables the city to go on impeccably, reliably, and efficiently, proving that ultimately, the rationale of a clearly readable urban form is but one of many.

EROS

"Tokyo is built on compacted layers of pornography" wrote Stephen Barber.[43] Many Japanese natives or perhaps even non-natives who have lived in Japan for a long time would perhaps strongly disagree with his suggestion that Japan is sex-driven. But as a starry-eyed outsider, Barber was referring among other things to the comic books, internet guides, and manga pamphlets that he observed Tokyo salarymen take in compulsively each day. He was quoting another starry-eyed outsider Romain Slocombe's full-page black-and-white photographs in "Tokyo Sex Underground" ranging from the faux-innocent naturalistic to the artfully kinky, and from demurely costumed nurses to fetish parties.[44] He was referring to the hospital rooms and the neon streets, where he had seen Slocombe's "Broken Dolls" in plaster-casts and

Figure 11.10 Top left: View from train window.

Figure 11.11 Top right: One of Shibuya's canals. These waterways lie between the backs of buildings, faced by utility and services areas. They bear the potential to become unique urban spaces through incremental revitalization.

Figure 11.12 Bottom: In-between spaces. Skate park, and bars next to train tracks near Shibuya Station. Note the vertical wall of buildings enclosing the space on both sides. In the far distance is the NTT Docomo Yoyogi Building.

Figure 11.13 Opposite page: Historic photo of Yoshiwara brothel, circa 1890.

bandages, as victims of unknown traumas in a city seething with undercurrents of sexual violence and bondage.[45]

The fact is that Tokyo like any city, reserves another world in its sexual enclaves. For me, the most Japanese of these are the *rabu hoteru* or love hotels that continue to enable Japanese couples to engage in acts of intimacy beyond their owned spaces. Here, you pay to have sex in two-hour units in a room of your selection. This trend runs deep in Japanese culture. Love hotels can be traced back to tea-places or *deai-chaya* during the Edo Period, where couples were served tea and cake before being left alone to engage in sexual activity. Later in the 20th century, *machiai*, small establishments with *tatami*-mat spaces, and *sobaya*, noodle shops with upper floors rented out usually for prostitution, became the new meeting places for *geishas*, clients and couples (fig. 11.13).

Unlike regular hotels that are usually situated in the core urban areas along arterials to increase visibility, love hotels are sequestered in the urban back streets. As Cybrisky notes, the physical framework of Japan's urban centers is distinguished between the *omote-dori* or front streets where skyscrapers and major shopping malls are situated, versus the *ura-dori*, or back streets or alleyways tucked behind the tall buildings – where love hotels are largely located.[46] Many hotels are built in concentrated clusters, such as "Love Hotel Hill" in Shibuya with approximately sixty hotels huddled in less than a quarter-mile radius of the Dogenzaka section behind the popular Shibuya 109 department store (fig. 11.14). The exterior architecture of love hotels displays thematic idioms – from bright and colorful paint, and fairy-tale castles to Victorian mansions, with signage navigating pedestrian flow to these discrete places (fig. 11.15, 11.16).[47] They stand out in their dependence on neon to reshape nondescript silhouettes into castles of the imagination, and in their attempt to transform the mundane into the magical.

Love hotels were once defined in the same category as massage parlors, pachinko parlors, and strip clubs, but in 1985, the Japanese government passed the Entertainment Law by regulating love hotels in an effort to address social issues. With Japan's lenient zoning regulations, love hotels were not only operated within red-light districts, but they could also be found next to a school or retirement home.[48] Some hotels were even located near religious areas. The law re-defined love

Figure 11.14 Top right: Plan of Love Hotel Hill.

Figure 11.15 Center left and right: Love Hotels on Love Hotel Hill.

Figure 11.16 Bottom: Display wall outside a bar in Shibuya.

Figure 11.17 Opposite page: Kinky Tokyo.

hotels as a place to rest for a short duration, and not a traditional hotel or *ryokan* (Japanese inn). In other words, as West notes, the Entertainment Law reclassified love hotels as a sex-related business because they were not operating for the purpose of guest lodging.[49] The law now regulates that hotels may not operate at least 200 meters from schools and libraries.

Meanwhile, incubating between Shinjuku's station and skyscrapers is Kabu-ki-cho, a neon-drenched enclave packed with sex shops, love hotels, clubs, bars, pachinko parlours, and pleasure houses catering to both sexes (fig. 11.17). It got its name from the originally planned and eventually abandoned *Kabuki* theatre in this district, and its proximity to the train station catalyzed the proliferation of forbidden pleasures as early as the seventies. Although prostitution is illegal in Japan, everyone seems to ignore what goes on behind these closed doors that are strictly bounded from the rest of the city with clear divisions between a shopping district and recreation area. Within the enclave, however, compared to other cities in the world, these shops are wide open to the public, some blatantly facing the main street with decorated neon sign boards that in fact render a street scene where one can easily pass by without feeling awkward.

There are three dimensions to this neon economy: The first is the *mizu sho-bai*, the women protagonists, mostly of Japanese descent but with an increasing number of foreigners from Vietnam, Thailand, Cambodia, and the Philippines, all part of a long-established sex trade. The second is the *sarariman* or white-collared worker that patronizes the mizu-shobai on his employer's account. The third is the *yakuza* that own and manage the business. With tattoos that stretch across their entire body, these members of organized crime groups maintain formal offices, but remain veiled in public life, operating behind brothel curtains, as the benefactors of Japan's counter-culture.[50] These aspects of Japanese culture stand out for many outsiders, perhaps more so than other cultures where they also exist, because of their unabashed contrast with what we immediately associate with Japan – the calm of a dry sand garden, the refined art on a *kimono*, the meditative silence of a tatami room.

Figure 11.18 Top: Government
shelters for the homeless,
Shibuya.

Figure 11.19 Opposite page:
Homeless in Ueno Park.

BLUE TENTS

We also do not immediately associate Tokyo with homelessness. Japan's reputation as a middle class paradise has led to a persistent myth that homelessness is rare or even non-existent in the country. The fact is that today, more than 15,000 people live on streets, with at least 10,000 in Tokyo alone. These numbers do not include residents of capsule hotels, or those that sleep overnight in 24-hour Internet cafes and saunas.[51] While these numbers may not seem significant compared to other cities around the world, for Japan, this is a new dimension not encountered in recent history. With the economic collapse, laborers that previously worked in the construction industry were immediately affected, and with many international businesses declaring bankruptcy, there was a parallel increase in younger homeless men in their twenties and thirties. The rise of homelessness is surfacing new issues in Tokyo that cannot be underestimated for the future of Japan.

In 1996, for instance, the homeless people of Shinjuku's cardboard town were forcibly evicted by private guards and police. Even as supporters were arrested, questions such as "who owns public space" or "what should be given priority: human lives or local regulations?" surfaced as dominant rubrics.[52] One needs a fixed address to qualify for welfare help, and be eligible to receive 78,000 yen a month and lodging to the value of 1,900 yen a night.[53] But many homeless in Tokyo as the rest of Japan choose not to claim state help. Tamae Ishiwatari has suggested that this is a political issue: "The welfare benefits are given in an attitude of condescending, patronizing charity. The laws, regulations, the pre-conditions required, the bureaucracy and the smug arrogance of officials all combine to act as a powerful deterrent." My own experiences in Shibuya (jotted in the spread before this chapter) have revealed another subtlety. Many homeless have in fact refused state stipends as a matter of personal pride. In turn they have formed micro-communities, of modest timber structures provide by the state, and launched micro-businesses such as collecting beer cans sold each week to the state for a price significantly less than the stipend they are entitled to.

Today, blue tents – in Ueno Park, Shinjuku or along portions of the Sumida River – are blatant symbols of Japan's homelessness phenomenon. Less blatant are

the capsule hotels.[54] Two decades ago, when Japan was pulling back from its bubble economy, the Capsule Hotel Shinjuku had opened its tiny 6 feet x 5 feet plastic cubicles as a night's refuge to salarymen who had missed the last train home. Today, these capsules offer an affordable option for people with nowhere else to go. Rents are more than the equivalent of 600 American dollars, but cheaper than anywhere else in Tokyo, with residents having reduced their possessions to only that which can be stored in a locker.

On May 18, 2013, the British magazine "Economist," featured a cover story on Japanese prime-minister Shinzo Abe's vision of a prosperous and patriotic Japan. Since he was elected for his second term, the stock market rose by 55%, and consumer spending pushed up growth in the first quarter to an annualized 3.5%.[55] How this will all eventually play out is another subject but as Japan endures its worst recession since World War II, such figures are crucial signs of optimism for a country of over 127-million inhabitants that is confronting new gripping realities.

As the global architecture and urbanist community continues to see Tokyo as a dynamic ground for new ideas on architecture and urbanism, we must not forget the deeper issues that this agglomeration now dives headlong into. They will also be the gauge of Tokyo's resilience, and ultimately of its evolving ethos as a global city (fig. 11.18, 11.19).

TOKYO – AS TOKYO

Where an outsider's and insider's Tokyo overlap is in its non-figural and accumulative urban form, and its dense, compact disposition on limited land. Where an outsider's and insider's Tokyo separate is in the manner in which this physical setup is understood and experienced. I for one would argue that Tokyo remains one of most livable and walkable cities in the world. Physically, its most dominant experience is its generic fabric of unpretentious architecture on equally unpretentious but perpetually active streets, with innumerable micro-enclaves of eating, shopping and socializing, all weaving together an impressive subterranean as well as elevated mobility infrastructure. It reminds us that cities can in fact be conceived, experienced and understood beyond the normative and dominantly Western parameters of physical

Figure 11.20 Opposite page: Diagram comparing urban expansion of Tokyo and Los Angeles in relation to population size. The timeline begins with the establishment of Tokyo in 1603 and continues to the 21st century, marking major events in Tokyo and Japan's history.

form, and that visually ambiguity should not be confused with the richness of daily urban life. Tokyo's seemingly visual cacophony might not be a model for other cities, but its livability quotient, impeccable efficiency, and diverse sociability are things every other city should aspire to.

As Asia's first global megalopolis, Tokyo pioneered what is now an evolutionary trajectory of many rapidly urbanizing Asian mega-cities – from Hong Kong to Shenzhen – where severe land pressure among other things forges process and forms of urban growth that are unheard of in the West. Additionally, Tokyo also typifies what is now being seen by many urban scholars as one of the most relevant lessons Asian cities are imparting to Western ones: the seamless coexistence and juxtaposition of aspirations, of globalization and quotidian life, or what Jeff Hou calls "vertical urbanism and horizontal urbanity."[56] For instance when one admires the Nakagin Capsule Tower, now long fallen into disrepair, one must not fail to notice the cacophony of restaurants and stores that occupy every inch of space beneath the Japan Railway tracks a walk away from the seventies architectural icon. As Hou observes, "much more than the iconic tower, these mundane structures and shops embody the vision and reality of (Tokyo's) urban metabolism, without singular architectural expressions."[57]

In Tokyo, like other Asian cities, compositional clarity is subservient to constant appropriation and change – leading many visitors to misread its hidden order as a visual chaos. When I look at Tokyo as an Indian native, I am tempted to compare its urban energy to Mumbai, and then just as quickly remove the colossal informal economy that dominates India's financial capital. Tokyo is also parallel to Mumbai in its apparently visually chaotic physical disposition, but it is far closer to a European city when we look at its cleanliness, order and daily efficiency. When in turn I look at Tokyo as a resident of Los Angeles, I am tempted to see them as contrasting parallels: their massive urban growth from modest settlements into global mega-cities, their visible urban infrastructure, their fragile disaster-prone natural geographies on the one hand, versus Los Angeles' vast horizontal explosion in contrast to Tokyo's land-pressure driven implosion on the other (fig. 11.20). The point is that Tokyo must ultimately be seen on its own terms – typical in many respects, unique in others.

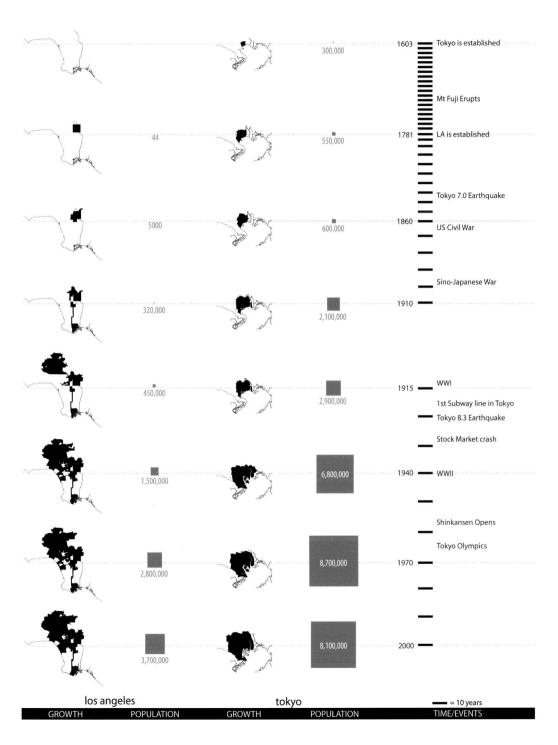

1603	Tokyo is established
	Mt Fuji Erupts
1781	LA is established
	Tokyo 7.0 Earthquake
1860	US Civil War
	Sino-Japanese War
1910	
1915	WWI
	1st Subway line in Tokyo
	Tokyo 8.3 Earthquake
	Stock Market crash
1940	WWII
	Shinkansen Opens
	Tokyo Olympics
1970	
2000	

los angeles   tokyo   ▬ = 10 years

| GROWTH | POPULATION | GROWTH | POPULATION | TIME/EVENTS |

As an event in time, Tokyo stands at a crucial juncture: On September 8, 2013, Tokyo was chosen over Madrid and Istanbul to host the Olympic Games in 2020.[58] Some 2,000 supporters who had gathered at a gymnasium near Komazawa stadium – originally built for the Tokyo Olympics in 1964 – cheered as the decision was relayed via a big screen. This was a landmark event, particularly because Tokyo's bid for the games appeared to be fading amid the slew of bad news from the Fukushima Daiichi nuclear power plant, 140 miles to the north. Eleventh-hour assurances from Japan's prime-minister Shinzo Abe, that radiation from the destroyed Fukushima plant posed no threat to Tokyo paid off.[59] But given the size of Japan's public debt – "now more than twice the size of its $6-trillion economy," there are those that have questioned Tokyo's decision to bid for the Olympics.[60] Those among the 160,000 people forced to evacuate after the March 2011 tsunami and Fukushima plant meltdown have argued that money would be better spent on fixing leaks and decontaminating towns.[61] While this debate will no doubt continue, the bill for the 2020 Games has been estimated at just under $8 billion, and the city already has $4.5 billion in an Olympic reserve fund.[62] And according to SMBC Nikko Securities, hosting the event is estimated to bring positive economic effects of more than $40 billion and create more than 150,000 jobs.[63] If this is an opportunity for Japan to make a significant global statement, then it has been here before: The 1964 Tokyo Games, held less than two decades after Japan's defeat in World War II, symbolized the country's re-emergence from its biggest military misadventure.

Tokyo then is an urban phenomenon where the term disaster translates into cyclic occurrence, where the term chaos translates into J. Saramago's definition of an "order to be deciphered" and where the term density translates into a mechanism for survival.[64] Tokyo's perception as an extreme city is a Western construct, an exaggeration born out of a comparative bias from the standpoint of the European and American polis. If therefore we as outsiders can shift our perceptions on rereading Tokyo – on its own terms – it may offer us significant takeaways to question our own preconceptions of what cities are or ought to be. I for one have not failed to notice the bowing ticket-collector in the Shinkansen bullet train, and I have admired as much the vista from the grounds of the Senso-ji temple in Asakusa juxtaposing its curved roof with a love hotel in the distance (fig. 11.21). This is why in Tokyo, my narrative ends as naturally as it began at Ise – because I have journeyed to Japan's cultural extremes; because I do not need to search for cultural threads anymore. Ise and Tokyo are in their own way equally Japanese and will always be – there is nothing like them anywhere else in the world.

Figure 11.21 Top: View from Senso-ji Temple, with Tokyo Skytree and a love hotel in the distance.

Epilog

Moving across Japan in time and space, the chapters in this book have traversed through numerous layers of history, tracing how cultural patterns and expressions were discovered, imported, assimilated, built on, interrogated, engaged with, and eventually made "Japanese" – in our case, specifically those of architecture and urbanism. They have simultaneously reflected on a wide range of factors that have shaped the Japanese built landscape – from historic epochs to recent crises; from individual buildings to entire cities; from ecological dilemmas to political challenges; and from philosophical concepts to physical places.

Readers who expected my "Reflections on Japanese Architecture and Urbanism" to celebrate the cutting-edge of contemporary Japanese architecture, architects or cities might be disappointed. Their disappointment, I would argue, stems from a stereotypical short-sighted understanding of the built world, of how to read it, and how in turn to see their role in shaping it. This book is a counterpoint to their fixed, highly biased, definitive – and therefore for me myopic – treatises on architecture and urbanism. The muddle of multifarious angles and themes in this book is my way of attempting to truly understand Japan on its own terms without any pretention or self-imposition to objectify it. My understanding of Japan is complex, not simplistic; multi-faceted, not linear. That is because it has evolved over multiple visits, stays, studies, projects, observations, readings, conversations with my Japanese hosts, discussions with Japanese and non-Japanese peers, etc. – indeed from an up and down, deeply personal – even spiritual – relationship with this culture for twenty years. I believe Japan deserves this kind of understanding.

As stated in the book's Introduction, I have attempted to shift the emphasis on how we choose to read Japanese architecture and urbanism. If "architecture" is the making of individual buildings, and "urbanism" the making of what is between them, then diffusing the boundaries of these two disciplines is only as natural as their separation is a convenient denial. Nothing in our built world exists in isolation: individual buildings are only parts of larger places and districts that nurture everyday life. These places in turn are ingredients of a city that in itself bears indelible relationships with the natural world within and around it. While this may seem like an obvious point, current dominant attitudes in architecture and urbanism seem far removed from this truism. Additionally, buildings and places are judged by both architects and citizens largely by how they look – that is as static end products. They are hardly read through how they have come to be or what they are becoming – that is as evolving entities in time; or how they contribute to something bigger than themselves – that is as agents for social reform and change.

In looking beyond stereotypes, this book calls for an alternative reading of the build landscape – as a complex evolving mosaic of criss-crossed issues and trajectories. The themes in the book's various chapters highlight this: There are ecological trajectories (Chapter 2 – the dilemmas surrounding the future of Ise shrine's reconstruction); social trajectories (Chapter 8 – street life); political trajectories (Chapter 10 – the meanings and manifestations of democracy); external influences (Chapter 9 – the East-West dialectic); deep religious and philosophical blueprints (Chapters 3 & 5 – Zen and the consciousness to temporality); cultural tastes and propensities (Chapters 4 & 6 – the aesthetics of rectilinear compositions and the propensity for dimness); populist forces (Chapter 9 – everyday Japanese objects); and circumstantial limitations (Chapter 11 – land scarcity or wars). In other words, the built environment is always an intertwined physical, political, social, cultural, ecological and anthropological compound.

As investors, shapers & recipients of the built environment, how do we situate ourselves in these dimensions? How do we engage with these numerous trajectories as we make singular or collective decisions about a culture's past, present and future? The book's multifaceted narrative suggests several pointers in this regard:

1) By Excavating Deep Histories – For instance, the book reveals how the perceived landscape of the Ise Shrine, one of Japan's most revered places, actually extends far beyond the shrine complexes into the pilgrimage path, surrounding forest and natural geography (Chapter 1). Thus, even though the complexes are meticulously preserved, the continuing ambivalence towards its adjacent town and macro-landscape is a degradation of the sacredness of the shrine itself. What places like Ise need is a deeper application of this knowledge-base towards real action – in other words a more reflective integration of deep scholarship with deep praxis.

2) By Probing Evolutionary Patterns – By tracing the evolution of Zen landscapes (Chapter 3), or the changing attitudes to traditional aesthetics of darkness (Chapter 6), or the shifts in patterns of publicness in post-war Japan (Chapter 10), or Tokyo's evolution from a feudal castle town to a global mega-city (Chapter 11), the book reminds us that cultural expressions and products are always evolving constructs. Assessing what has endured, what has changed, and what has precipitated these shifts, is not a passive anthropological exercise, but an essential part of responsible intervention and decision-making.

3) By Tracing Cross-Cultural Currents – The book demonstrates this in several ways: First, by tracking the contemporaneous trajectories of other cultures – such as the comparative chronological analysis of Kyoto and Renaissance Rome (Chapter 7). Second, by identifying parallel themes – such as the aesthetics of Mondrian paintings and the shoin interior (Chapter 4). Third, by investigating cultural symbiosis – in this case the reciprocal influences of Japan and the West soon after the Meiji Era (Chapter 9). Fourth, by studying the results of insinuated or imposed external influences – in this case, the advent of Western democracy and beyond (Chapter 10). Such trans-cultural examinations offer us refreshing lenses to probe deeper into how and where cultural propensities overlap, and where they truly separate.

4) By Rethinking Heritage and Heritage Conservation – Not too many people know about the Japanese idea of Ningen Kokuho (Living National Treasure). It refers not to buildings but individuals certified as Preservers of Important Intangible Cultural Properties. As such, Japan expands the mainstream global rhetoric of heritage conservation through several counterpoints: First, Ise Shrine's cyclic reconstruction offers a direct challenge to conventional notions of building preservation globally (Chapter 1 & 2). Second, the demolition of major Modern icons such as the Imperial Hotel by Frank Lloyd Wright, or the dialog surrounding the potential demolition of the Nakagin Capsule Tower reveals the difficulties of preserving a recent past in the wake of other pressing issues such as land pressure (Chapter 9 & 11). And third, by showing how several Japanese historic wooden landmarks are being painstakingly restored and preserved (Chapter 1 & 2), this study also dispels the stereotype that historic preservation – in the Western sense – is non-existent in Japan.

5) By Balancing Populist Expression and Formal Design – Shibuya, Shinjuku, Ginza, and Takeshita-dori are not experienced as formally designed places, but as complex urban ensembles juxtaposing populist appropriation, improvisation and flux (Chapter 8), leading to the common impression that formal urban design has no place in Japanese cities. But as this study shows, it is in fact around the framework of carefully designed places, from Omotesando to Ueno Park; and landmarks, from the Senso-ji Temple to Tokyo Tower, that a city like Tokyo spins and thrives (Chapter 8 & 11). It is the juxtaposition of these contrasts, and the diversity of choices that makes it so compelling. The question therefore is: where should a city demand and embrace formal design, where in turn should it step back?

6) By Engaging with Power and Administrative Structures – The built landscape of any culture, at any point in its history is a reflection of its extant governance entities and regimes. For instance Nara and Kyoto's urban form as a grid without any apparent plaza or square was a direct reflection of a non-egalitarian, non-democratic society with the diamyo at its apex (Chapter 8). The uncomfortable introduction of the Western plaza as a symbol of post-war democracy is an extension of this rubric (Chapter 10). Thus, the current urban forms, trends and workings of Japanese cities must also be understood as manifestations of their current decision-making processes. If the lynch-pin for urban transformation is not architecture or urban design but the specific power and administrative structures of a place, how do we create the conduits to engage with them?

7) By Interrogating "Ideal City" Barometers –The book shows how Tokyo for instance represents an urban conundrum when seen from the West. Its compact footprint, mobility efficiency, and pedestrian density are things many Western cities would aspire to. On the other hand, its seemingly ad-hoc urban form or spatial density per person would be considered un-livable by Western standards. The book discusses the dilemmas surrounding homelessness in Japan, and also highlights the resilience of Japanese cities to recurrent disasters and crises (Chapter 11). Particularly for a Western onlooker, the Japanese city poses a mind-boggling question: Who ultimately defines "livability", "sustainability", "democracy" or "social equity"? While there are certain fundamental concepts that cannot be disputed, the eventual subtleties of how we choose to understand each of these terms remain subjective.

Thus, while the content of this book is focused on Japan, the message of this book goes far beyond it: Eventually, all cultures are both unique and typical; they all have traits that set them apart, versus those that remain common. Reading a culture is always a relative exercise of negotiating histories, impressions and personal biases. For example, India (where I was born and raised) from a Japanese standpoint can be compared to a palimpsest: Mohenjodaro, the Aryan influx, the Golden Age of the Guptas, the glory of the Mughals, the British Raj, and post-independence is a historic continuum of constant revisionism, rewriting a new script right upon the one before. In turn, Japan, looked at from India, is comparable to a pearl: I think of the more-than-a-thousand years in which the seed of Buddhism that reached this sequestered archipelago from India was recurrently coated with cultural interpretations – from the massive temples of Nara, to the sand gardens of Zen – all hardly known to or influenced by the rest of the wider world. When I think of Japan and India together, I see the contemporaneous emergence of two born-again nations, two industrial democracies that both got there through two tumultuous events – India's freedom struggle with the British rule, and Japan's defeat in World War II. I think of how different our histories are, and yet how they overlap in so many ways.

As architects and urbanists, as well as other actors who play a role in shaping built environments, especially in a time when cross-cultural fluidity is less viscous than ever before, the final takeaway of this study is to strive to read, understand, and intervene with cultures on their own terms. To do this, we need to be far more open minded and empathetic, and far more inclusive and expansive in our knowledge-base to understand the complex cultural threads that weave deep histories and contemporary aspirations. We need to characterize our relationship with a culture not as a static one-way outlook, but as a flowing two-way discourse that enriches both sides: I like to believe that I am all the more rich for engaging in a dialog with Japanese architecture and urbanism, as much as Japan benefits from keen observers like me. My approach to understanding Japan is only part of a fluid process that will continue to evolve long after this book is published. This book, twenty-years in the making, is thus but a stopping point on a continuing journey – an important stopping point, but a stopping point nonetheless.

Shinkansen bullet train with Mount Fuji in the background.

Endnotes

INTRODUCTION

[1] See Keim Kevin (editor), You Have to Pay for the Public Life: Selected Essays of Charles W. Moore, "Impressions of Japanese Architecture," Cambridge, Massachusetts: MIT Press, pp 279-282

[2] A *koan* is a paradoxical statement or question to be meditated upon by Zen Buddhist monks. It is used as part of their training to abandon dependence on reason and to force them into gaining sudden intuitive enlightenment.

[3] Sadler A. L., Short History of Japanese Architecture, Tokyo: Charles E. Tuttle Company, 1962, pp 1

[4] Drexler Arthur, The Architecture of Japan, New York: Museum of Modern Art, 1955, pp 240

CHAPTER 1 – BETWEEN ISE AND KATSURA

[1] Isozaki Arata, Japan-ness in Architecture, Cambridge, Massachusetts: MIT Press, 2006, Chapter 8, pp 130

[2] Ibid

[3] Ibid, Chapter 8, pp 120

[4] See Hearn Lafcadio, Glimpses of Unfamiliar Japan, Book Jungle, 2008

[5] http://www.japantimes.co.jp/culture/2012/08/16/arts/izumo-the-myths-and-gods-of-japans-history/#.UczfxTvkvuo, accessed July 2013

[6] Nishi Kazuo & Hozumi Kazuo, What is Japanese Architecture, USA: Kodansha, pp 41

[7] Ibid

[8] Ueda Atsushi, The Inner Harmony of the Japanese House, USA: Kodansha, 1990, pp 11

[9] It is possible that the existence of Japanese architecture in which pillars are lined up in a single row in the center of the building is related to the significance of the yorishiro. The yoroshiro also eventually became the original shape of the Shinto shrine. The shin no mihashira (esteemed pillar of the heart) under the center of the floor of the main temple at Ise is significant because it is regarded as a yorishiro in which the Gods reside.

[10] For more on this, see Nishi Kazuo & Hozumi Kazuo, What is Japanese Architecture, pp 17

[11] For more on this, see Sadler A. L., Japanese Architecture: A Short History, Tuttle, 2009.

[12] For more on the Shoso-in, see Drexler Arthur, The Architecture of Japan, New York: The Museum of Modern Art, 1955, pp 82-85

[13] For more on the Byodo-in, see Fukuyama Toshio, Heian Temples: Byodo-In and Chuson-Ji (The Heibonsha Survey of Japanese Art, V. 9), New York: John Weatherhill, Inc.; first English edition, 1976, Chapter Two: "Temples of the Fujiwara," pp 46 – 71

[14] Ibid, pp 101

[15] For more on this, see Sadler A. L., Japanese Architecture: A Short History,

[16] Ibid

[17] The Katsura Villa has been extensively studied and written about. For one of the more sophisticated and interpretative accounts see Isozaki Arata, Japan-ness in Architecture, Part IV – "A Diagonal Strategy: Katsura as Envisioned by "Enshu Taste," pp 245 - 291

[18] Nishi Kazuo & Hozumi Kazuo, What is Japanese Architecture, pp 124-125

[19] Nishi Kazuo & Hozumi Kazuo, What is Japanese Architecture, pp 9

[20] These five attitudes stem from my own analysis of traditional Japanese architecture. Other scholars have indicated similar observations, though not necessarily spelt out five of them. For example, Kisho Kurokawa has talked about the eclecticism of Edo-era buildings. See Kurokawa Kisho, Rediscovering Japanese Space, Tokyo: John Weatherhill Inc.; first edition, 1988, pp 47-52. Arata Isozai had used the term "constructive" to describe the Nandaimon of Todai-ji. See Isozaki Arata, Japan-ness in Architecture, pp 243

[21] Kurokawa Kisho, Rediscovering Japanese Space, pp 50. In the section titled "Reappraising the Edo Period" Kurokawa surveys the eclecticism of Edo-period culture from the 1793 five-story pagoda of the Kanoji Temple and the roof-lines of the Hiunkaku – Flying Cloud Pavilion- of the

Nishi Honganji Temple, to the cross-section of the Sazaedo – Conch Hall, with its trompe l'oeil, to the "baroque" aesthetic of the Yodomiseki tea room of the Saioin subtemple.

[22] Ibid, pp 57

[23] Ibid, pp 71

CHAPTER 2 – BEHIND THE CULTURE OF WOOD

[1] Diamond Jared, Collapse: How Societies Choose to Fail or Succeed, Penguin Books; Revised edition, 2011, "Why Japan Succeeded" pp 304

[2] Ito Chuta, "Horyu-ji Kenchiku Ron" (On the Architecture of Horyu-ji), in Kenchiku Zasshi (Architecture Journal), November 1893

[3] For more on the Japanese timber bracket, see Nishi Kazuo & Hozumi Kazuo, What is Japanese Architecture, USA: Kodansha, pp 36-37

[4] Ibid, pp 23

[5] For more on this, see Ibid, pp 32-33 and 49-52

[6] King Ross, Brunelleschi's Dome: How a Renaissance Genius Reinvented Architecture, Penguin Books; Reprint edition, 2001

[7] Isozaki Arata, Japan-ness in Architecture, Cambridge, Massachusetts: MIT Press, 2006, Chapter 18-21, pp 212-229

[8] Ibid, pp 219

[9] Ibid, pp 220

[10] Diamond Jared, Collapse: How Societies Choose to Fail or Succeed, "Why Japan Succeeded," pp 294 - 305

[11] Ibid, pp 297

[12] For more on the Tokugawa policies and an excellent overview of this period in Japanese history, see Ibid, pp 299-300

[13] For more on Shikinen Sengu rituals, see Nitschke Gunter, From Shinto to Ando: Studies in Architectural Anthropology in Japan, Great Britain: Academy Editions, 1993, Chapter 1: "Daijosai and Shikinen Sengu: First Fruits Twice Tasted", pp 9-31

[14] Saeki Yoko, unpublished thesis "Behind the Shikinen Sengu: Re-examining the Urban and Ecological Dimensions of the Ise Shrine," University of Southern California School of Architecture, August 2013

[15] Ibid

[16] For more on the Izumo shrine, see Noboru Kawazoe, Ki to mizu no kenchiku isejingu, Tokyo: Chikuma Shobou, 2010, pp 59. Also see Nishi & Hozumi, What is Japanese Architecture, pp 40

[17] For more on how various Shinto shrines have changes their originating rituals, see official Website of Katori Shrine, Accessed March 1, 2013, http://www.katori-jingu.or.jp/. Also see Nitschke From Shinto to Ando: Studies in Architectural Anthropology in Japan, pp 18-20

[18] From field observations by the author in June 2013.

CHAPTER 3 – A VIEW FROM THE ZEN SHOIN

[1] For more, see Suzuki Daisetz T., Zen and Japanese Culture, Princeton University Press, Reprint edition, 2010

[2] Nitschke Gunter, Japanese Gardens, Taschen, 2002, pp 65

[3] All karesansui gardens after the Muromachi period trace their origin to this rock garden, although an early type of the ka-resansui style is to be seen in the famed moss garden of Saihoji Temple of the 14th century, and even in some gardens prior to this.

[4] The manual classifies four types of shakkei: distant borrowing enshaku, adjacent borrowing rinshaku, upward borrowing gyoushaku and downward borrowing fushaku.

[5] The garden is believed to have been made in the early part of the 17th century. Shoden-ji was removed to the present site overlooking downtown Kyoto in 1282 from a place near the center of the city. The garden is said to have been designed by Kobori Enshu, noted artist-tea master, but the fact has not yet been established.

[6] For more on Tenryu-ji garden, see Nitschke Gunter, Japanese Gardens, pp 76-78

[7] The temple belonging to the Rinzai (Zen) sect was established by the then ruler Ashikaga Takauji to the memory of Emperor Godaigo who had been exiled in Yoshino, Nara.

8 Process Architecture 116: "Kyoto – Its Cityscape Traditions and Heritage," Tokyo: Process Architecture Publishing Co. Ltd., pp 20-21

9 Many scholars consider this episode to mark the beginning of Zen. Among Zen adherents, the origin of Zen Buddhism is ascribed to the fable "nengemisho" (literally "pick up flower, subtle smile"). In the story, the Buddha gives a wordless sermon to his disciples by holding up a white flower. No one in the audience understands the sermon except Mahakasyapa, who smiles. Within Zen, the Flower Sermon communicates the ineffable nature of tathata (suchness) and the smile signifies the direct transmission of wisdom without words. For more, see Welter, Albert, "Mahakasyapa's Smile: Silent Transmission and the Kung-an (Koan) Tradition" in "The Koan: Texts and Contexts in Zen Buddhism," edited by Steven Heine & Dale S. Wright; Oxford and New York: Oxford University Press, 2000, pp 75–109

10 Slawson David A., Secret Teachings in the Art of Japanese Gardens Design Principles, Aesthetic Values, USA: Kodansha, 1991, Chapter 3: "The Art We See: Sensory Effects," pp 122

11 Ibid, pp 76 - 122

12 Ferras George, Frontal Perception in Japanese Architectural Space, in Process Architecture 25 – "Japan: Climate, Space, Concept"; Tokyo: Process Architecture Publishing Co. Ltd., pp

13 For more on Zen, see Suzuki Daisetz T., Zen and Japanese Culture. Also see Osho, Zen: The Path of Paradox, St. Martin's Griffin; First Edition, September, 2003

14 For more in the Tea Ceremony see Sadler A. L., The Japanese Tea Ceremony: Cha-No-Yu, Tuttle Publishing; Original edi-tion, 2008

15 Ibid. Sadler provides an elaborate account of the cultural roots of the Tea Ceremony in Chapter 1 – "Origins"

16 Ibid, pp 10-11. Sadler notes how Tea-rooms are classified according to the position of the hearth as well as the number of mats. There are eight kinds, besides some other modifications. The eight are, the Four-and-a-half mat; the Daime; the Muko-giri (or Opposite Hearth); and the Sumi-giri (or Corner Hearth), each in two styles, Normal and Reverse.

17 Kurokawa Kisho, Rediscovering Japanese Space, Tokyo: John Weatherhill Inc.; first edition, 1988, pp 71

18 Ibid, pp 74

19 Ibid

20 There are numerous such words explaining the essence of the Tea Ceremony by tea masters. This one may be attributed to Sen-no-Rikyu. For more on the words and episodes of tea-masters see Sadler, The Japanese Tea Ceremony: Cha-No-Yu, Chap-ter II : "Tea Masters" pp 93 - 230

21 The emulation of the hermit's hut stems from the Vimalakirti Sutra, a Buddhist fable related to the monk Vimalakirti, who miraculously hosted thousands of Boddhisatvas in his ten-foot-square hut. For more on this see Suzuki Daisetz T., Zen and Japanese Culture, Appendix II:"The Vimalakirti Sutra," pp 410-414

22 Sadler A. L., The Japanese Tea Ceremony: Cha-No-Yu, pp 2

23 Nitschke Gunter, Japanese Gardens, pp 233

24 Ibid

25 Ibid

26 For more on these gardens, including photographs, see Ibid, pp 226-232

27 Ibid pp 27

28 Slawson David A., Secret Teachings in the Art of Japanese Gardens Design Principles, Aesthetic Values, pp 16

29 Mariani Fosco, Ore Giapponesi. Bari" Leonardo da Vinci Editrice, 1957. Quoted in Sacchi Livio, Tokyo: City and Architecture, USA: Universe Publishing, 2004, pp 121

CHAPTER 4 – THE MONDRIAN IN THE JAPANESE ROOM

1 Tange Kenzo, Ishimoto Yashiro and Gropius Walters, Katsura: Tradition and Creation in Japanese Architecture, Yale University Press; first edition, 1960

2 De Stijl (Dutch for "The Style"), also known as neoplasticism, was a Dutch artistic movement founded in 1917. In a narrower sense, the term De Stijl is used to refer to a body of work from 1917 to 1931 founded in the Netherlands. Proponents of De Stijl sought to express a new uto-pian ideal of spiritual harmony and order. They advocated pure abstraction and universality by a

reduction to the essentials of form and colour; they simplified visual compositions to the vertical and horizontal directions, and used only primary colors along with black and white. For more see De Stijl Jaffe H. L. C., De Stijl 1917-1931: The Dutch Contribution to Modern Art, Belknap Press; First Edition, 1986

[3] Tange et al, Katsura: Tradition and Creation in Japanese Architecture, pp v

[4] Ibid

[5] The method of Okosheizu involved the composing of walls on the ground as planar compositions that were then manifested vertically. In this sense the Japanese room was like a paper box, made of various folds of paper. For more on Okosheizu, see Ferras Gorge, Frontal Perception in Japanese Architectural Space, published in Process Architecture 25 - Japan: Climate, Space, Concept; Process Architecture Publishing Co. Ltd., Tokyo.

[6] See Drexler Arthur, The Architecture of Japan, New York: Museum of Modern Art, 1955, pp 66

[7] For more see Ibid, pp 71

[8] Ibid, pp 68

[9] Ibid

[10] For more on tengo-nageshi, see Ibid, pp 68-73

[11] Ferras Gorge, Frontal Perception in Japanese Architectural Space, published in Process Architecture 25

[12] Drexler in-fact use the term "Mondrian-like" in his book. See Drexler Arthur, The Architecture of Japan, pp 68

[13] Ibid pp 55-56

[14] For more on Ozu, see Bock Audie, "Yasujiro Ozu" in Japanese Film Directors, Kodansha, 1978, pp. 69–98.

[15] http://www.paralumun.com/zenquotes.htm, accessed July 2013

[16] http://quote.robertgenn.com/auth_search.php?authid=65, accessed July 2013

[17] Neo-plasticisme is a term coined by Piet Mondrian and first used in 1919 as the title of a collection of his writings published by the dealer Léonce Rosenberg. Mondrian published Le Néo-plasticisme while in Paris, having become convinced that his theories, published in De Stijl, were almost unknown beyond his native country. A collection of his articles was translated into German and published in 1925 as Neue Gestaltung as the fifth in the series of Bauhausbücher. His theories were published in English for the first time in 1937 under the title of 'Plastic Art and Pure Plastic Art' in Circle: An International Survey of Constructivism. For more on Mondrian, see Bax, Marty, Complete Mondrian, Aldershot (Hampshire) and Burlington (Vermont): Lund Humphries, 2001

CHAPTER 5 – CELEBRATING TIME

[1] Though this argument bears the risk of oversimplifying Western architectural history, it has been made before. For instance, see Giedion Siegfried, Space, Time & Architecture, Harvard University Press, Seventeenth Printing, Fifth Edition 1970, pp. 1v – 1vi, "Three Space Conceptions". Giedion notes how "Interior space was disregarded" in the early architecture of Egypt, Sumer and Greece, how interior space started to become the highest aim of architecture" in the Roman period, and how the beginning of the nineteenth century saw a new optical revolution that abolished the single viewpoint of perspective.

[2] For more on this see Giedion, Space, Time & Architecture, pp 443

[3] Ibid, pp 444

[4] For more on this see Ibid pp 436-448

[5] The period from 1868 until 1912 in Japan is called the Meiji era – after the name chosen by the young prince Mutsuhito, when he followed his father to the throne. Meiji in Japanese means "the enlightened rule". During the Meiji period, Japan underwent a transformative development from a medieval society to a leading Asian economic and military power. For more on these events see Satow Ernest, A diplomat in Japan: An inner history of the critical years in the evolution of Japan, C.E. Tuttle Co; 1st Tuttle edition (1983).

[6] Isozaki Arata has explained that "ma does not describe the West's recognition of time and space as different serializations, suggesting instead that it "coincides with present day theories that equate space and time." See Isozaki Arata et al, ed., Ma: Space-Time in Japan, New York: Cooper-Hewitt

Museum, 1979, pp 12. For further reading on the concept of ma, also see Nitschke Gunter, "Ma: The Japanese Sense of Place", Architectural Design, vol. 36, March 1966, pp 116-156.

[7] With Buddhist scriptures containing explications of the chain of causation introduced to Japan by the 7th or 8th century CE, Japanese literature gradually came to be marked by an increasingly large number of references to mujo, the "transience" of life and to the operation of inga, the "karmic force". Such concepts exerted an increasingly deep influence on historical works written between 1086 and 1221, such as the Heike Monogatori. For more on this see Brown Delmer, "Buddhism and Historical Thought in Japan before 1221", in Philosophy East and West, Vol. 24, no. 2, pp 215-225, University of Hawaii Press, 1974.

[8] Satori (literally "to understand") is the Zen term for enlightenment. The Zen Buddhist experience recognizes enlightenment as transitory, similar to the English term epiphany. Because all things are transitory per Zen philosophy, the fleeting nature of satori is not regarded as a limitation in the way that a fleeting epiphany would be in Western understandings of enlightenment.

[9] Nitschke Gunter, From Shinto to Ando: Studies in Architectural Anthropology in Japan, Great Britain: Academy Editions, 1993, Chapter 1: "Daijosai and Shikinen Sengu: First Fruits Twice Tasted", pp 9

[10] Ibid

[11] Ibid, pg 10

[12] See Nitschke Gunter, "Transience and Renewal in Japanese Form", Kyoto Journal 50: Transience – Perspectives on Asia, June 2002

[13] The Ise Shrine's Shikinen Sengu incorporates some thirty Shinto rituals that mark important milestones in its reconstruction process every 20 years. The last reconstruction took place in 1993. For more on this see Adams Cassandra, "Japan's Ise Shrine and its Thirteen-Hundred-Year-Old Reconstruction Tradition" Journal of Architectural Education, Vol. 52 No. 1, pp. 49-60, MIT Press, 1998.

[14] Nitschke, From Shinto to Ando: Studies in Architectural Anthropology in Japan, pp 15

[15] Originating as a Zen meditation technique, the Cha-no-yu or tea ceremony is a traditional ritual in which powdered green tea, or matcha, is ceremonially prepared by a skilled practitioner and served to a small group of guests in a tranquil setting. Elaborate rules of tea culture and etiquette have been created over the ages by various Japanese Tea masters and Zen priests. For more see A.L. Sadler, Cha-no-yu - The Japanese Tea Ceremony, Tuttle Publishing, 2001.

[16] Hanami (Literally "flower viewing") is the Japanese traditional custom of contemplating the beauty of flowers, mainly cherry blossoms, from late March to early April. The cherry blossom season is relatively short – mankai (full bloom) is usually reached within about one week after kaika (the opening of the first blossoms) with the blossoms falling from the trees a week later. Thus the delicate flowers are seen as a metaphor for the fleeting nature of life. The custom is said to have started during the Nara Period (710–784) through Chinese Tang Dynasty influences.

[17] Wabi meaning humble, refers to a way of life ordinarily associated with simplicity, implying an abstinence from social fashions. Sabi refers to the beauty of aging, wherein individual objects and the environment imbibed an archaic imperfection through patina. For more on this, see Leonard Koren, Wabi-Sabi for Artists, Designers, Poets & Philosophers, Stone Bridge Press, Berkeley, CA, 1994.

[18] Noh or Nōgaku is a major form of classical Japanese musical drama that has been performed since the fourteenth century. It is unique in its slow, spartan grace and use of distinctive masks, tracing its roots back to Chinese Nuo theater, Sarugaku, and folk theatricals. It was brought into its present day form by Kan'ami and his son Zeami during the Muromachi period (1392-1573) under the patronage of the powerful Ashikaga clan. It would later influence other dramatic forms such as Kabuki and Butoh.

[19] Chirari stems from the word Chira-Chira, implying the voyeuristic peep into something private while walking along the lattice window or the slight curve of the eaves in a Japanese roof as compared to its Chinese or Indian counterpart – providing a gentle glimpse of the underside and implying an indirect voyeurism.

[20] During the Edo Period, the Tōkaidō referred to one of the major Tokugawa-era roads connecting Edo (modern-day Tokyo) to Kyoto. The famous artist Hiroshige depicted the Tōkaidō in his work Fifty-three Stations of the Tōkaidō (1833 – 1834).

[21] For more on this, see Nitschke Gunter, Japanese Gardens, Taschen, 2003, pp. 146- 155.

[22] See Giedion , Space, Time & Architecture.

[23] For more on the Metabolist movement and its projects, see Michael Franklin Ross, Beyond Metabolism, McGraw Hill, 1978.

[24] Ibid

[25] *Ukiyo* or "The Floating World" is a term used to describe – but not limited to – the pleasure seeking lifestyle and culture of Edo Period Japan (1600-1867). Though its epicenter was Yoshiwara, the culture of this licensed red-light district, with brothels, teahouses and kabuki theatres frequented by Japan's growing middle class, also arose on other cities such as Osaka and Kyoto. The famous Japanese woodblock prints known as ukiyo-e, or "pictures of the Floating World", depict scenes of geisha, kabuki actors, sumo wrestlers and samurai.

[26] See Ito Toyo, "Collage and Superficiality in Architecture", A New Wave of Japanese Architecture, Kenneth Frampton ed., IAUS, New York, 1978

[27] Bognar Botond, "What Goes Up Must Come Down: Recent Urban Architecture in Japan", in Harvard Design Magazine, Vol. 3 Cambridge: Harvard University Press, Fall 1997, pp 33-43

[28] Nitschke, From Shinto to Ando: Studies in Architectural Anthropology in Japan, Ch. 2 – "Time is Money, Space is Money," pp 35

CHAPTER 6 – DELIBERATE DUSK

[1] See Tanizaki Jun'ichiro – In Praise of Shadows (In'ei Raisan), translated by Thomas J. Harper and Edward G. Seidensticker, New Haven: Leete's Island Books, Inc., 1977

[2] The Western influence on Japanese culture began with the end of the Tokugawa Era and the beginning of the Meiji Restoration in 1867-68. The new government aimed to make Japan a democratic state with equality among all its people. In order to transform the agrarian economy of Tokugawa Japan into a developed industrial one, many Japanese scholars were sent abroad to study Western science and languages, while foreign experts taught in Japan. On the political sector, Japan received its first European style constitution in 1889.

[3] Tanizaki, In Praise of Shadows, pp 31

[4] Ibid, Harper Thomas J. "Afterword," pp 47

[5] Japan is no exception in its affinity to darkness. Darkness has remained a central cultural trait in ancient cultures like India and Egypt: One thinks of the garbagriha, the most sacred chamber of a Hindu temple that like its Egyptian counterpart is bathed in absolute dark.

[6] For more on Ise Shrine's rituals, see Nitschke Gunter, From Shinto to Ando: Studies in Architectural Anthropology in Japan, Great Britain: Academy Editions, 1993, Chapter 1: "Daijosai and Shikinen Sengu: First Fruits Twice Tasted", pp 9-31

[7] Tsurezuregusa ("Essays in Idleness", alternatively: "The Harvest of Leisure") is a collection of Japanese essays written by the monk Yoshida Kenko between 1330 and 1332. The work is widely considered a gem of medieval Japanese literature and one of the three representative works of the zuihitsu genre, along with Makura no Soshi and the Hojoki. For more, see Chance Linda H., Formless in Form: Kenko, Tsurezuregusa, and the Rhetoric of Japanese Fragmentary Prose, Stanford: Stanford University Press, 1997

[8] The *Roji* (literally dewy path) is a garden through which one traverses in order to reach the Chashitsu (Tea Hut) where the Cha-no-yu (Tea Ceremony) is performed. For more see Sadler A. L., The Japanese Tea Ceremony: Cha-no-yu, Tuttle Publishing; Original edition, 2008

[9] Tanizaki, In Praise of Shadows, pp 20

[10] Ibid, pp 21

[11] Ibid, pp 17

[12] Ueda Atsushi, The Inner Harmony of the Japanese House, Tokyo & New York: Kodansha, 1990, pp 25

[13] See Kurokawa Kisho, Rediscovering Japanese Space, Tokyo: John Weatherhill, Inc., 1988, Chapter 2 – "Rikyu Gray: An Open-Ended Aesthetic," pp 61

[14] Ibid, pp 62

[15] See Cram Ralph Adams, Impressions of Japanese Architecture and the Allied Arts, Charles E. Tuttle Company, 1981, pp 83

[16] See Tanizaki, In Praise of Shadows, pp 10

[17] See Kurokawa, Rediscovering Japanese Space

[18] See Tanizaki, In Praise of Shadows, pp 20

[19] For more on Japanese lacquer, see Dees Jan, Facing Modern Times - The Revival of Japanese Lacquer Art 1890-1950, Rotterdam: Optima Grafische Communicatie, 2007, http://www.kunstpedia.com/PDFArticles/Facing%20Modern%20Times%20%20The%20Revival%20of%20Japanese%20Lacquer%20Art%201890-1950.pdf, accessed August 2013

[20] See Tanizaki, In Praise of Shadows, pp 26

[21] Ibid, pp 14

[22] The number 33 is sacred in Buddhism, for it is believed that Buddha saves mankind by disguising himself in 33 different forms.

[23] See Drexler Arthur, The Architecture of Japan, New York: The Museum of Modern Art, 1955, pp 130

[24] Ibid, pp 65

[25] See Tanizaki, In Praise of Shadows, pp 14

[26] For more in the history of neon in Japan, see http://www.neon-jp.org/98/eng/enkaku.html, accessed August 2013

[27] Ibid

[28] See Tanizaki, In Praise of Shadows, pp 42

[29] Ibid, Harper Thomas J., "Afterword," pp 48

CHAPTER 7 – KYOTO: A VIEW FROM ROME

[1] Mumford Lewis, The City in History: Its Origins, its Transformations & its Prospects, Harvest Books, Harcourt Inc., 1989 Ch. 9 – " Cloister and Community," pp 243

[2] In ancient Roman city planning, a Cardo or Cardus Maximus was a north-south-oriented street in cities, military camps, and colonia lined with shops, merchants, and vendors serving as the center of economic life. Most Roman cities also had a Decumanus Maximus, an east-west secondary main street that sometimes due to varying geography, served as the main street. The Forum was normally located at the intersection of the two.

[3] This was the initial plan for Kyoto. However, a three-meter-high odoi or defensive barrier was constructed by Toyotomi Hideyoshi at the end of the sixteenth century, clearly delineating the boundary between the central part of the city and its immediate surroundings.

[4] For more on this see Schulz Christian Norberg, "Genius Loci of Rome," published in "Roma Interotta," Architectural Design, Academy Editions, 1979, Vol. 49, No. 3-4

[5] In "easing" the path to enlightenment from the Shingon method of ritual and gesture to faith in the Amida and repetition of the formula of appeal to him, Amida Buddhism introduced to Heian Japan the symbolism of a Pure Land Paradise in the West. This is where the Amida dwelled, and where the faithful would be united with him after death.

[6] The Onin War was a civil war from 1467 to 1477 during the Muromachi period in Japan. A dispute between Hosokawa Katsumoto and Yamana Souzen escalated to nationwide proportions involving the Ashikaga shogunate and various daimyo. By September 1467, Kyoto's northern parts were in ruin, and its citizen's were abandoning the city.

[7] For more on Rome's reawakening, see Mumford Lewis, The City in History, Chapter 9 – "Cloister and Community," pp 244-248

[8] See Giedion Siegfried, Space, Time & Architecture, Cambridge, Massachusetts: Harvard University Press, Fifth Edition, 1967, Sixtus V (1585-1590) and the Planning of Baroque Rome, pp 17-106

[9] "Kyoto – Its Cityscape Traditions and Heritage," in Process: Architecture No. 116, Tokyo: Process Architecture Co. Ltd., 1994, pp 38

[10] This is the Nishi Honganji Temple we see in Kyoto today. The Higashi Hongan-ji is not only a temple but also the Mausoleum of Shinran, founder of Jōdō-Shin Buddhism. For more see http://www.wa-pedia.com/japan-guide/nishi_higashi_honganji.shtml, accessed August 2013

[11] Ibid

[12] As contemporaries of the Renaissance, this genre of screens apparently appeared for the first time around 1525 in the Sanetaka koki, the diary of the courtier Sanjonishi Sanetaka (1455-1537). While the existence of this pair of screens was never confirmed, the oldest existing Rakuchu rakugai zu was the Machida-ke bon (Machida Family version), named after its former owners

and depiction of Kyoto between the years of 1530 to 1540. The National Museum of Japanese History also has another early edition, known as the Takahashi version by Kano Naonobu, the father of the famous Kano painter Eitoku (1543-90). The finest example, known as the Uesugi version, which was passed down in the Uesugi clan for generations, was by Eitoku, who served as an official painter for the warlord Oda Nobunaga (1534-82), who gave this painting to the renowned warrior Uesugi Kenshin (1530-78).

[13] For instance, the Machida Ryakuchu Ryakugai zue depicts the Heian cityscape in the first half of the 16th century; the Funaki Ryakuchu Ryakugai zue depicts the Kyoto townscape in the early 17th century; and the two six-paneled sections of the Ikeda Ryakuchu Ryakugai zue show Kamigyo and Shimogyo, Nijojo and the Daibutsuden in close proximity. For more, see "Kyoto – Its Cityscape Traditions and Heritage," in Process: Architecture No. 116, pp 38

[14] The Meiji Restoration also known as the Meiji Ishin, was a series of events that led to a change in Japan's political and social structure. A direct response to the opening of Japan by the arrival of the Black Ships of Commodore Matthew Perry, it occurred from 1866 to 1869, traversing both the late Edo period (often called Late Tokugawa Shogunate) and beginning of the Meiji Era. For more on these events see Satow Ernest, A diplomat in Japan: An Inner History of the Critical Years in the Evolution of Japan, C.E. Tuttle Co; first edition, 1983

[15] Caron Bruce R., "Heritage Management in Kyoto: History, Place & Festivity," in Kyoto Journal No. 27, Kyoto: Harada Shokei, 1994; "The Death and Resurrection of Kyoto," pp 44

[16] Kyoto Journal No. 27, pp 13-17

[17] Ibid, pp 84

[18] Salastie Riitta, Living Tradition or Panda's Cage? An Analysis of the Urban Conservation in Kyoto; Case Study: 35 Yamahoko Neighborhoods, Academic dissertation for the degree of Doctor of Technology, Helsinki University of Technology, 1999, Chapter 9 – "Historic Preservation in Kyoto up to the Present Day, pp 83-84. http://lib.tkk.fi/Diss/199X/isbn9512253895/isbn9512253895.pdf, accessed August 2013

[19] See "Entombing the Tomb of the Gladiator: Who Will Save the Roman Ruins?" http://world.time.com/2013/01/23/entombing-the-tomb-of-the-gladiator-who-will-save-the-roman-ruins/#ixzz2VpuxXFpd, accessed on June 10, 2013

CHAPTER 8 – THE JAPANESE STREET IN SPACE AND TIME

[1] The Heian Capital (Kyoto) resembled that of its predecessor Heijo (Nara) in its basic grid layout, but was completely regular in plan. The blocks too were a uniform 120 metres on a side and were not affected by varying street widths as they had been at Heijo, where it was the distance from street centerlines that remained a constant 120 metres. The Heijo Capital was built at the height of a period of international commerce and exchange throughout Asia that centered on the Tang Court and the Silk Road. It was amidst these exchanges that Heijo was designed as a copy on a smaller scale of the Tang-dynasty capital of Changan.

[2] See Nishi Kazuo & Hozumi Kazuo, What is Japanese Architecture, USA: Kodansha, pp 57, 62,63

[3] For more on Japanese Premodern town types, see Ibid, pp 86-91, and 102-103

[4] Ibid, "The Edo Metropolis," pp 90-91

[5] Nagaya implies a series of attached townhouse types that made smallest unit of community in a traditional Japanese town.

[6] Engel Heino, Measure and Construction of the Japanese House, Charles E. Tuttle Co., first edition, 1989

[7] Shoji are sliding latticed doors with washi rice paper panels that admit diffused light; Amado are sliding or removable opaque wooden doors that are intended for security and weather protection.

[8] Kurokawa Kisho, Rediscovering Japanese Space, Tokyo: John Weatherhill Inc.; first edition, 1988, pp 90

[9] The Garden City movement is a method of urban planning initiated in 1898 by Sir Ebenezer Howard in the United Kingdom. Garden cities were intended to be planned, self-contained communities surrounded by "greenbelts", containing proportionate areas of residences, industry and agriculture. His idealized garden city would house 32,000 people on a site of 6,000 acres (2,400 ha), planned on a concentric pattern with open spaces, public parks and six radial boulevards, 120 ft (37 m) wide, extending from the centre. The garden city would be self-sufficient and when

it reached full population, another garden city would be developed nearby. Howard envisaged a cluster of several garden cities as satellites of a central city of 50,000 people, linked by road and rail. For more see Howard, Ebenezer, Garden Cities of Tomorrow, second edition, London: S. Sonnenschein & Co, 1902, pp 2–7.

[10] For more see Oshima Ken Tadashi,"Denenchōfu: Building the Garden City in Japan" in Journal of the Society of Architectural Historians, Vol. 55, No. 2, 1996), pp 140-151

[11] Kurokawa Kisho, Rediscovering Japanese Space, pp 28

[12] Ibid

[13] Kyoto Journal No. 27 - "The Death and Resurrection of Kyoto," Kyoto: Harada Shokei, 1994; pp 7

[14] Based on field observations by the author in June 2013

[15] Ibid

[16] For more see http://www.japanvisitor.com/japan-city-guides/daidogei, accessed July 2013

[17] Gion Matsuri is one of the largest festivals in Japan. The origins of the festival can be traced back more than 1100 years, to a procession led by a Shinto priest in 869 CE to try and appease the gods and halt an outbreak of the plague that was devastating the city. The plague stopped soon after, but the procession remained a popular event and was repeated year after year. In 970 CE it was institutionalized and became an official festival of the city. It is held from the 1st to the 31st of July and consists of various major and minor events. However, the highlight of the celebration takes place on the 17th, with 32 colorful floats (Yamaboko in Japanese) forming a long procession pulled through the main streets of the city.

CHAPTER 9 – THE WESTERN GENOME

[1] See Venturi Robert, Complexity and Contradiction in Architecture, New York: The Museum of Modern Art, second edition, 2002

[2] Venturi Robert and Scott Brown Denise, "Two Naifs in Japan", Architecture and Decorative Arts: Two Naifs in Japan (Tokyo: Kajima Institute Publishing Co., 1991), pp 16

[3] Ibid, pp 18

[4] This political revolution "restored" the emperor to power, but he did not rule directly. He was expected to accept the advice of the group that had overthrown the shôgun, and it was from this group that a small number of ambitious, able, and patriotic young men from the lower ranks of the samurai emerged to take control and establish the new political system. At first, their only strength was that the emperor accepted their advice and several powerful feudal domains provided military support. They moved quickly, however, to build their own military and economic control. By July 1869 the feudal lords had been requested to give up their domains, and in 1871 these domains were abolished and transformed into prefectures of a unified central state.

[5] With an internal deadline approaching, the government enlisted Ende and Bockmann associate Adolph Stegmueller and Japanese architect Yoshii Shigenori to design a temporary structure. The building, a two-story, European-style wooden structure, opened in November 1890 on a site in Hibiya. Bockmann associate, Oscar Tietze, joined Yoshii to design its replacement. The second building was larger than the first, but followed a similar design: it housed the Diet until 1925.

[6] Morse Edward S., Japanese Homes and Their Surroundings, Tokyo: Charles E. Tuttle Company Inc. Eighteenth Printing 1997, pp 6

[7] In the 1850s, several modern-minded artists in France discovered the Japanese woodblock print. By the 1860s, nearly all the French artists who developed Impressionism were collecting Japanese prints. The first modernist to incorporate elements of the Japanese pictorial grammar was Edouard Manet. Shocking the French cultural establishment, Manet created several paintings in flat, unmodulated colors, paying only lip-service to the rules of "modeling" objects in clair-obscure. Van Gogh, perhaps alone among his contemporaries, realized that the Japanese print had liberated European art from its optical straitjacket. He spent nearly two years adjusting his painterly technique, discarding his old palet and learning to use flat, pure (rather than "naturalistic") colors. This involved the study of new color phenomena like "simultaneous contrast" and "complimentary contrast".

[8] Condor's Landscape Gardening in Japan was originally published by Msrs. Kelly & Walsh in 1893, some 16 years after he arrived in Japan. Because Condor left for Japan just before the Modern

movement began in Europe, it is difficult to ascertain the influences that particularly affected him. However the evidence of theorist John Ruskin could be seen in Condor's book, The Floral Art of Japan (Kelly and Walsh, Limited, Yoko-hama, 2nd Ed. 1899), in which he quoted him. For more on Condor's Mitsui Building see Leonardo Benevolo, History of Modern Architecture, Vol. 1; The Modern Movement Cambridge, Massachusetts: MIT Press, 1960, pp 171

[9] See Mrs. Frank Lloyd Wright, The Work of Frank Lloyd Wright, Horizon Press, 1965, pp 139

[10] See Isozaki, pg 8-9 see Isozaki Arata, Japan-ness in Architecture, Cambridge, Massachusetts: MIT Press, 2006

[11] For more on this, see Isozaki Arata, Japan-ness in Architecture, pp 15-17

[12] Nute Kevin, "Frank Lloyd Wright and Japanese Architecture: A Study in Inspiration," Journal of Design History, Vol. 7, No. 3, Oxford University Press, 1994, pp 170

[13] Ibid, pp 169-185

[14] Ibid, pp 180

[15] The scandal of Schindler's exclusion from the exhibition becomes clearer when one examines the accompanying catalogue, book and illustrations. Barr, Hitchcock and Johnson, the exhibition curators, attacked the 'Modernistic or half-Modern' decorative style, and Expressionism, along with all of the traditional styles. (See Barr, "Foreword", in Modern Architecture : International Exhibition, pp 13.) The book advocated three principles: "architecture as volume rather than as mass"; "regularity rather than axial symmetry serves as the chief means of ordering design"; and the prohibition of "arbitrary applied decoration". It propounded that "anyone who follows the rules, who accepts the implications….can produce buildings which are at least aesthetically sound" (See Hitchcock and Johnson, The International Style, 20, 68.)

[16] Taut Heinrich, Bruno Taut, "Bruno Taut in und uber Japan," pp 133. Also quoted in von Moos Stanislaus, Venturi Scott Brown & Associates: Buildings and Projects 1986-1998, USA: The Monacelli Press Inc., 1999, pp 60

[17] Taut Bruno, House and People of Japan, Tokyo: Sanseido, 1973

[18] The museum would be completed as late as 1959 by his students Mayekawa, Sakakura and Yoshizaka

[19] See Kenzo Tange, et al, Katsura: Tradition and Creation in Japanese Architecture, New Haven: Yale University Press, 1960; and Ise: Prototype of Japanese Architecture Cambridge: MIT Press, 1965. Also see Boyd Robin, Kenzo Tange, George Braziller, 1962; and Boyd Robin, New Directions In Japanese Architecture, George Braziller, 1968

[20] See Giedion Siegfried, Space, Time and Architecture, Fifth Edition, Cambridge, Massachusetts: Harvard University Press, Seventeenth Printing, Fifth Edition, 1970

[21] For more on Metabolism, see Ross Michael Franklin, Beyond Metabolism,McGraw Hill, 1978.

[22] For more on this plan, see Lin Zhongjie, Kenzo Tange and the Metabolist Movement: Urban Utopias of Modern Japan, London: Routledge, 2010

[23] Frampton Kenneth, Modern Architecture : A Critical History (Thames & Hudson, 1980), 284-285

[24] The Osaka Expo Theme was 'Progress and Harmony for Mankind'. It was held from March 15 - September 13, 1970 (183 days) in the Senri Hills, Osaka, Japan. This was the first International Exposition to be held in Asia.

[25] See Maki Fumihiko 1979-1986, Tokyo: Space Design 1, 1986. Quoted in Frampton Kenneth, Modern Architecture: A Critical History, London: Thames & Hudson, Third Edition, 1980, pp 340

[26] Ibid

[27] Frampton Kenneth, Modern Architecture: A Critical History, pp 284-285

[28] For more on this shift, see Frampton Kenneth, Modern Architecture : A Critical History, pp 284

[29] Bognar Botond, "What Goes Up Must Come Down: Recent Urban Architecture in Japan", in Harvard Design Magazine, Vol. 3 Cambridge: Harvard University Press, Fall 1997, pp 33-43

[30] The essay was originally published in The Japan Architect in 1978. See Keim Kevin (editor), You Have to Pay for the Public Life: Selected Essays of Charles W. Moore, Cambridge, Massachusetts: MIT Press, 2001, pp 279-282

[31] See Frampton Kenneth, Modern Architecture : A Critical History, pp 324

[32] Ibid

[33] Ibid

[34] Sacchi Livio, Tokyo: City and Architecture, USA: Universe Publishing, 2004, pp 192

[35] Ibid pp 192 & 195

[36] Ibid pp 208

[37] For more on the Tokyo Metropolitan Tower, see Chapter 10

[38] Sacchi Livio, Tokyo: City and Architecture, pp 218

[39] For more on the Pritzker Prize, see http://www.pritzkerprize.com/

[40] Ito Toyo, "Tarzan nella giungla dei media" (Tarzan in the Media Jungle), Domus 835, March 2001, Servizi/Features pp 36-59

[41] For more on the work of Ban, see Jodidio Philip (ed.), Shigeru Ban: Complete Works 1985-2010, Taschen, 2010

[42] See von Moos Stanislaus, Venturi Scott Brown & Associates: Buildings and Projects 1986-1998, pp 320-321

[43] See Benedict Ruth, The Chrysanthemum and the Sword: Patterns of Japanese Culture, Houghton Muffin & Company, 1946

[44] See von Moos Stanislaus, Venturi Scott Brown & Associates: Buildings and Projects 1986-1998, "The City as Kimono," pp 60

[45] Venturi and Scott Brown, "Two Naifs in Japan," pp 16

[46] Venturi Robert, Scott Brown Denise & Izenour Steve, Learning from Las Vegas, Cambridge, Massachusetts: The MIT Press, Third Printing, 1978

[47] Isozaki Arata, Japan-ness in Architecture, Cambridge, Massachusetts: MIT Press, 2006, Chapter 18-21, pp 103

[48] Ibid, pp 65

CHAPTER 10 – MANIFESTING DEMOCRACY

[1] Ishida Takeshi & Krauss Ellis S., Democracy in Japan, University of Pittsburg Press, 1989, pp 3

[2] Dower John W.,"The Bombed: Hiroshimas and Nagasakis in Japanese Memory" in Hiroshima in History and Memory, Edited by Hogan Michael J., Cambridge: Cambridge University Press, 1996, pp 116-142.

[3] Isozaki Arata, Japan-ness in Architecture, MIT Press, 2006, pp 65 & 66

[4] The Congrès International d'Architecture Moderne (CIAM) (or International Congress of Modern Architec-ture), founded in 1928 and disbanded in 1959, was a series of international conferences of modern architects. The organization was hugely influential not only in formalizing the architectural principles of the Modern Movement, but also in projecting architecture as an economic and political tool that could be used to improve the world through the design of buildings and through urban planning. In 1951, CIAM VIII was held in Hoddesdon, England, with the theme "The Heart of the City."

[5] For more, see Isozaki Arata, Japan-ness in Architecture, pp 56

[6] Kurokawa Kisho, Rediscovering Japanese Space, pp 107

[7] Ibid, pp 107

[8] For more on this, see Ibid, "The Symbiosis of Interior and Exterior," pp 19-22. Also see "An Intermediary and the Spec Time Continuum," pp 106-110

[9] Ibid, pp 107

[10] Isozaki Arata, "Ka (Hypothesis) and Hi (Spirit)" in Japan-ness in Architecture, pp 75

[11] Ibid, pp 75

[12] Ibid, pp 75

[13] Ibid, pp 76

[14] Eckersall, P., "The Emotional Geography of Shinjuku: the case of Chikatetsu Hiroba (underground plaza, 1970)", in Japanese Studies, 31(3), 2011, pp 333-343.

[15] Ibid

[16] Ibid

[17] Isozaki Arata, Japan-ness in Architecture, pp 80

[18] Ibid

[19] Ibid

[20] The planning and development was carried out jointly by The Housing and Urban De-

velopment Corporation, Tokyo Metropolitan Housing Supply Corporation and Tokyo Metropolitan Government.

21 Tokyo Disneyland for instance was owned and operated by the Oriental Land Company (OLC), a post World War II corporate conglomerate whose initial goal had simply been the reclamation of the shallow areas of Tokyo Bay as valuable real estate investment. A subsequent government policy mandating exclusively "leisure" purposes had compelled the OLC to send study teams around the world to determine the best solution, and one team had returned from Anaheim, California with the idea of Disneyland. Negotiations with The Walt Disney Company in the mid 60's just prior to Walt Disney's death and during the development of the Orlando, Florida park, had been unsuccessful, but the OLC would returned again in the late 70's agreeing to a handsome licensing contract with Tokyo Disneyland eventually opening on April 15, 1983.

22 Charles Moore, "You Have to pay for the Public Life," published in Perspecta, No. 9-10, Yale University Press, 1965, pp 57-97.

23 Caballero Jorge Almazán and Tsukamoto Yoshiharu, "Tokyo Public Space Networks at the Intersection of the Commercial and the Domestic Realms," published in Journal of Asian Architecture and Building Engineering, vol.5 no.2 November 2006, pp 301

24 Ibid

25 The third place (also known as third space) is a term used in the concept of community building to refer to social surroundings separate from the two usual social environments of home and the workplace. For more see Ol-denburg Ray, The Great Good Place, New York: Paragon Books, 1989

26 Caballero and Tsukamoto "Tokyo Public Space Networks at the Intersection of the Commercial and the Do-mestic Realms," pp 304

27 Caballero and Tsukamoto, "Tokyo Public Space Networks at the Intersection of the Commercial and the Do-mestic Realms (Part II): Study on Urban Content Space," published in Journal of Asian Architecture and Build-ing Engineering, vol.6 no.1 May 2007, pp 145

28 For more, see Ibid, pp 147-149

29 The term "deliberative democracy" was originally coined by Joseph M. Bessette, in "Deliberative Democracy: The Majority Principle in Republican Government," in 1980, and he subsequently elaborated and defended the notion in "The Mild Voice of Reason" (1994). Jurgen Habermas remains one of the most prolific advocates of this theory. For more see Habermas Jurgen, The Structural Transformation of the Public Sphere, 1962.

30 For more on Mouffe's concept, see Mouffe Chantal, "Deliberative Democracy or Agonistic Pluralism," in Politi-cal Science Series # 72, Institute for Advanced Studies, Vienna, 2000.

31 Ibid

32 For example Japan imported many of its cultural ideals in religion, art, and architecture from China, and then 'refined' them through its own context to create a unique and specific cultural identity. So also in a more modern context, Japan 'imported' the automobile and electronic industry ideas from the West and revolutionized them in its own right.

33 Isozaki Arata, in Japan-ness in Architecture, "Japanese Taste and its Recent Historical Construction" pp 3

CHAPTER 11 – REREADING TOKYO

1 Alberto Arbasino quoted in Mariani Fosco, Ore Giapponesi, Milan: Corbaccio, 2000, pp 60

2 Sacchi Livio, Tokyo: City and Architecture, USA: Universe Publishing, 2004, pp 96

3 Brandi Cesare, Budda sorride, Turin: Einaudi, 1973, quoted in Sacchi Livio, Tokyo: City and Architecture, pp 13

4 Bognar Botond, "What Goes Up Must Come Down: Recent Urban Architecture in Japan", in Harvard Design Magazine, Vol. 3 Cambridge: Harvard University Press, Fall 1997, pp 33-43

5 Barber Stephen, "Tokyo Pornography;" Tokyo Vertigo, USA: Creation Books, 2001, pp 83

6 Sacchi Livio, Tokyo: City and Architecture, pp 32

7 For more on Tokyo statistics, see http://en.wikipedia.org/wiki/Tokyo. Also see Ibid

8 See Bestor Theodore, Neighborhood Tokyo, Stanford University Press, March 1990. The book was based on two years of fieldwork, from 1979-81, when the author and his wife were residents there, along with subsequent trips.

[9] Ibid

[10] Kelly William W., Neighborhood Tokyo – Book Review, Journal of Japanese Studies, Volume 16, No. 1 (Winter 1990), The Society for Japanese Studies, pp 195

[11] Kelly William W., Neighborhood Tokyo – Book Review, Journal of Japanese Studies, pp 196

[12] Sacchi Livio, Tokyo: City and Architecture, pp 45

[13] Ibid, pp 52

[14] For more on this, see Allison Gary D., Japan's Postwar History, Cornell University Press; second edition 2004

[15] Barthes Roland, Empire of Signs, Hill and Wang; writing edition, 1983, pp 30

[16] For more, see Rowe Peter G., East Asia Modern: Shaping the Contemporary City, London: Reaktion Books, 2005, pp 98-102

[17] Ibid, pp 99

[18] For more on the Heisei Boom and immigrant flows, see Sacchi Livio, Tokyo: City and Architecture, pp 65-69

[19] Ibid, pp 65

[20] Sacchi Livio, Tokyo: City and Architecture, pp

[21] Ibid, pp 170

[22] For more, see http://world.time.com/2013/03/10/two-years-after-fukushima-japan-worries-about-the-next-big-quake/, accessed July 2013

[23] Ibid

[24] See "Tokyo fire hydrants to serve as emergency water stations after earthquake" in Japan Daily Press, September 27, 2012; http://japandailypress.com/tokyo-fire-hydrants-to-serve-as-emergency-water-stations-after-earthquake-2713623/ (accessed September 2013)

[25] Ibid

[26] Ibid

[27] Fackler Martin, "Japan Weighed Evacuating Tokyo in Nuclear Crisis," The New York Times, February 27, 2012; http://www.nytimes.com/2012/02/28/world/asia/japan-considered-tokyo-evacuation-during-the-nuclear-crisis-report-says.html?_r=0 (accessed September 2013)

[28] See Hays Walter, "Earthquake Resilient City Being Planned for Tokyo: A Backup in case of Disaster" www.pitt.edu/~super7/44011-45001/44421.ppt□ (accessed September 2013)

[29] Ibid

[30] Chakrabarti Vishaan, "The Ultimate Country of Cities," http://urbanomnibus.net/2011/03/the-ultimate-country-of-cities/, accessed in June 2103

[31] Adapted from the title of a book by Inam Aseem, Planning for the Unplanned – Recovering from Crisis in Megacities, Routledge, 2005.

[32] Solomon Erez Golani, Morris Brian & Dimmer Christian, "4 Hours: Orchestration of Timespace," Modern- Re-appropriating Asia's Urban Heritage: Modern Asia Architecture Network (mAAN) 6th International Conference, Proceedings, University of Tokyo, Muramatsu, S., Ed., mAAN Publishing, Tokyo, 2006, pp 192

[33] Ibid, pp 191

[34] For more in this, see Hirooka Haruya, "Evolution of Urban Railways: The Development of Tokyo's Rail Network, in Japan Railway & Transport Review, Vol. 23, 22-3, 2000; http://www.jrtr.net/jrtr23/F22_Hirooka.html (accessed September 2013)

[35] For more on the history of Japan's trains, including a timeline, see http://en.wikipedia.org/wiki/Rail_transport_in_Japan (accessed September 2013)

[36] For more see, Hood, Christopher, Shinkansen: From Bullet Train to Symbol of Modern Japan, London and New York: Routledge, 2006, pp 25

[37] See Hirooka, H. "The Development of Tokyo's Rail Network", pp 25. Also see Takatsu Toshiji, "The History and Future of High-Speed Railways in Japan" in Japan Railway and Transportation Review, Vol. 48, 2007, pp 9

[38] JR Central Railway Company. Annual Report 2012, http://english.jrcentral.co.jp/company/ir/annualreport/_pdf/ annualreport2012.pdf, accessed May 2013

[39] The Kanto region around Tokyo, for instance, has had over 100 historical rail lines, and over 2000 stations.

[40] Barber Stephen, Tokyo Vertigo, pp 9

41 Ibid, pp 29

42 Sacchi Livio, Tokyo: City and Architecture, pp 91-92

43 Barber Stephen, Tokyo Vertigo, pp 83

44 See Slocombe Romain, Tokyo Sex Underground, USA: Creation Books, 2001

45 Ibid

46 For more on this , see Cybriwsky R., Tokyo: The Changing Profile of an Urban Giant, Boston: G.K. Hall & Co., 1991

47 From conversations with Winnie Fong, based on her field observations in Tokyo during Spring 2013. Also see Fong Winnie, unpublished paper "Tokyo Eros: Love Hotels as a part of Japan's Urban Landscape," written for PPD 531L, Japan Lab, Price School of Public Policy, University of Southern California, Spring 2013

48 For more on regulations, see West, M., Law in Everyday Japan: Sex, Sumo, Suicide, and Statutes, Chicago: University of Chicago Press, 2005

49 Ibid

50 From conversations with Jeffrey Khau, based on his field observations in Shinjuku during Spring 2013. Also see Khau Jeffrey, unpublished paper "Tokyo Noir: Planning and the Informal Economy," written for PPD 531L, Japan Lab, Price School of Public Policy, University of Southern California, Spring 2013

51 http://www.nytimes.com/2010/01/02/business/global/02capsule.html?em&_r=0, accessed July 2013

52 Ishiwatari Tamae, "Homelessness in Japan: Cardboard Village and the Shogun's Law," in Share International Archives, http://www.share-international.org/archives/homelessness/hl-ticardboard.htm (accessed September 2013)

53 Ibid

54 http://www.nytimes.com/2010/01/02/business/global/02capsule.html?em&_r=0, accessed July 2013

55 http://www.economist.com/news/leaders/21578044-shinzo-abe-has-vision-prosperous-and-patriotic-japan-economics-looks-better, accessed July 2013

56 Hou Jeff, "Vertical Urbanism, Horizontal Urbanity" in The Emerging Asian City: Concomitant Urbanities and Urbanisms, Bharne Vinayak (editor), London: Routledge, 2012

57 Ibid pp 241

58 McCurry Justin, "Tokyo 2020 Olympics: hugs, tears and shouts of 'banzai' greet news of victory;" in The Guardian; September 8, 2013; http://www.theguardian.com/sport/2013/sep/08/tokyo-2020-olympics-jubilation-relief (accessed, September 9, 2013)

59 Ibid

60 Ibid

61 Ibid

62 Ibid

63 Ibid

64 Saramago J., L'uomo duplicato, Turin: Einaudi, 2003, pp 88

Bibliography

BOOKS

- Barber Stephen, Tokyo Vertigo, USA: Creation Books, 2001
- Bax Marty, Complete Mondrian, Aldershot (Hampshire) and Burlington (Vermont): Lund Humphries, 2001
- Benevolo Leonardo, History of Modern Architecture, Vol. 1; The Modern Movement; Cambridge, Massachusetts: MIT Press, 1960
- Bestor Theodore, Neighborhood Tokyo, Stanford University Press, March 1990
- Bharne Vinayak (ed.) The Emerging Asian City: Concomitant Urbanities and Urbanisms, London: Routledge, 2012
- Bock Audie, Japanese Film Directors, USA: Kodansha, 1978
- Chance Linda H., Formless in Form: Kenko, Tsurezuregusa, and the Rhetoric of Japanese Fragmentary Prose, Stanford: Stanford Unversity Press, 1997
- Cram Ralph Adams, Impressions of Japanese Architecture and the Allied Arts, U.S.A: Cybriwsky R., Tokyo: The Changing Profile of an Urban Giant, Boston: G.K. Hall & Co., 1991
- Diamond Jared, Collapse: How Societies Choose to Fail or Succeed, Penguin Books; Revised edition, 2011
- Hogan Michael J. (ed.), Hiroshima in History and Memory, Cambridge: Cambridge University Press, 1996
- Drexler Arthur, The Architecture of Japan, New York: The Museum of Modern Art, 1955
- Engel Heino, Measure and Construction of the Japanese House, Charles E. Tuttle Co., first edition, 1989
- Frampton Kenneth (ed.), A New Wave of Japanese Architecture, IAUS, New York, 1978
- Frampton Kenneth, Modern Architecture : A Critical History; (London)Thames & Hudson, 1980
- Fukuyama Toshio, Heian Temples: Byodo-In and Chuson-Ji (The Heibonsha Survey of Japanese Art, V. 9), New York: John Weatherhill, Inc.; first English edition, 1976
- Giedion Siegfried, Space, Time & Architecture, (Cambridge, Massachussettes) Harvard University Press, Seventeenth Printing, Fifth Edition 1970
- Habermas Jurgen, The Structural Transformation of the Public Sphere, 1962
- Hearn Lafcadio, Glimpses of Unfamiliar Japan, Book Jungle, 2008
- Heine Steven & Wright Dale S.; The Koan: Texts and Contexts in Zen Buddhism, Oxford and New York: Oxford University Press, 2000
- Hood Christopher, Shinkansen: From Bullet Train to Symbol of Modern Japan, London and New York: Routledge, 2006, pp 25
- Inam Aseem, Planning for the Unplanned – Recovering from Crisis in Megacities, (London & New York) Routledge, 2005.
- Ishida Takeshi & Krauss Ellis S., Democracy in Japan, University of Pittsburg Press, 1989
- Isozaki Arata, Japan-ness in Architecture, Cambridge, Massachusetts: MIT Press, 2006
- Isozaki Arata et al, (ed.), Ma: Space-Time in Japan, New York: Cooper-Hewitt Museum, 1979
- Jaffe H. L. C., De Stijl 1917-1931: The Dutch Contribution to Modern Art, Belknap Press; First Edition, 1986
- Jodidio Philip (ed.), Shigeru Ban: Complete Works 1985-2010, Taschen, 2010

- Keim Kevin(ed.), You Have to Pay for the Public Life: Selected Essays of Charles W. Moore, Cambridge, Massachusetts: MIT Press, 2001
- King Ross, Brunelleschi's Dome: How a Renaissance Genius Reinvented Architecture, Penguin Books; Reprint edition, 2001
- Kurokawa Kisho, Rediscovering Japanese Space, Tokyo: John Weatherhill Inc.; first edition, 1988
- Koren Leonard, Wabi-Sabi for Artists, Designers, Poets & Philosophers, Berkeley, CA, Stone Bridge Press, 1994.
- Lin Zhongjie, Kenzo Tange and the Metabolist Movement: Urban Utopias of Modern Japan, London: Routledge, 2010
- Morse Edward S., Japanese Homes and Their Surroundings, Tokyo: Charles E. Tuttle Company Inc. Eighteenth Printing 1997
- Mumford Lewis, The City in History: Its Origins, its Transformations & its Prospects, Harvest Books, Harcourt Inc., 1989
- Noboru Kawazoe, Ki To Mizu No Kenchiku Ise Jingu, Tokyo: Chikuma Shobou, 2010
- Nishi Kazuo & Hozumi Kazuo, What is Japanese Architecture: A Survey of Traditional Japanese Architecture, USA: Kodansha, 1983
- Nitschke Gunter, *From Shinto to Ando: Studies in Architectural Anthropology in Japan*, Great Britain: Academy Editions, 1993,
- Oldenburg Ray, The Great Good Place, New York: Paragon Books, 1989
- Ross Michael Franklin, Beyond Metabolism, McGraw Hill, 1978.
- Sacchi Livio, Tokyo: City and Architecture, USA: Universe Publishing, 2004
- Sadler A. L., A Short History of Japanese Architecture, Tokyo: Charles E. Tuttle Company, 1962
- Sadler A. L., *The Japanese Tea Ceremony: Cha-No-Yu*, Tuttle Publishing; Original edition, 2008
- Satow Ernest, A Diplomat in Japan: An Inner History of the Critical Years in the Evolution of Japan, C.E. Tuttle Co; 1st Tuttle edition,1983
- Slawson David A., Secret Teachings in the Art of Japanese Gardens: Design Principles, Aesthetic Values; USA: Kodansha, 1991
- Slocombe Romain, Tokyo Sex Underground, USA: Creation Books, 2001
- Suzuki Daisetz T., *Zen and Japanese Culture*, Princeton University Press, Reprint edition, 2010
- Tange Kenzo, Ishimoto Yashiro and Gropius Walters, Katsura: Tradition and Creation in Japanese Architecture, Yale University Press; first edition, 1960
- Tanizaki Jun'ichiro, In Praise of Shadows (In'ei Raisan), translated by Thomas J. Harper and Edward G. Seidensticker, New Haven: Leete's Island Books, Inc., 1977
- Taut Bruno, House and People of Japan, Tokyo: Sanseido, 1973
- Ueda Atsushi, The Inner Harmony of the Japanese House, USA: Kodansha, 1990
- Venturi Robert and Scott Brown Denise, "Two Naifs in Japan", Architecture and Decorative Arts: Two Naifs in Japan, Tokyo: Kajima Institute Publishing Co., 1991
- Venturi Robert, Scott Brown Denise & Izenour Steve, Learning from Las Vegas, Cambridge, Massachusetts: MIT Press, Third Printing, 1978
- Venturi Robert, Complexity and Contradiction in Architecture, New York: The Museum of Modern Art, second edition, 2002
- Von Moos Stanislaus, Venturi Scott Brown & Associates: Buildings and Projects 1986-1998, The Monacelli Press, 2000
- West, M., Law in Everyday Japan: Sex, Sumo, Suicide, and Statutes, Chicago: University of Chicago Press, 2005

JOURNALS & JOURNAL ARTICLES

- Adams Cassandra, "Japan's Ise Shrine and its Thirteen-Hundred-Year-Old Reconstruction Tradition" Journal of Architectural Education, Vol. 52 No. 1, MIT Press, 1998.
- Bognar Botond, "What Goes Up Must Come Down: Recent Urban Architecture in Japan", in Harvard Design Magazine, Vol. 3, Cambridge: Harvard University Press, Fall 1997
- Brown Delmer, "Buddhism and Historical Thought in Japan before 1221", in Philosophy East and West, Vol. 24, no. 2, pp 215-225, University of Hawaii Press, 1974
- Caballero Jorge Almazán and Tsukamoto Yoshiharu, "Tokyo Public Space Networks at the Intersection of the Commercial and the Domestic Realms," published in Journal of Asian Architecture and Building Engineering, vol.5, no.2, November 2006
- Caballero and Tsukamoto, "Tokyo Public Space Networks at the Intersection of the Commercial and the Domestic Realms (Part II): Study on Urban Content Space," published in Journal of Asian Architecture and Building Engineering, vol.6, no.1, May 2007
- Caron Bruce R., "Heritage Management in Kyoto: History, Place & Festivity," in Kyoto Journal No. 27, "The Death and Resurrection of Kyoto," Kyoto: Harada Shokei, 1994
- Eckersall, P., "The Emotional Geography of Shinjuku: the case of Chikatetsu Hiroba (underground plaza, 1970)", in Japanese Studies, 31(3), 2011
- Ferras George, Frontal Perception in Japanese Architectural Space, in Process Architecture 25 – "Japan: Climate, Space, Concept"; Tokyo: Process Architecture Publishing Co. Ltd
- Hirooka Haruya, "Evolution of Urban Railways: The Development of Tokyo's Rail Network, in Japan Railway & Transport Review, Vol. 23, 22-3, 2000
- Takatsu Toshiji, "The History and Future of High-Speed Railways in Japan" in Japan Railway and Transportation Review, Vol. 48, 2007
- Ito Chuta, "Horyu-ji Kenchiku Ron" (On the Architecture of Horyu-ji), in Kenchiku Zasshi, November 1893
- Mouffe Chantal, "Deliberative Democracy or Agonistic Pluralism," in Political Science Series # 72, Vienna: Institute for Advanced Studies, 2000
- Nitschke Gunter, "Ma: The Japanese Sense of Place", Architectural Design, Vol. 36, March 1966
- Nute Kevin, "Frank Lloyd Wright and Japanese Architecture: A Study in Inspiration," Journal of Design History, Vol. 7, No. 3, Oxford University Press, 1994
- Oshima Ken Tadashi,"Denenchōfu: Building the Garden City in Japan" in Journal of the Society of Architectural Historians, Vol. 55, No. 2, 1996
- Process Architecture 116: "Kyoto – Its Cityscape Traditions and Heritage," Tokyo: Process Architecture Publishing Co. Ltd.
- Saeki Yoko, unpublished thesis, "Behind the *Shikinen Sengu*: Re-examining the Urban and Ecological Dimensions of the Ise Shrine," University of Southern California School of Architecture, August 2013
- Salastie Riitta, "Living Tradition or Panda's Cage? An Analysis of the Urban Conservation in Kyoto; Case Study: 35 *Yamahoko* Neighborhoods," Academic dissertation for the degree of Doctor of Technology, Helsinki University of Technology, 1999
- Schulz Christian Norberg, "Genius Loci of Rome," published in "Roma Interotta," Architectural Design, Academy Editions, 1979, Vol. 49, No. 3-4
- Solomon Erez Golani, Morris Brian & Dimmer Christian, "4 Hours: Orchestration of Timespace," Modern- Re-appropriating Asia's Urban Heritage: Modern Asia Architecture Network (mAAN) 6th International Conference, Proceedings, University of Tokyo, mAAN Publishing, Tokyo, 2006

Image Credits

COVER IMAGES
- Michael McDermott

BLACK & WHITE SPREADS
- *Ise Naiku main shrine covered during reconstruction* – Yoko Saeki
- *Close-up of Buddha state in Kamakura* – Michael Greenhalgh (Courtesy of ArtServe)
- *Cha-no-yu: tea and sweet snack* – Michael McDermott
- *Kimono-clad ladies on the path to Kiyomizu Temple* – Vinayak Bharne
- *Cherry Blossoms in bloom at Ueno Park* – Vinayak Bharne
- *Adashino Nenbutsu-ji, Kyoto* – Noboru Asano
- *Chinese character Dai lit annually on the Kyoto mountain* – J_o, Wikimedia Commons
- *Ishizawa's Home* – Vinayak Bharne
- *Buddha statue in the Todai-ji Temple, Nara* – Michael Greenhalgh (Courtesy of ArtServe)
- *Farmers Market in front of the Yoyogi Stadium* – Yoko Saeki
- *Tokyo Night* – Vinayak Bharne

INTRODUCTION
- View of Mount Fuji from Hikone – Thiago Valente
- Painting of Daruma – Michael Greenhalgh (Courtesy of ArtServe)
- Landscape in Hikone – Thiago Valente
- Nightscape in Shinjuku – Vinayak Bharne

EPILOG
- Shinkansen bullet train with Mount Fuji in the background – Tansaisuketti, Wikimedia Commons

CHAPTER 1
- Title Image (Nanzen-ji Temple, Kyoto); 1.5; 1.13; 1.14; 1.17; 1.18; 1.19; 1.20; 1.23; 1.24; 1.25 - Michael Greenhalgh (Courtesy of ArtServe)
- 1.1 – research and diagrams by Yoko Saeki
- 1.2; 1.7; 1.16 – Michael McDermott
- 1.3; 1.9(top); 1.12; 1.22 – Vinayak Bharne
- 1.4 – main image: National archives of Japan, Wikimedia Commons; inset: Jnn, Wikimedia Commons
- 1.8 – main image: Wikimedia Commons; inset: Ignis, Wikimedia Commons
- 1.11 – Bernard Gagnon, Wikimedia Commons
- 1.6 – diagrams by Vinayak Bharne & Yoko Saeki
- 1.9 (bottom); 1.10; 1.15; 1.21 – Noboru Asano

CHAPTER 2
- Title Image (Kiyomizu Temple Pagoda) – Vinayak Bharne
- 2.1; 2.2; 2.3; 2.4; 2.5; 2.6; 2.7 – Michael Greenhalgh (Courtesy of ArtServe)
- 2.8; 2.11 – Noboru Asano
- 2.9 – both images: N yotarou, Wikimedia Commons
- 2.10 – Research and diagrams by Yoko Saeki; Photo by Vinayak Bharne

CHAPTER 3

- Title Image (Ginkaku-ji, Kyoto) – Thiago Valente
- 3.1; 3.2; 3.4; 3.6; 3.7; 3.8(Top); 3.10; 3.11, 3.12; 3.13; 3.14 – Michael Greenhalgh (Courtesy of ArtServe)
- 3.3; 3.8(Bottom) – Noboru Asano
- 3.5 – Ken Rodgers
- 3.15; 3.16 – Vinayak Bharne

CHAPTER 4

- Title Image (Nanzen-ji Shiro Shoin wall); 4.2 (top); 4.3; 4.4; 4.5;4.6; 4.7; 4.9 – Michael Greenhalgh (Courtesy of ArtServe)
- 4.1; 4.10 – Diagrams by Jennifer Bailey
- 4.2 (bottom); 4.8 – Noboru Asano

CHAPTER 5

- Title Image (Kinkaku-ji); 5.3 – Noboru Asano
- 5.1; 5.4; 5.5(photos) – Michael Greenhalgh (Courtesy of ArtServe)
- 5.2; 5.6 – Michael McDermott
- 5.5 (Diagrammatic plan); 5.8 – Vinayak Bharne
- 5.7 – Intercitylife, Wikimedia Commons

CHAPTER 6

- Title Image (Paper lanters and neon signs) – Thiago Valente
- 6.1 – Brian McMorrow
- 6.2 – WmPearl, Wikimedia Commons
- 6.3; 6.4; 6.5; 6.7; 6.8 – Michael Greenhalgh (Courtesy of ArtServe)
- 6.6 – diagrams by Vinayak Bharne
- 6.9 – Yoko Saeki

CHAPTER 7

- Title Image (View of Kyoto cityscape from Kiyomizu Temple); 7.1 (Kyoto evolution diagrams); 7.2; 7.12; 7.13; 7.14 – photos by Vinayak Bharne. Diagrams by Vinayak Bharne & Nicole Friend
- 7.1 (Kyoto plan diagram) – Iku Simomura & Vinayak Bharne
- 7.3 – Wikiwikiyarou, Wikimedia Commons
- 7.11 – Wikimedia Commons
- 7.2 (photo of Daimon-ji), 7.4; 7.5; 7.6; 7.15 (Philosopher's Walk) – Michael Greenhalgh (Courtesy of ArtServe)
- 7.7 – Stanislav Traykov, Wikimedia Commons
- 7.8 – Kevin J. Brown (Geographicus Rare Antique Maps)
- 7.9 – diagrams by Vinayak Bharne & Nicole Friend
- 7.10 – Malcolm Fairley (Malcolm Fairley Ltd.)
- 7.15 (Kyoto cityscape with Nishi Hongan-ji Temple complex in foreground) – Noboru Asano
- 7.15 (Streetscape at night with temple gate in background) – Yoko Saeki

CHAPTER 8

- Title Image (Gion Festival annual parade); 8.15 (Gion Festival photos) – Noboru Asano

- 8.1 – Kevin J. Brown (Geographicus Rare Antique Maps)
- 8.2 – Wikimedia Commons
- 8.3; 8.8; 8.9; 8.10; 8.11; 8.12 – Photos by Vinayak Bharne. Diagrams by Vinayak Bharne & Nicole Friend
- 8.4 – Iku Shimomura
- 8.5 – diagrams by Iku Shimomura and Vinayak Bharne
- 8.6; 8.7 – Steve Sundberg
- 8.13; 8.14; 8.15 (diagram) – Yoko Saeki
- 8.16 – analysis and diagrams by Yining Tang

CHAPTER 9

- Title Image (View of Tokyo Tower); 9.15; 9.16 – Brian McMorrow
- 9.1; 9.3 – Steve Sundberg
- 9.2 (Diet Building) - Brian McMorrow
- 9.2 (Kyoto City Hall); 9.8; 9.9; 9.10; 9.14 – Michael Greenhalgh (Courtesy of ArtServe)
- 9.4; 9.5; 9.6; 9.7; 9.13; 9.17; 9.18; 9.19; 9.20 – Vinayak Bharne
- 9.11 – Hillside Terrace Complex: Wiiii, Wikimedia Commons; Spiral: Chris73, Wikimedia Commons (http://commos.wikimedia.org)
- 9.12 – Bergmann, Wikimedia Commons

CHAPTER 10

- Title Image (Nightscape, Shinjuku), 10.9 (photo)- Vinayak Bharne
- 10.1; 10.2 – Tange Associates
- 10.3; 10.6 – Isozaki, Aoki & Associates
- 10.4; 10.8; 10.11 – Vinayak Bharne
- 10.5 – Michael Greenhalgh (Courtesy of ArtServe)
- 10.7 – Stefan Zwanzger
- 10.9 (vending machine diagram) – Analysis and diagram by Avni Shah
- 10.10 – Yoko Saeki

CHAPTER 11

- Title Image: (Tokyo Cityscape); 11.5 (The *ango-kawa* configuration) – Brian McMorrow
- 11.1 (left page); 11.5 (photo showing the dramatic grain of high and low rise development); 11.7 (Shinkansen bullet train) – Michael Greenhalgh (Courtesy of ArtServe);
- 11.1 (right page); 11.2; 11.6; 11.8; 11.9; 11.10; 11.11; 11.12; 11.16; 11.17; 11.18; 11.19; 11.21 – Vinayak Bharne
- 11.3 (Evolution of Tokyo) – Analysis and diagrams by Amber Churches Hathaway;
- 11.3 (Map of Tokyo) – Kevin J. Brown (Geographicus Rare Antique Maps)
- 11.4 – Analysis and diagrams by Xin Xin
- 11.5 (Figure field diagram) – Avni Shah
- 11.7 (train network diagram) – Nicole Friend
- 11.13 – Steve Sundberg
- 11.14 (Plan of Love Hotel Hill); 11.15 – Winnie Fong
- 11.20 – Research and diagram by Nicole Friend

Index